AF470894

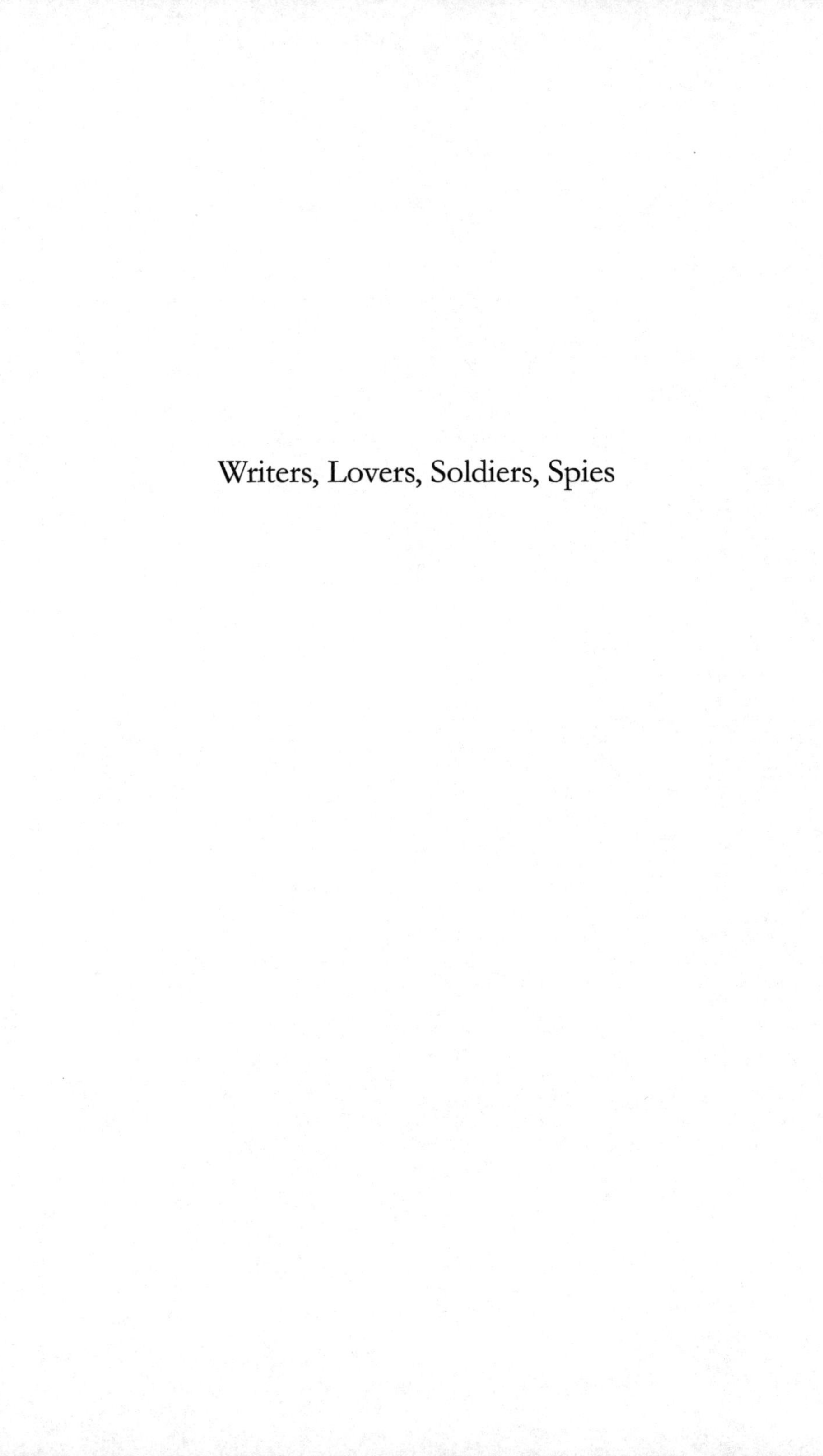

Writers, Lovers, Soldiers, Spies

Writers, Lovers, Soldiers, Spies

A History of the Authors' Club of London,

1891–2016

C. J. Schüler

Authors' Club
LONDON
2016

First published in the United Kingdom in 2016 by
The Authors' Club,
1 Whitehall Place,
London SW1 2HE

info@authorsclub.co.uk
www.authorsclub.co.uk

ISBN 978-1-5272-0168-2

British Library Cataloguing in Publication Data:
A catalogue record for this book is available from the British Library.

Typeset in 11/14 Garamond
Printed in the United Kingdon by Bell & Bain Ltd, Glasgow

Contents

Sympathetic though I am to the Groucho Marx view of clubs – why belong to one that would have me as a member? – the Authors' Club might change even Groucho's mind. It's certainly swayed mine. I've loved it in three locations: the very grand Dover Street Arts Club; the charmingly snug Georgian townhouse where it settled for a time within the Soho premises of Blacks – and best of all, back in its former home: at the stupendous National Liberal Club.

To those who haven't visited it, the NLC might sound a touch dull for bohemian spirits. They'd be wrong. Short of the jaw-droppingly showy Reform and perhaps the more classically restrained Athenaeum – I may not belong to clubs, but that doesn't preclude visiting them – there's nothing to beat the exuberant sensation of walking up the National Liberal Club's grand swirl of a staircase for a peep into the great shadowy library where Gladstone's bag and axe still lie out on display (the NLC's founder was an ardent woodchopper) before settling into the cosier auspices of the Authors' Club's present – and former – home.

Back in time – the club began in 1891, the year that two of its most renowned members, Arthur Conan Doyle and Thomas Hardy, introduced Sherlock Holmes and Tess Durbeyfield to their readers – it formed the social arm of the Society of Authors. Its presidents were illustrious – Meredith was the first, followed by Hardy and J.M. Barrie – and the speeches were short. (More clubs could introduce the AC's tradition of ringing a silver bell to rescue the audience from a garrulous orator.) Food isn't much mentioned in C.J. Schüler's splendidly informative and engrossing history, but I somehow doubt that the cuisine was ever quite so enjoyable as the conversation. How could it have been, when club members were the first to hear Oscar Wilde raging at the censoring of his new play, *Salomé,* when they were not being treated to after-dinner talks by the likes of P.G. Wodehouse, Jerome K. Jerome and Mark Twain?

To me, the most engrossing aspect of the Author's Club history as recounted here is its use in wartime. The reasons should appear obvious. Whitehall was at the heart of Secret Service operations and many of the senior figures in MI5 and MI6 had flats in Whitehall Court, of which the Authors' Club then formed a part. The First World War saw government officials joining the club in order to recruit writers who could serve as propaganda-penmen. The Second World War found it utilised in much the same way by Maxwell Knight, the man who might have caught the Cambridge Five had he not been tarnished by his embarrassing attempt to implicate Graham Greene's Quaker cousin, Ben, as a Nazi sympathiser.

It was over dinner at a table in the Authors' Club that Knight recruited Ian Fleming to the Secret Service; a few years later, Graham Greene was doing much of his work as a commissioning editor for Eyre & Spottiswoode around the same table. (It was entirely typical of Greene, as Schüler rightly observes, to mock the unnamed but clearly identifiable Authors' Club as a 'seedy club' for failing diehards in *The End of the Affair*, while he himself was using its premises to sign up writers of the calibre of Mervyn Peake and François Mauriac.)

The Author's Club only just escaped being drawn into Ribbentrop's coils as part of the Anglo-German Brotherhood during the pre-war years that W.H. Auden, who later became a member, memorably described as 'a low dishonest decade'. A persistent resistance to membership for anybody who was not – in a chilling phrase lodged in the club's records for 1942 – a gentleman 'of pure European descent', did the club scant credit at a time when even the stuffy Athenaeum was more enlightened on the subject. In the case of women, however, the Author's Club can hold its head high. It may have taken its time – Schüler cites the occasion on which Brigid Brophy wittily beseeched the club's male members to abandon a terror of 'authoresses' that would vanish if they could only change their name to the Writers' Club – but it got there. In 1971, the Authors' Club became the first major London club to accept women. From 1971 to 1979, its annual Best First Novel prize was awarded to female authors.

Monthly speaker's lunches and Authors' Club prizes – they include the prestigious Stanford Dolman Travel Book of the Year and a long-running award for writing on art or architecture that was presented, back in the 1950s, to both a youthful Kenneth Clark and to Nikolaus Pevsner – have helped the club to maintain its identity and to keep up its membership. Dwindling from an impressive 1438 members in 1920 to a few hundred in the early Sixties (a period that saw all the major clubs fretting about their shrinking numbers), and then to just 50 by 1992, the club has since recovered its equilibrium under the vigorous presidency of John Walsh and dedicated chairmanship of C.J. Schüler.

Back in 1945, Anthony Powell sniffily dismissed this splendid organization as 'an odd little backwater'. The Authors' Club has never aspired to be a mighty river, but its original spirit remains. If J.M. Barrie and G.B. Shaw (an honorary life member) were to visit it today, they'd feel both welcome and at home. We all do: that's the secret charm of it.

C.J. Schüler has done a marvellous job of weaving the archival resources into a narrative that brims with startling facts, quirky anecdotes and unexpected information. My personal favorite? Perhaps, the news that it was here, at the Authors' Club, that Ford Madox Hueffer finally, in 1919, signed off as a German and became the English prose master Ford Madox Ford. The club served 'Fordie' in another and less noble way: he used its address to protect himself when escaping from one of the numerous affairs by which his life seemed perpetually bedevilled.

And yet, throughout his life, Ford would remain genuinely faithful to the spirit – and perhaps this might be seen as the implicit emblem – of that sociable, welcoming, intelligent club of which he proved such a proud and devoted member: he never stopped writing.

Miranda Seymour

Introduction:
Elusive Histories

Surprisingly for an organisation made up of writers, journalists and publishers, no complete history of the Authors' Club has been written during the 125 years of its existence. There have been several attempts. Before he took his life by wading into the sea at Ramsgate in the dead of night in 1928, the theological writer Victor Leuliette compiled an account of all the club dinners from 1908; the four stout volumes are still in the Authors' Club archive. In 1959, Robin Goodfellow, then Secretary, was instructed to approach members with a view to collecting material for a club history. Nothing seems to have come of this.

At the 1980 Annual General Meeting, a member requested that a history of the club be compiled for members and potential members. To facilitate this, Edward Walsh, a former Secretary, was asked to retrieve a trunk of papers that had been left behind at the National Liberal Club when the Authors' moved to the Arts Club. However, Walsh resigned from the club before this was achieved, and it was not until the following year that the Chair, Lesley Weissenborn, went to the NLC to locate the missing records. In 'a room leading from the "print room", where Mrs Bonner used an electric torch to provide a little light', she found a number of items 'covered in thick dust', including a framed letter from the club's founder, Sir Walter Besant, the Authors' Club cricket shield and some photographs of past dinners. Of the 'black trunk', however, there was no trace.

At the time of his death in 1983, Kenneth Garside, a distinguished librarian and former Authors' Club Chairman, was said to be writing a history, but we do not know what became of his manuscript. In June 1994, the committee approached the writer George Bruce with a view to his producing a history of the club, but it was soon decided that the cost of printing it would be prohibitive.

In 2000, his successor Reay Tannahill compiled an inventory of the archive, which included the following item:

> THE AUTHORS' CLUB by Ernest Short
> *Quarto typescript of c. 80 unnumbered pages, 10⅝" x 8", bound navy pebbledash* Dated December 7th, 1955, this is part history, part recollections of talks, part anecdote, part scrapbook, written by and presented to the club by an art historian who had been a member since 1910. Useful stuff; although a few more dates would have been helpful.

When my fellow committee members and I examined the archive in 2011, we found Tannahill's inventory to be a thorough and accurate catalogue of its contents – except for this one item, which had disappeared without trace. The loss of these previous drafts is frustrating – their authors had access to the memories of people now long in their graves, and to documents now lost. But they may also, constrained by the proprieties of their times, have seen fit to omit much that a modern reader would find interesting.

The Authors' Club archives contain few records prior to the reconstruction of 1908: just a couple of quarter-bound, marbled exercise books recording the minutes of the House, Library and Entertainment sub-committees in spidery black ink, in which the literary lions of late Victorian London debate such lofty matters as the replacement of a gas mantle in the lavatory and the purchase of some shilling cigars.

Then, through a search of the National Archives, I discovered a cache of material in Richmond Local Studies Library. It turned out that Douglas Sladen, one of the club's first secretaries, had kept a great deal of paperwork at home. When he died in 1947, aged 91, it all went to the local library. One summer afternoon, in a sunlit room overlooking the Thames, I went through the files. Here it all was: prospectuses from the 1890s, with lists of members such as Thomas Hardy, Henry Irving and Bram Stoker; memoranda about the formation of the club; letters to prominent writers inviting them to join; invitation cards blackened by mildew…

From 1908, the records in the club's archives offer a continuous – if at times laconic – record of its affairs, bound in large, burgundy morocco-backed ledgers with green moiré boards, redolent of the dust of a century, or stuffed haphazardly into modern document wallets. There is one frustrating omission, however: the entire run of minutes from 1966 to 1978 is missing. Perhaps it was in the mysterious black trunk.

Fortunately, several members wrote memoirs that add anecdote and colour to the dry official transactions. These are listed in the bibliography at the end of this book, but worth mentioning here are Sladen's *Twenty Years of My Life*, Francis Gribble's *Seen In Passing*, Anthony Powell's *Faces in My Time*, Douglas Jerrold's *Georgian Adventure*, and Sir Charles Petrie's *A Historian Looks at His World*. I have also relied extensively on the articles that the late Edwin Robertson wrote on the Authors' Club history for the *Arts Club Journal* and *The Author*.

There can be no such thing as a definitive history. Tastes and opinions change, and this is inevitably a very different account from any my predecessors might have written. While the object of this book is to record and celebrate 125 years of literary and social fellowship, I have no desire to compile an anodyne, self-congratulatory catalogue of honours and achievements. I have omitted much that earlier chroniclers might have thought worthy of record, but which a modern reader would find tedious, and have made no attempt to downplay crises and controversies that they would perhaps have chosen to gloss over.

One final observation. The history of the Authors' Club is studded with famous names: Arthur Conan Doyle, Thomas Hardy, Rider Haggard, Ford Madox Ford, Graham Greene. Yet in the course of writing this history, I have learned that the life, the culture, and often the very survival of the club have depended on others who are not so well remembered today. A healthy literary culture is not sustained by a handful of greats alone; it requires a significant number of dedicated, skilful practitioners who may not achieve critical accolade or vast commercial success yet persist in writing worthwhile, interesting books.

C.J. Schüler,
Whitehall Court,
London 2016

1

A Club for Writers

*Novelists are not associated as are painters; they hold no annual
exhibitions, dinners, or conversazioni…*

Walter Besant, 'The Art of Fiction', 1884

London, 1891: capital of an empire covering a fifth of the land area
of the globe, with a population of more than 370 million. The sprawl-
ing metropolis, which has swollen exponentially since the coming of the
railways in the 1840s, is the largest the world has ever seen, and home
to more than 5 million people.[1] Queen Victoria, having survived eight
assassination attempts, is in the 53rd year of her reign. The Conservative
Prime Minister, the formidable Robert Cecil, 3rd Marquess of Salisbury
(his ancestor and namesake was Queen Elizabeth's spymaster), staunchly
resists the octogenarian Liberal leader William Ewart Gladstone's demands for Irish Home Rule. Both stand firm in their resistance to the
growing campaign for women's suffrage.

Electric arc lights are slowly supplanting gas lamps on the London
streets, on which the first motorcars, limited to 4 mph, are starting to
appear amid the crush of horse-drawn traffic. The first electric trains
have come into service on the London Underground the previous year.
At the eastern edge of the City, where the Pool of London throngs with
shipping, a strange new structure is rising above the Thames – a massive
iron skeleton that, when clad in Cornish granite and Portland stone, will
assume the now familiar shape of Tower Bridge. Still further east, beyond the river's serpentine loop around the Isle of Dogs, construction
of the Blackwall Tunnel is beginning.

In January, a 33-year-old Polish seaman, Józef Teodor Konrad
Korzeniowski, having spent the previous year visiting relatives in his
homeland and captaining a steamer on the Congo River, rents two rooms

4

at 17 Gillingham Street, Victoria. He has with him the manuscript of a novel, *Almayer's Folly*, on which he has been working for years, and which will finally be published in 1895. By February, he has been admitted to hospital suffering from fever and rheumatism. At 43 Villiers Street, the narrow thoroughfare that runs down the side of Charing Cross Station to the Embankment, lives a young writer recently returned from India. 'From my desk,' Rudyard Kipling wrote his semi-autobiographical first novel *The Light That Failed*:

> I could look out of my window through the fanlight of Gatti's Music-Hall entrance, across the street, almost on to its stage. The Charing Cross trains rumbled through my dreams on one side, the boom of the Strand on the other, while, before my windows, Father Thames under the Shot Tower walked up and down with his traffic.

In the small hours of 13 February, a young woman named Frances Coles is found with her throat slashed in Swallow Gardens, Whitechapel. She may or may not have been the 11th and final victim of Jack the Ripper. The pleasant spring weather of early March is abruptly dispelled on the 9th by a blizzard that continues for four days, causing snowdrifts in the country and havoc in the towns. Roads and railways become impassable, telephone and telegraph lines are taken out of commission. Ships are lost at sea and more than 200 people perish across the country. The public is incensed by the inadequacy of the steps taken to combat the conditions. On the 11th, *The Times* reports:

> The night and day that followed are not likely to be forgotten for a long time. In London we had all the pleasant concomitants of a snow storm; no cabs or omnibuses at work for many hours, the streets first deep in muddy snow and then a pool of slush, which no man seemed even to wish to remove…

On 20 March, the first London to Paris telephone link was established and, on 1 April, it opened to the general public. On 20 April, the curtain went up on Ibsen's *Hedda Gabler* at the Vaudeville Theatre, less than a month after its Oslo premiere. The *Pall Mall Gazette* found it 'brilliant and powerful throughout' while the American actress Elizabeth Robins was 'all versatility, expressiveness, and distinction' in the title role. That same month, Oscar

Wilde's novel *The Picture of Dorian Gray* was published by Ward Lock, after appearing in *Lippinscott's Magazine* the previous year. To the critics who had denounced his story as 'decadent' and 'unmanly', Wilde responded defiantly in his preface: 'There is no such thing as a moral or an immoral book. Books are well written, or badly written. That is all.'

April also saw the publication by Smith, Elder & Co. of the 33-year-old George Gissing's *New Grub Street,* a tragi-comic novel about the precarious existence of the men and women who earn a living in 'the valley of the shadow of books'. On 25 June, Conan Doyle's detective Sherlock Holmes made his debut in the *Strand Magazine,* and in July, Thomas Hardy's *Tess of the d'Urbervilles* began its serialisation in *The Graphic.*

On Thursday 16 July, the Society of Authors held a dinner at the Hotel Metropole in Whitehall to celebrate the passing of the US Copyright Act, which finally resolved a long-standing dispute by allowing British authors to receive royalties on American sales of their work. The chairman was Lord Monkswell and the guest of honour Robert Todd Lincoln, son of Abraham Lincoln and US minister to the Court of St James. Among those present were Besant, Conan Doyle, Wilde, Hardy, Rider Haggard, Bret Harte and Walter Pater.[2]

Robert Collier, second Baron Monkswell, was a lawyer, radical Liberal politician, London County Councillor and a prominent member of the Society of Authors. If his novels, such as *Kate Grenville* (1896), are forgotten today, all those who earn a living by the written word owe him a debt of gratitude, for it was he who, in 1897, introduced in to Parliament the Bill that would become the Copyright (Amendment) Act of 1900.[3]

Conan Doyle's unlikely friendship with Wilde dated back to August 1889, when Joseph Stoddart, the editor of the Philadelphia monthly *Lippincott's Magazine,* had invited them both to dinner at the Langham Hotel. 'His conversation left an indelible impression on my mind,' Doyle recalled. 'He towered above us all, and yet had the art of seeming to be interested in all that we could say.' The result of the dinner was the commissioning of two novellas for *Lippincott's*: Doyle's Sherlock Holmes story *A Study in Scarlet* and Wilde's *The Picture of Dorian Gray.*[4]

A week after the American copyright dinner, on Thursday 23 July, a group of literary men met at the Society of Authors' offices in Portugal Street, Holborn, with Besant presiding. Among them were Howard

Collins, the publisher W.M. Collins; Egmond Hake, the author of *The Death of General Gordon at Khartoum*, Arthur Montefiore, and the actor-manager Vagg Walter, who took the role of Honorary Secretary *ad interim*. They resolved 'to found a club to be named the Authors' Club… whose first condition of membership shall be a *bona fide* connexion with the life of Letters'. The prospectus went on to state that 'the Club shall admit not only authors of books, but also dramatists, journalists, authors of papers in reviews and magazines, editors of newspapers, journals and magazines, professors, lecturers and Fellows of colleges, men of science, scholars, and all gentlemen who in their public or private capacity shall advance the cause of Letters…'[5]

Although he was the author of some 30 novels and numerous historical works, Besant is best remembered for two things: his lecture 'The Art of Fiction', delivered at the Royal Institution on 25 April 1884, which provoked rejoinders from Henry James and Robert Louis Stevenson; and his work on behalf of authors' intellectual property rights. That same year, he had founded the Society of Authors to reform domestic and international copyright to protect writers from pirate editions for which they received no payment. That has remained the objective of the Society ever since, and it continues to fulfil it admirably.

The son of a Portsea wine merchant, Besant was an indefatigable activist and organiser who campaigned for free public libraries, fought for the rights of sweatshop workers in the East End, promoted the work of the Salvation Army, the Ragged School Union and the London Hospital, and founded the Home Arts Association, which ran evening schools up and down the country to promote handicrafts. If that were not enough, he was treasurer of the Palestine Exploration Fund, president of the Hampstead Antiquarian Historical Society and vice-president of the Hampstead Scientific Society and the Hampstead Arts Society. He was also a passionate historian of London, and an inveterate reader, a man who could write in his diary, 'Day wasted. Read nothing.'

'He was an extraordinary little man to look upon,' the Authors' Club's first secretary, Herbert Thring, recalled:

His outward appearance carried with it little evidence of his power and character. He was short, rather below middle height;

broad in shoulder and strong. Just the figure to push for all he was worth in a Rugger scrum, but he was no athlete. His head was square and his face florid and hairy with a spade-shaped beard. There was one feature, however, that stood out – not to the casual observer – but to one who knew him well. His eyes, which were dreamy, flashed with fire when his mind was stirred with a tale of injustice as if lit by a spark within. A feature that escaped many, for his 'pince-nez' obscured his eyes. In London he usually wore a frock coat.[6]

Despite his pride in the achievements of the Society of Authors, Besant believed that writers needed something more sociable than a professional organisation to support them. In 1880, even before creating the society, he had set up the Rabelais Club, whose members included Thomas Hardy, Robert Louis Stevenson and Henry James, but by 1889 it had petered out. In 1890, he founded the society's journal, *The Author,* to increase the sense of unity among members, but the Portugal Street offices had none of the facilities for social gatherings that most London clubs offered. While many clubs, including the Athenaeum and the Savile, had a number of literary figures among their numbers, none was specifically aimed at them. For an example of what he was trying to achieve, Besant had to look across the Atlantic to New York, where an Authors' Club had been founded in 1882, and included Mark Twain, Theodore Roosevelt and Andrew Carnegie among its members.

Besant first mooted the idea of starting a club in the pages of *The Author* in December 1890. At this stage, he was still undecided whether to set up an Authors' Club or an Authors' House. A house, he explained, would be a relatively modest affair, with just a dining room and a library with writing tables, and a number of rooms that members could use as working space. A club would be more ambitious and more oriented towards socialising, with a dining room, reading and writing rooms, a library, a billiard room, a smoking room for men and a conversation room for women.[7] Besant – brother-in-law to the pioneering feminist and Theosophist Annie Besant – was a staunch supporter of the rights of women, and had ensured that the Society of Authors' statement of purpose made clear that it was an organisation devoted to the interests of literary men *and women*. The Authors' Club, he wrote, 'would have to be a club of men and women', citing the Albemarle

Club – which numbered both Oscar and Lady Constance Wilde among its members – as a model.

Besant issued members of the Society of Authors with cards on which to state their preference. Of the members who voted, 60 percent wanted a club, while 30 percent wanted a house. The women members were split between the club and the house options. 'More than one-third of those who have voted for the house were ladies; more than five-sixths of those who have voted for a club were men,' Besant wrote. The male members, moreover, overwhelmingly preferred the club to be open to men only. 'The ladies who voted for a club,' he added, 'did not raise a word against the admission of men, but many of the men, speaking for a club, urged strongly upon us the necessity of excluding ladies.'[8]

In response, a group of women members of the Society of Authors held a meeting at its offices in September 1891, chaired by the novelist Henrietta Stannard, with the aim of starting their own club. They decided to call it the Writers' Club, that the subscription should be fixed at one guinea, and that a committee should be appointed to seek premises. Florence Fenwick Miller, the writer and campaigner for women's suffrage, was chosen as President.[9] Within two months, the club had more than 100 members, including Lady Isabel Burton, writer and wife of explorer Sir Richard Francis Burton; Isabella Banks, the women's rights activist; the publisher Emily Faithfull; and Mrs Forrester, the popular author of *Dearest* and *Mignon*. Besant was said to be taking a 'very sympathetic interest'.[10] By 1894, this club had outgrown its Fleet Street premises and its new rooms in Norfolk Street, off the Strand, were inaugurated in May.[11]

Besant's partner in his own new enterprise was the diplomat and writer Oswald Crawfurd, a rich, well-connected Old Etonian 'of melancholy but distinguished aspect'.[12] Crawfurd had been British consul at Oporto, Portugal, where he enjoyed a leisurely existence playing polo, seducing the local beauties and penning elegant travel sketches. Then, in 1891, Britain and Portugal clashed over the borders of their East African colonies, provoking fierce anti-British demonstrations. Although rioters stoned his house, Crawfurd stuck to his post until the furore had died down, and was rewarded with a CMG before retiring to London to devote himself to a literary life. Though writing had been largely a leisure activity for Crawfurd, fitted into the spare hours between hunting, shooting, fishing, fencing and bridge, he was a prolific author, producing novels, detective stories, travel sketches, plays and poetry under a bewildering plethora of pseudonyms, including John Dangerfield, Archibald Banks, Alex Freke Turner, Joseph Strange, Humphrey St Kaine, George Windle Sandys, and John Latouche.[13] Having invested money in his friend Frederic Chapman's publishing house, Chapman & Hall, he became a director of the company and editor of *Chapman's Magazine* and the *New Quarterly Magazine*.

Crawfurd was an unlikely foil for the kindly, earnest Besant. With his dyed black hair, imperial beard, disconcertingly penetrating eyes and astrakhan-trimmed coat, he appeared every inch the Victorian stage villain. Appearance, in his case, was not deceptive. Crawfurd was a notorious womaniser, a dedicated libertine who had honed his powers of seduction to a fine art. Then in his mid-fifties, with an invalid wife at home, he was already conducting an affair with Frederic Chapman's young wife when he met the aspiring novelist Violet Hunt, daughter of the painter Alfred Hunt and model for Burne-Jones's *King Cophetua and the Beggar Maid*. In this self-professed 'female rake', he encountered his equal in disregard for Victorian propriety, and their turbulent relationship was to last for most of the 1890s. Crawfurd fostered Hunt's career, publishing her writing in *Chapman's Magazine*, while adding a frisson to their affair by taking her to watch the prostitutes at work in Hyde Park. Years after they parted company, she discovered that he had infected her with syphilis.

Although Crawfurd was widely regarded as a dilettante, what he lacked in literary eminence he made up for in wealth, worldliness and charisma. His powers of persuasion and his ambition to be taken seriously as a writer served the Authors' Club well. Douglas Sladen, the Club's Honorary Secretary, recalled that he 'used his influence, his energy and his money, prodigally, in making the new club go. He entertained possible members both at the club, in his home and at favourite restaurants; he wrote an enormous number of persuasive letters; he kept the thing going generally. The club was his protégé as much as Besant's.'[14]

Using Crawfurd's apartment at Queen Anne's Mansions in Petty France – where the Ministry of Justice now stands – as a temporary office, they set about looking for premises for the new club. Vagg Walter reported that he had visited many houses to let, in and around

Piccadilly, submitting plans and drawings, with estimates for furniture and installation and the day-to-day management of the club. 'The balance of opinion was in favour of going west, and the house will be taken speedily in Piccadilly.'[15]

At a final meeting on Tuesday 24 November, rules were adopted and a prospectus drawn up for a joint stock company. The annual subscription was set at 4 guineas.[16] On Monday 23 May 1892, the Authors' Club opened its doors to members in temporary premises in a hotel at 17 St James's Place,[17] the former home of Lord Hertford – alleged to be the model for the Marquis of Steyne in Thackeray's *Vanity Fair* – which was demolished 1899 to make way for the Stafford Hotel.[18] Hertford's decorations were still intact in the drawing room used for club nights.[19] The 'moot point of the admission of ladies,' noted the *Daily Graphic,* had 'been settled in the negative'.[20] They would, however, 'be admitted either on ladies' nights or ladies' afternoons, or to concerts or entertainments organised by the committee'.[21]

Besant was never fully reconciled to that decision. The writer Laura Hain Friswell raised the subject when she met him at the publisher A & C Black's in Soho Square shortly before his death:

> We talked of the Authors' Society and the Authors' Club. I told him that women should belong to the latter, as there should be no sex in literature. He quite agreed, but said it had been put forward before the club was started, and it was thought that the subscription was too heavy for literary women. I said I had seen something of the sort in *The Author,* and thought it a singular idea; I also remarked that the entrance fee and subscription should not be too heavy for either men or women, for literary people were not rich as a class.
>
> 'But men are paid in that, as in everything, much better than women,' said Sir Walter.
>
> I knew this was true, but felt annoyed, for it is so scandalously unfair, and I said so.
>
> 'It is the same in government offices, and everywhere: women are underpaid as they can live on less than men.'
>
> 'Because they are less extravagant than men, it is no reason why they should take less money for the same work, especially as I have heard it said that they often do their work more conscientiously.'

Sir Walter admitted he had heard the same thing, but that did not do away with the fact that women were underpaid.

'It only aggravates it,' I returned, and then I said that the Authors' Club could not be considered a representative club when it excluded women from its membership. To this he agreed, and said he had thought the same, but there were difficulties; however, he 'was glad to hear a woman's views on the subject and he would see what arrangement could be made; for, as the Authors' Club was an offshoot of the society, it certainly should admit the women members.'[22]

Both Laura Friswell and Sir Walter would be long in their graves before their ambition was realised.

As the club was intended to be the social arm of the Society of Authors, many early members were drawn from its ranks. The club's Secretary, George Herbert Thring, was also secretary of the Society of Authors. Then in his early thirties, he was the son of Edward Thring, the celebrated headmaster of Uppingham School. Trained as a solicitor, he was an expert in copyright law, about which he advised many of the leading authors of the day and on the subject of which he published extensively. Though sceptical at first – 'My advice to those about to join literary clubs,' he had once written, 'is don't'[23] – he soon threw himself wholeheartedly into the venture.

Among the original members were Thomas Hardy, Rudyard Kipling, George Moore, and E.W. Hornung, whose 'gentleman thief' Raffles first appeared in *Cassell's Magazine* in 1898. Known to his friends as Willie, Hornung married Conan Doyle's sister Connie in September 1893. Several others were contributors to *The Idler*, a humorous literary magazine edited by Jerome K. Jerome. Its stable of writers ranged from the Anglo-Jewish novelist and campaigner Israel Zangwill to the prolific author, poet and dramatist Eden Phillpotts and the Canadian-born Gilbert Parker, who won acclaim for the romance *Pierre and his People,* the first of a series of novels on the lives of French Canadians. Handsome and nattily dressed, with a neat beard and intense eyes, Parker took a prominent role in the club's affairs and was elected Chairman in 1920, subsequently serving as its librarian.

Douglas Sladen, the Honorary Secretary, had settled in Australia as a young man, where he became the first lecturer in modern history at the University of Sydney. On his return to England in 1884, he compiled an immensely popular anthology, *Australian Ballads and Rhymes* (1888). His wide-ranging travels gave him the material for numerous books, including *Queer Things About Japan* (1903), *Queer Things About Persia* (1907) and *Queer Things About Egypt* (1910); he also compiled the first *Who's Who* in 1897. Clubbable and well connected, he was a key figure in the early years of the Authors' Club, and his autobiography *Twenty Years of My Life* (1913) contains reminiscences of many major literary figures of the late 19th and early 20th centuries.

Francis Gribble was the editor of *Phil May's Annual,* a contributor to the *Fortnightly Review* and a prolific novelist and biographer. Having hit on a winning formula with *Madame de Staël and her Lovers,* he followed it up with *George Sand and her Lovers, Rousseau and the Woman he Loved, The Love Affairs of Lord Byron* (1910) and *The Romantic Life of Shelley* (1911). He served on both the Executive Committee and, later, on the General Council, and remained a member of the club until the end of his long life. His memoir *Seen In Passing* (1926) contains a valuable chapter on the early days of the Authors' Club.

The club also welcomed men who, if not primarily known for their literary efforts, brought experience in public affairs and administration. In his capacity as chief registrar of the Royal Commission on friendly societies, Edward Brabrook was an ardent supporter of the Co-Operative movement, about which he wrote extensively, in addition to holding fellowships of several learned societies including the Society of Antiquaries, the Anthropological Society of London and the Royal Society of Literature.

Henry Tedder, the secretary and librarian of the Athenaeum and treasurer of the Libraries Association, was also a prolific contributor to the *Encyclopaedia Britannica* and the *Dictionary of National Biography.* Sir Henry Wolff, diplomat and Conservative politician, served as British ambassador in Madrid. Frederick Pollock, barrister and celebrated writer on jurisprudence, was a friend of Leslie Stephen and co-founder of his Sunday Tramps, a group of artists, scientists and thinkers who would go for long walks in the countryside around London, and whose numbers included Lord Monkswell's brother, the painter John Collier, and the novelist and poet George Meredith.

In addition to Sladen, the general committee – 'probably the strongest of any club in London except the Athenaeum'[24] – included Lord Pembroke, Sir Robert Morier (another diplomat friend of Crawfurd), Sir Henry Wolff, Thomas Hardy, Arthur Conan Doyle, Rider Haggard, author of *King Solomon's Mines* and pioneer of the Lost World literary genre, the composer Charles Villiers Stanford, the philologist W.W. Skeat and the actor-manager Herbert Beerbohm Tree.

The club's inaugural dinner was held at 17 St James's Place on 30 June 1892.[25] Wilde's play *Salomé* was then in rehearsal at the Palace Theatre, with Sarah Bernhardt in the title role. Towards the end of the month, it was refused a licence by the Lord Chamberlain's inspector on the ostensible grounds that it depicted Biblical figures on stage. At an Authors' Club dinner soon afterwards, Wilde, sporting a spray of lilacs in the buttonhole of his evening dress, launched into a vehement denunciation of the idiocies of the censors before sweeping from the room in a rage. Phillpotts was unimpressed by the performance:

> He applied none of his gifts of humour, satire and irony to the incident and was not concerned to make his speech a work of art. He spoke in passionate earnest as one suffering under personal and brutal blows. The Censor had attacked an outstanding man of Letters, and Wilde poured out his sense of assault and battery committed upon himself and laid his spirit bare and bruised before us. Having finished, he did not sit down again but swept from the company still overwhelmed by the weight of his wrongs.[26]

The first of the club's regular dinners took place at St James's Place at 7.30 pm on Thursday 10 November. It was followed by a soirée entitled 'Uncut Leaves', at which members read unpublished stories, essays and poems. For those who skipped dinner and arrived after 9 pm for the readings, sandwiches and whisky and soda were laid on free of charge. The readers were Jerome K. Jerome and the poet Richard Le Gallienne, and their audience included Conan Doyle, the American novelist Henry Harland, the poet Arthur Symons, C.J. Cutcliffe Hyne, author of *The Lost Continent* and the highly popular Captain Kettle novels, and a few others. It was a very foggy night, and the London correspondent of the *New York Times* was unimpressed with the turnout, noting that the dinner coincided with the opening night of Henry Irving's *King Lear* at the Lyceum.[28]

At the dinner, Crawfurd announced that the club had secured permanent premises at Whitehall Court, a vast, French Renaissance-style block of serviced apartments at the southern end of Northumberland Avenue, overlooking the Embankment, and would be moving in the New Year. The eastern third of the building was by Alfred Waterhouse, the architect of the Natural History Museum, and was occupied by the National Liberal Club, while the rest was the work of Thomas Archer and Arthur Green. The building's gabled and pinnacled roofscape remains one of the glories of the Thames skyline, but its origins were murky. The project had been financed by the speculator Jabez Balfour. A former Liberal MP and mayor of Croydon, Balfour had founded the Liberator Building Society to lend money to 'the deserving poor' to purchase their own properties. In reality, the funds were diverted to speculative building projects such as Whitehall Court, completed in 1887. After the building society collapsed and Balfour was discovered to have been cooking the books, he fled to Argentina, where he was arrested three years later, extradited to Britain and sentenced to 14 years' hard labour.

In fact, the details of the lease on Whitehall Court had not yet been finalised. On 28 November, Crawfurd dashed off a memo to Sladen:

> Whitehall Court want a six year lease: on other points – except electric installation – they agree – I am in correspondence with them & hope to make a compromise… Sir E Arnold comes into the committee, so does Conan Doyle who also becomes a member of the club – so Lord Pembroke who takes 2 shares.
>
> We should print the list now in a day or two in time for the dinner & when we get the two or three others I have asked to join. Sincerely, O Crawfurd.
>
> PS They now accept 3 year lease. Letter just come. Lewis Morris comes on the committee.[29]

At the second Uncut Leaves on Thursday 8 December, Conan Doyle, tiring of Sherlock Holmes, read a macabre and melodramatic medical story entitled 'The Curse of Eve', which described a distraught father's reaction to a difficult childbirth. According to Gribble, who was present that night, the wife died and the bereaved father tried to kill the baby, shout-ing 'You little beast, you've murdered your mother!'[30] Ralph Blumenfeld, a journalist with the *Daily Express* (he went on to become the newspa-per's editor) recalled the occasion:

> I sat between Mr F. Frankfort Moore, then a leading story writer, and Sir Walter Besant, the father of the Author's Club.
>
> Dr Conan Doyle rose to read from a new story which he had just completed. It was all about obstetrics and the terror of a household in which a woman was about to become a mother; all about the husband's agonies, the doctor's embarrassments and professional distress – I forget the details, but my mind jumps across to that evening in St. James', with a hundred men in evening dress sitting uneasily under the monotonous flow of the Scottish-Northumbrian phrases, with not a sign of light, just a long, gloomy ghastly dissertation which, if I remember rightly, made me feel unhappy and cold.
>
> Finally the big man with the rough voice stopped talking and sat down abruptly. Walter Besant turned to me and said, 'Have you ever heard worse?' I had not. [31]

Sladen took a more favourable view. 'Your story has made a profound impression,' he told Conan Doyle. 'Two or three men have told me that they couldn't sleep after it. I can't personally recall anything in fiction more lifelike than the husband. He was a masterpiece.'[32] But when the story appeared in *The Idler* soon afterwards, Doyle, chastened by its re-ception, had, on Jerome's advice, revised the piece to give it a happy ending, with mother and child doing well and the father radiant.

Jerome attempted to dispel the gloom that night by reading a hu-morous story. Israel Zangwill, whose *Children of the Ghetto* had appeared in 1892, read an essay 'Unnatural History', 'which is about to come out in book form'. The proceedings concluded with a performance by the famous ventriloquist and conjuror Robert Ganthony.[33]

That same month, in a bid to increase the membership, Thring, on behalf of the directors, wrote to a number of 'gentlemen whose liter-ary and social position entitles them to the distinction of being invited to join the Authors' Club without going through the formality of an election'.[34] Among those approached were dramatist and actor Harley

Granville Barker, the writers Max Beerbohm, Hilaire Belloc, Joseph Conrad and W. Somerset Maugham, and the poet and essayist A.C. Benson, who was for a time Master of Magdalene College, Cambridge.

The New Year found the Authors' Club still in St James's Place, and the directors issued a circular to members explaining that 'the new rooms… are not yet ready for occupation by the club, owing to the considerable alteration that it has been found necessary to make in them'.[35] The third Uncut Leaves, therefore, was held at the old premises on Monday 9 January 1893. Both Besant and Crawfurd were indisposed that night, but Doyle and Jerome were there, as was Sladen, who took the chair. Arthur Symons read a poem, Barry Pain read 'a sketch depicting in somewhat cynical fashion the annoyances and ambitions of "an ugly girl"', and Morley Roberts read from 'The Man-Eater' ('a powerful study of wild life').[36]

Pain, a contributor to *Punch* and the *Daily Chronicle* who was to succeed Jerome as editor of *Today* in 1897, was one of the most gifted humourists of his day. His most popular work, the charming domestic comedy *Eliza*, would appear in 1900, and was followed by several sequels. Its wry, low-key humour arises from the lack of self-awareness of its narrator, Eliza's husband, who unwittingly reveals his own incompetence and pomposity, while Eliza emerges as an intelligent, good-humoured and long-suffering woman who is forever extricating him from the scrapes he gets into. The poet Alfred Noyes once complained that Pain wasted his talent on railway bookstalls, but that even then his work 'had more genius in it than ninety percent of the solemn "Art" of the day'.

They were joined that night by a short, slightly built young Scotsman, with a high, broad forehead, pallid complexion and a long, straggly moustache.[37] A friend of Conan Doyle and Jerome K. Jerome, James Matthew Barrie was 32 years old and had already made a name for himself with his stories for the *St James's Gazette* and three novels of small-town Scottish life. He resisted all attempts to persuade him to read, but sat listening and smoking a cigar, before entertaining the company with an anecdote. Apologising for his late arrival, he explained that he had asked a policeman the way. On account of his Scots accent, the policeman misheard, and directed him to Arthur's, an august establishment at 69 St James's Street. Barrie, as was his habit, was casually dressed, and the porter at

Arthur's had looked him up and down before informing him that 'The servants' entrance is round the corner.'[38]

In March 1893, the Authors' Club finally moved to No. 3 Whitehall Court. Behind the ornately historicist facade with its finials, canopies and arched loggias, the building was equipped with the most-up-to-date technology, including electric light, central heating, telephones, lifts and sound-proofing. Yet it was also subject to an ancient historical anomaly. Because it stood within the former precincts of the Palace of Westminster, it had to apply for a license to sell alcohol not to the local authority but to the Board of Green Cloth – a mediaeval institution that met around a green-baize-covered table in a back room of Buckingham Palace – a distinction it shared with the four pubs that line the northern end of Whitehall: the Silver Cross, the Old Shades, the Clarence and Old Ship.[39]

The club's suite of 10 rooms included dining and morning rooms on the ground floor, looking on to Embankment Gardens, and beneath them, in the basement, a billiard room, smoking room and offices opening on to a small paved court 'which, when arranged with tables and seats and decorated with shrubs, will make an agreeable adjunct to the smoking room in warm weather. The list of members of the club now numbers three hundred and is rapidly increasing'.[40] The premises offered 'everything required for a first class and comfortable club… run as cheaply as is consistent with reasonable comfort'. The Club even had its own printing telegraph: address, 'Azyrites, Parl'. There was also a small reference library and 'three quiet writing rooms where members may work undisturbed'.[41]

2

AESTHETES AND HEARTIES

*The hearties wore huge woollen scarves and had enormous muscles and
drank beer. Aesthetes went about by themselves and wore elaborately
expensive clothes and had very elaborate pansy manners. So when the
hearties met aesthetes, they tended to want to beat them up.*

Isaiah Berlin, Letters

English literature in the 1890s was divided into two camps, often characterised as aesthetes and hearties, and the club's early membership reflected this. The aesthetes gathered around Oscar Wilde, and many were his
personal friends. Among them was the great Shakespearian actor Henry
Irving, who brought with him his business manager, Bram Stoker. A protégé of Wilde's mother Jane Francesca, Lady Wilde (known as Speranza),
Stoker had known the playwright since spending the Christmas of 1875
at the family home in Dublin when Wilde was on vacation from Oxford.
The theatrical contingent also included the playwright Arthur Wing
Pinero, author of *The Second Mrs Tanqueray*, who had acted in Irving's
Lyceum company; the actor-manager Herbert Beerbohm Tree, then run-
ning the Haymarket Theatre where he staged Wilde's *A Woman of No
Importance* in 1893; and Henry Arthur Jones, of whom Wilde once said,
'There are three rules for writing plays. The first is not to write like Henry
Arthur Jones; the second and third rules are the same.'

Another early member, Dr John Todhunter, a Dublin Quaker and
former GP, was a playwright and friend of W.B. Yeats, known for his
translations of Goethe's *Faust* and Heine's *Book of Songs*. His most popular play, *A Sicilian Idyll*, a verse pastoral, was first performed in 1890 in
the artists' colony at Bedford Park, Chiswick, where he lived. Constance
Wilde had acted in one of his plays and he was also acquainted with
Stoker. Wilde's old friend Thomas Hall Caine, a former secretary to

Dante Gabriel Rossetti, was the author of *The Christian,* the first novel to sell more than a million copies in Britain.

The great-grandson of William Wordsworth, Robert Harborough Sherard had lived in Paris since 1882. The author of such novels as *A Bartered Honour* (1883), *The American Marquis* (1888) and *After the Fault* (1906), he became Wilde's first biographer (his *Oscar Wilde: The Story of an Unhappy Friendship* was privately printed in 1902), and also wrote lives of Zola, Daudet and Maupassant. The ranks of the aesthetes also included the journalist, publisher and sexual adventurer Frank Harris, whose explicit memoir *My Life and Loves,* first published in the 1920s, would be banned in Britain and the United States for 40 years.

The novelist Henry Harland was a cosmopolitan American expatriate, inveterate traveller and protégé of some of the leading literary tastemakers of his time, including Henry James. With the controversial young illustrator Aubrey Beardsley, he went on to found *The Yellow Book,* a quarterly that ran for 13 issues from 1894 to 1897 and became the standard-bearer for the aesthetes of the *fin de siècle,* publishing work by Tree's half-brother Max Beerbohm and the poet Ernest Dowson. Harland's own contributions (under his nôm-de-plume The Yellow Dwarf) took the form of short, stylised tales and waspish commentary on the London literary scene.

The Symbolist poet Arthur Symons was also a contributor to *The Yellow Book* and an associate of Irving, having edited a number of plays for the Irving edition of Shakespeare. His collections *Days and Nights* (1889), *Silhouettes* (1892), *London Nights* (1895) and *Amoris victima* (1897) capture the fevered brilliance and heady eroticism of *fin de siècle* bohemia with the evocative precision of a Dégas or a Toulouse-Lautrec, and provoked the ire of Victorian moralists.

If anyone fitted the 'aesthetic' mould it was the poet Richard Le Gallienne, the author of *My Ladies' Sonnets* and *The Book-Bills of Narcissus,* and another contributor to *The Yellow Book.* For the novelist Llewelyn Powys, who knew him in his old age after he had settled in the United States, Le Gallienne was 'the last of the great figures of the Nineties; and in truth, because of a certain look of fatality he wore over his shoulders, like Caesar's cloak, one was constantly being reminded that one was talking with a man who had sat at meat with Swinburne, with Dowson, with Lionel Johnson, and with Oscar Wilde'.[1]

Caesar's cloak hung less comfortably on the shoulders of James Rennell Rodd. The young poet had known Wilde since their Oxford days, and Wilde had thought highly enough of Rodd's first collection, *Rose Leaf and Apple Leaf* (1881), to write a glowing *Envoi*. Rodd returned the compliment with a copy inscribed *To Oscar Wilde – Hearts Brother – These few songs and many songs to come.* By the time the US edition appeared the following year, Rodd, sensing perhaps that he was destined for a diplomatic rather than a literary career, was becoming embarrassed by the association. The dedication, he wrote to his American publisher, though 'kindly meant', was 'too effusive... I have written to Mr Wilde on this score, but if he does not write to you, I must ask you as a personal favour to see to it. I want to have it removed from all copies that go out for the future... It did not occur to me at the time that I should be so completely identified with a lot of opinions with which I have no sympathy whatever.'[2] A note in the London magazine *The Academy* spells out just what those opinions were: 'We understand that Mr Rennell Rodd has a new volume of poems in the press. He is anxious to disclaim any connection with the "Aesthetic" school, with which he has been identified.'[3]

In the hearty contingent were the stalwart purveyors of stirring tales of Empire and derring-do: Rudyard Kipling, Rider Haggard, Anthony Hope Hawkins, the author (under the name Anthony Hope) of *The Prisoner of Zenda,* and C.J. Cutcliffe Hyne. Morley Roberts was a much-travelled adventurer and raconteur whose sociability earned him many friends at the club; his account of his experience as a down-and-out in California, *The Western Avernus,* was a bestseller on publication in 1887, and was followed by a series of successful novels. For E.H. Lacon Watson, Roberts *was* the Authors' Club – his spirit 'pervaded the place' and his voice was 'audible as soon as the door of the smoking-room was opened'.[4]

Kipling, that quintessential poet of the British Empire, was in fact a strangely ambivalent case. The nephew of the painter Edward Burne-Jones, he was brought up in a lushly pre-Raphaelite environment, and his study at school was richly decorated with pictures, antiques and curios. His 1889 poem 'In Partibus' – the title means 'in heathen lands' – offered a sharp rejoinder to the aesthetes, but also hinted that his professed revulsion might smack of embarrassment or even self-loathing:

> But I consort with long-haired things
> In velvet collar-rolls,
> Who talk about the Aims of Art,
> And 'theories' and 'goals,'
> And moo and coo with women-folk
> About their blessed souls...
>
> It's Oh to meet an Army man,
> Set up, and trimmed and taut,
> Who does not spout hashed libraries
> Or think the next man's thought
> And walks as though he owned himself,
> And hogs his bristles short.

Such broad categorisations inevitably oversimplify a complex web of social and literary allegiances. While Caine was a close friend of both Wilde and Stoker, his sturdy tales of Manx life can scarcely be said to exude bohemian decadence, while Eden Phillpotts, an old friend of Conan Doyle, was a follower of R.D. Blackmore whose many romantic novels set on Dartmoor enjoyed vast popularity well into the 20th century.

On 28 September 1893, the club held a dinner in honour of Emile Zola, who was then visiting London, at the Hotel Metropole, immediately opposite Whitehall Court. Among those present were Crawfurd, in the chair, Besant, who acted as vice-chair, Thring, Zola's British publisher Henry Vizetelly, George Moore, also published by Vizetelly, Jerome K. Jerome, Frank Harris, the American hotel magnate W.W. Astor, Besant's publisher Andrew Chatto of Chatto & Windus, and Frederic Chapman of Chapman & Hall.

After toasts to the Queen, the royal family and the President of the French Republic, Crawfurd hailed Zola as the 'evangelist of realism'. The novelist's reply, delivered in French, was anodyne enough: thanks to his hosts for their kindness and the growing recognition afforded his works, culminating in a toast to 'all authors in our universal republic of letters'.[5] The significance of the event lay less in what was said than in the fact that it happened at all – it was a considered gesture of solidarity for a writer who, while increasingly recognised as one of the giants of European literature, remained fiercely controversial. It was also a closing of ranks around his embattled publisher. In 1888, Vizetelly, a former

Paris correspondent of the *Illustrated London News*, had been prosecuted for obscene libel for publishing a translation of Zola's *La Terre*, and fined £100. When he reissued Zola's works the following year, he was fined £200 and imprisoned for three months. He was then almost 70, and many believed that the harsh custodial sentence had undermined the old man's health.

The dinner could not have been more timely, for Vizetelly died on 1 January 1894, little more than three months later. On learning of the publisher's death, the eminent literary critic Sir Arthur Quiller Couch raged against his treatment in the pages of the liberal weekly *The Speaker*:

> A jury decided that the books were obscene, and Mr Vizetelly went to gaol. Since then M. Zola has visited London, where he was entertained by the Lord Mayor, surely the representative of respectability, if ever there was one, by the Authors' Club, and by the Institute of Journalists… What is the consistency of this attitude towards M. Zola with the punishment which broke the health and destroyed the trade of his English publisher?… The Lord Mayor was not impeached in the name of outraged virtue. The Authors' Club was not called to account for doing honour to the prophet of obscenity. Yet the verdict of a British jury cannot be reconciled with the distinctions offered to the French novelist by his brethren of letters, including men who cannot be suspected by any stretch of suggestion of a desire to poison the public mind with foul literature… A literal translation of Rabelais, if submitted to the same tribunal, would no doubt receive the same judgment; so would many scenes in Shakspere, in Fielding, and even in Richardson…

The battle between the Authors' Club and the forces of censorship had only just begun. In March 1894, George Moore published the novel that would seal his reputation. *Esther Waters* tells the story of a kitchen maid who, made pregnant by a footman who then abandons her, decides to raise her child alone. Esther's decency, stoicism and resilience invite the reader's admiration. When the novel was reissued in 1920, Virginia Woolf praised it as 'vivid, truthful, so lightly and yet so firmly constructed', a book that 'will go on being read and re-read' and which, if falling short of greatness, nevertheless 'holds a very distinguished place in English fiction'.[6]

Its gritty realism – influenced by both Hardy and Zola – fell foul of

W.H. Smith, which banned the novel from its station bookstalls. Conan Doyle sprang to its defence, writing numerous letters to the press. 'If a book errs in morality let the law of England be called in,' he argued. 'But we object to an unauthorised judge, who condemns without trial, and punishes the author more heavily than any court could do…'[7] It was not Conan Doyle's energetic advocacy, however, but the approval of Gladstone, writing in the *Westminster Gazette*, that got the ban lifted.[8]

Not every significant writer of the 1890s succumbed to the Authors' Club's charms. On 19 November 1894, George Gissing, having resisted his friend Morley Roberts's previous attempts to bring him to the club, agreed to attend a dinner in honour of Anthony Hope. While he was glad to meet the author of *The Prisoner of Zenda*, he was not impressed by the 40 or so other writers gathered there that evening.

'To mingle with these folk is to be once and for ever convinced of the degradation that our time has brought upon literature,' he fumed in a letter to the social reformer Clara Collett. 'What an assembly on the whole! Respectable tradesmen… Well literature is now on all fours with the butter trade.' In his diary, he criticised the speech by Crawfurd, who was in the chair, as 'ludicrously feeble'. In the club doorway he bumped into Sherard, who was about to cross Northumberland Avenue to Charing Cross Station to catch the boat train back to Paris.

'Oh, Robert Sherard, is it?' Gissing said. 'I've wanted to meet you for so long.' Before the hapless Sherard could respond to the apparent flattery, Gissing added: 'You knew Daudet, and I've so much wanted to meet somebody who knew him.'

Afterwards, Gissing noted that Sherard (who would outlive him by 40 years) looked like 'a walking skeleton, tall, upright, ghastly, with warts on face and neck'. [9]

On 9 July 1894, the members turned out in force for the Authors' Club summer dinner at the Holborn Restaurant. The guests of honour were Rudyard Kipling and the explorer, writer and colonial administrator H.H. Johnston. Besant, Anthony Hope, Egmont Hake, the publisher J.A. Blackie and Sladen were all there. Also present was Lockwood Kipling, the writer's artist father and illustrator of the *Jungle Book*. After the toast to the Queen and the royal family, Crawfurd, in the chair, said that 'a well-known foreign critic' had remarked that 'the greatest mark of a great creative genius was that he should be able to make men speak who had never spoken before, and that Mr Kipling had done. He had found the voice of the British private soldier in "Soldiers Three" and made it eloquent for all time.'

Kipling, who was received with loud cheers, replied that calling upon him to respond was 'a clear case of making a man speak who did not speak before... They had done him a very peculiar honour, and he did not know in what words he could thank them. They were men of his own business and of his own trade, and they knew how very much a man valued the good opinion of his fellow-professionals. They also knew that the little things that brought a man luck, that made his work successful, came from the outside. Men could take no credit for their best work: it came from without, and they could only say that they did not know how they did it.'[10]

By the end of the year, Besant was satisfied that 'the Club, which is now two years old, may be looked upon as established. The members are all connected with literature.'[11] He can have had little idea of the storm that was about to break.

On 18 February 1895, the Marquis of Queensberry, enraged by Oscar Wilde's relationship with his son Lord Alfred Douglas, left a card – 'To Oscar Wilde posing as a somdomite' [sic] – at the Albemarle Club. The subsequent events are too well known to require more than the briefest summary here. Wilde brought charges for libel, and Queensberry was arrested and tried at the Old Bailey. The prosecution case collapsed, and a warrant was then issued for Wilde's arrest. His criminal trial opened at Old Bailey on 26 April, and on 1 May the foreman of the jury announced that they could not agree on a verdict. After being held in custody for a week, Wilde was released on bail to enjoy three weeks of freedom until the start of his second trial. Sherard and Harris both tried, unsuccessfully, to persuade him to flee to France. Wilde's second trial began on 24 May and ended the following day, when he was convicted of 'acts of gross indecency with men' and taken directly to Pentonville prison.

What was the reaction of Wilde's friends at the Authors' Club? Irving – knighted on the same day that Wilde was convicted – and his theatrical partner Ellen Terry remained staunch supporters. Hall Caine was profoundly shaken. His friend – and Wilde's copy-editor – Coulson Kernahan recalled:

> I met [Wilde's] friend and mine, Mr Hall Caine, immediately after the verdict and sentence. I have seen Caine ill, and I have seen him deeply moved, even distressed, but I remember always to his honour (for Wilde not seldom made Caine's writing the butt of his wit) the anguish in his face as he said:
>
> 'God pity him in this hour when human pity there seems none! To think of it! That man, that genius as he is, whom you and I have seen feted and flattered! Whose hand we have grasped in friendship! A felon, and come to infamy unspeakable! It haunts me, it is like some foul and horrible stain on our craft and on us all, which nothing can wash out. It is the most awful tragedy in the whole history of literature.'[12]

Hornung was defiant in his support of Wilde, and in March, a month after Queensberry's accusation, he named his newborn son Arthur (after Doyle) Oscar. Conan Doyle was out of the country during the critical months, at Davos (the scene of Holmes's disappearance at the Reichenbach Falls). His view of the case, that 'a hospital rather than a police court was the place for its consideration',[13] would not find favour today, but had at least the merit of the 'human pity' of which Caine had bemoaned the absence. Kipling was also out of the country, living in Vermont. 'I've never cared for his work,' he blustered many years later. 'Too scented.'[14]

Bram Stoker was benumbed. He had been close to Wilde for many years, and as a young man had written an emotional letter to Walt Whitman, that American evangelist of love between men, declaring, 'You have shaken off the shackles and your wings are free. I have the shackles on my shoulders still,' and thanking him for 'all the love and sympathy you have given me in common with my kind.' Willie Wilde wrote to Stoker, begging him to intercede on his brother's behalf – we do not know if he replied. Just weeks after Wilde's conviction, however, he took himself to Cruden Bay on the Aberdeenshire coast, where he began writing *Dracula*, a novel whose imagery of corruption and contagion eerily echoes the language of the press reports that accompanied the trial.

The public humiliation of one of its most famous members seems to have punctured the club's élan somewhat. In June, it staged a dinner for women writers, presided over by Moberly Bell, the managing director of *The Times*. The New Zealand paper the *Putanga Star* sent its London correspondent, who was not impressed by the 'so-called banquet'. 'The arrangements were wretched,' she reported, 'the menu badly served, and some stupid blunders about seats combined to put many of us out of temper… The speeches, too, were long and dull… Sir Walter Besant enlivened us somewhat, but taken as a whole, the evening was a failure.'

Sherard visited Wilde in both Wandsworth and Reading gaols. The two men fell out after Wilde's release in September 1897. Exasperated by Wilde's resumption of his relationship with Lord Alfred Douglas – whom he held responsible for Wilde's misfortunes – Sherard gave vent to his feelings in the Authors' Club smoking room. The American novelist Vincent O'Sullivan sprang to Wilde's defence. Wilde heard of the incident and wrote to both men from Naples, excoriating Sherard and telling O'Sullivan that he was 'deeply touched' by his loyalty. By the time *The Ballad of Reading Gaol* appeared the following year, however, Wilde had forgiven Sherard sufficiently to send him a copy inscribed 'In memory of an old and noble friendship'.

Symons also visited Wilde in prison, and Frank Harris campaigned energetically on his behalf. In 1896, Harris tried to get Wilde's sentence commuted by appealing to the chairman of the Prisons Commission, Sir Evelyn Ruggles Brise, who advised him that a petition signed by a dozen leading literary men might have the desired effect. Harris first approached Meredith, who flatly refused, expressing his abhorrence of Wilde's 'vile, sensual self-indulgence'. Harris had no more success with any other writer. One, whom he kindly refrained from naming, told him: 'Of course Wilde ought to get out… The sentence was a savage one and showed bitter prejudice; but I have children, and my own way to make in the world… I cannot afford to do it.' Crushed by Meredith's refusal, Harris neglected to ask the one writer who might have been willing to help, and whose name could have made a difference. 'I have been informed since,' he admitted, 'that if I had begun by asking Thomas Hardy, I might have succeeded.'[15]

But Hardy was himself in the firing line of the moral backlash that followed Wilde's conviction. In November 1895, his novel *Jude the Obscure* appeared in book form, to be savagely denounced for obscenity and publicly burned by the Bishop of Wakefield. The *Pall Mall Gazette* dubbed it 'Jude the Obscene',[16] while the *Morning Post* damned it as 'a farrago of miscellaneous miseries', adding that 'the whole tone of the book is morbid and unreal to a degree, and for the sake of his own reputation and the pleasure of his readers it is to be hoped that if Mr Hardy imagines any more such entanglements as he has given us in *Jude the Obscure* he will leave them in their obscurity.'[17]

Shaken by the vilification heaped on his work, and on him, Hardy took the advice to heart.

'I was in the little writing room of the Savile Club,' Rider Haggard recalled:

> Presently Thomas Hardy entered and took up one of the leading weekly papers in which was a long review of his last novel. He read it, then came to me – there were no others in the room – and pointed out a certain passage.
>
> 'There's a nice thing to say about a man!', he exclaimed. 'Well, I'll never write another novel.'
>
> And he never did.[18]

Symons also fell foul of the climate of censoriousness. When his collection of poems *London Nights* was published that autumn, it was received with a torrent of abuse. 'Mr Arthur Symons is a very dirty-minded man,' declared the *Pall Mall Gazette*, 'and his mind is reflected in the puddle of his bad verses. It may be that there are other dirty-minded men who will rejoice in the jingle that records the squalid and inexpensive amours of Mr Symons, but our faith jumps to the hope that such men are not.'[19]

This troubled year closed with a sinister incident that could have come from the pages of Joseph Conrad. On 23 December 1895, the Russian émigré Sergei Mikhailovich Stepniak-Kravchinsky, who had recently addressed an Authors' Club dinner, was killed by a railway engine at a level crossing near his home in Chiswick. Known in London revolutionary circles as Sergius Stepniak, the anarchist had assassinated the chief of the Russian secret police, General Nikolai Mezentsov, with a dagger on the streets of St Petersburg in 1878. Settling in England, he established the Society of Friends of Russian Freedom and edited its journal, *Free Russia*. Jerome K. Jerome spent some time in Stepniak's company, and was with him a few days before his death:

> Joseph Hatton had a house with a big garden in the Grove End Road, and gave Sunday afternoon parties. One met a motley crowd: peers and painters, actors, and thought-readers, kings from Africa, escaped prisoners, journalists and socialists. It was there that I first heard prophecy of labour governments and votes for women. Stepniak, the Russian Nihilist, was a frequent visitor; a vehement dark man, with an angelic smile. I met him one Sunday afternoon in an omnibus. We walked together from Uxbridge Road to Bedford Park. We were bound for the same house. The way then was through a dismal waste land, and the path crossed the North London Railway on the level. We had passed the wicket gate. Stepniak was deep in talk, and did not notice an approaching train, till I plucked him by the sleeve. He stood still staring after it for quite a time; and was silent – for him – the rest of the way. The following Sunday he was killed there by the same train. He had betrayed some secret, it was said, to the Russian Police, and had been given the choice between suicide or denunciation. The truth was never known.[20]

3

Reconstruction

We had a kettle; we let it leak:
Our not repairing made it worse.
We haven't had any tea for a week...
The bottom is out of the Universe.

Rudyard Kipling, 'Natural Theology'

One of the happier events of 1895 was the granting of a knighthood to Walter Besant for his services to literature and philanthropic work. On 27 June, club members gathered for a banquet at the Holborn Restaurant to pay tribute to their founder. Haggard, Hope, Jerome, Crawfurd, Zangwill, Sladen, Thring were all present, and the guests included Mrs Humphry Ward, best know for her book of *Robert Elsmere*, Moncure Conway, the American abolitionist, and the travel writer Mrs Alec Tweedie. Hall Caine, in the chair, proposed Besant's health, and read out a telegram of congratulation from John Ruskin.[1] Barrie published a poem in *The Sketch* entitled 'The Two Sir Walters', comparing Besant to Sir Walter Scott:

> His burden is of London Town,
> And scarce its glories.
> The folk who ne'er achieve renown
> Create his stories.
> He paints the dirty, squalid east,
> Its crowded alleys;
> To tell us how their flocks are fleeced
> On sweaters' galleys.
> And ever from his pages rise
> The plaints of pity
> For those who live 'neath smoky skies
> In sordid city.

30

It is his aim to seek to right
The living Present.
Had Chivalry so brave a Knight?[2]

In July of the following year, at an Authors' Club dinner in his honour, Conan Doyle defended his decision to kill off Sherlock Holmes at the Reichenbach Falls: 'I hold that it was not murder, but justifiable homicide in self-defence, since, if I had not killed him, he would certainly have killed me.'

In August 1896, the club held a dinner in honour of the novelist Frances Hodgson Burnett at the Holborn Restaurant. The author of *Little Lord Fauntleroy* (1885) was a Vice President of the Writers' Club, so the invitation – and her acceptance of it – was widely seen as a gesture of reconciliation. Burnett was clearly aware of the significance of the occasion. After Crawfurd had praised her achievements as a novelist and proposed her health, she told her audience, 'I am a pioneer in a new country… the first woman guest of a society of distinguished men.'

> I have never yet discovered a good quality or a bad one which seemed to have a gender… If a man can be selfish, a woman (by paying strict attention to business) can be selfish, also; if a man can break his word, there are women who do not always keep theirs to the letter; that if there are women who are weak and illogical, there exist men who do not exactly embody perfect strength of mind and infallibility of reason…
>
> Still, I believe people are more logical and just-minded than they used to be – in the time, for instance, when they burned each other alive for differences of opinion, religious or otherwise. They use their brains more; and the more human beings use their brains the more just and fair they are likely to become to each other in their efforts to solve the problem of life.
>
> In thanking my hosts for the kindness of the compliment they have paid me, I will express a thought which came to me yesterday. It is this:
>
> I think it probable that, say, a hundred years from now, a woman may stand as I do in some such place as this, the guest of the men who have done the work all the world has known and honoured, and she will be the outcome of all the best and most logical thinking of all the most reasonable and clear-brained men and women, women and men, of these seething years.

> She will know all the things I have not learned, and she will be
> a woman so much wiser and more stately of mind than I could
> ever hope to be… And of this woman I say, 'Good luck to her,
> great happiness, fair fortunes, and all the fullest joyousness of
> living; all kind fates attend her, all good things to her and the men
> who will be her friends.'

This rousing conclusion was met by loud applause.[3]

On 13 June 1899, the guest of honour was no less a figure than Mark Twain. 'I will now confess,' he told the club, 'that I have been engaged for the past eight days in compiling a publication. I have brought it here to lay at your feet. I do not ask your indulgence in presenting it, but for your applause.

'Here it is: "Since England and America may be joined together in Kipling, may they not be severed in Twain."'[4]

The dinners continued to attract a distinguished roster of speakers. In 1900, the publisher John Murray addressed the members, Leslie Stephen made a speech in praise of literature and, on 12 November, Conan Doyle gave a vivid eyewitness account of the Boer War and his work in a field hospital in Bloemfontein, for which he was subsequently knighted. The American steel magnate and philanthropist Andrew Carnegie joined in 1902, and in 1904 P.G. Wodehouse became a member. Soon he was playing cricket with Conan Doyle and Barrie in an Authors' XI,[5] which would play the Actors and Publishers each year at Lord's until 1912.

But if the Authors' Club sailed into the Edwardian era with the magnificent assurance of a great liner ablaze with lights, its ballroom thronged with glittering company, few noticed that, below deck, it was badly holed and shipping water at a dangerous rate. Problems had become apparent as early as 1897. An Extraordinary General Meeting was held at 5.15 pm on Thursday 14 January, with Crawfurd in chair; Tedder and Monkswell were present, along with several shareholders. Crawfurd described the club's financial position (the minutes, sadly, offer few details) and, referring to the possibility of changing the location of the club, stated that the majority wished to remain where they were. Despite his reassurance, rumours persisted. In December of that year, the *Illustrated London News* ran a story to the effect that the Authors' Club was to leave Whitehall

Court for 'some small, cheap premises near Fleet Street', only to publish a retraction the following week.[6]

In May 1899, Crawfurd and Besant resigned as directors after a letter of complaint from Ralph Blumenfeld about the way the club was managed. Doyle was elected Chairman, and Crawfurd bowed out of the club's affairs. Ever the ladies' man, he had been conducting an affair with a married woman, Lita Browne. After Crawfurd's wife died and Lita had obtained a divorce from her husband, the couple married and went to live abroad. On 9 June 1901, the 'brave knight' Sir Walter Besant died at his home in Hampstead. Hope, Hardy, Haggard and Thring were all present at his funeral.[7] Hope also paid tribute to the club's founder at the next dinner.

No doubt the club suffered from the loss of its founders and guiding spirits. Those who succeeded them were able, energetic and well-connected men, but they spread their talents thinly across a wide array of committees, clubs, charities and causes. When not writing Sherlock Holmes stories, Conan Doyle was travelling the world, reporting on the Boer War, campaigning for the release of George Edjali, an Indian solicitor wrongfully convicted of mutilating livestock, giving evidence before Parliamentary committees, and playing cricket for the MCC. Douglas Sladen, when not in Japan, was channelling his energies into the New Vagabonds Club and building a second career as a literary agent; Henry Tedder was preoccupied with stocking the library of the Athenaeum; while Herbert Thring was finding that his duties at the Society of Authors allowed him time for little else.

By 1905, the club was drifting towards the rocks. It had never managed to recruit many more than 200 members, which would have allowed it to meet the rent on the Whitehall Court premises. Thring and Sladen frequently discussed ways of remedying the situation, but encountered staunch resistance from regulars who feared that bringing in more members would make the club too busy to offer a relaxing haven to writers.[8] The premises and furniture were becoming dilapidated and, without money to renovate them, the directors had to appeal to the membership for contributions. There were frequent complaints about the quality of the food provided by Whitehall Court. The press, which had avidly reported club events throughout the 1890s, was losing interest, and members were beginning to drift away.

At the Annual General Meeting on Monday 23 April 1906, with Conan Doyle in the chair, Tedder drew attention to the fact the rent on No. 3 Whitehall Court was 'at least £100 a year more than the club could afford to pay'. Negotiations were under way to overcome this difficulty, he said, and alluded to the generous response to the directors' appeal for funds to repair the club premises. Herbert Thring, he announced, who had been Secretary since the club was founded, had reluctantly tendered his resignation because of the pressure of his work for the Society of Authors. George Burgin was elected in his place.

On Friday 8 June, an Extraordinary General Meeting was called, with Conan Doyle again in the chair, to consider exchanging premises with the Westminster Club, which occupied a smaller suite of rooms next door at No. 4 Whitehall Court. The motion was carried unanimously. In September, the club's directors were obliged to write to Barclay's Bank asking for an advance of £350 against the next year's subscriptions. In January 1907, Burgin wrote to members to announce that they had found new premises at 4 Whitehall Court, at a much lower rent. Putting a brave face on necessity, he described the new premises as 'much more compact and comfortable'. He assured them that the fortnightly dinners, which had fallen into abeyance, 'will be resumed after the commencement of the New Year'. [9]

By the time the next AGM assembled at No 4 on 15 April 1907, Conan Doyle felt able to congratulate the members that 'the experiment of moving into the present premises at a reduced rent had turned out very well'. In September that year, the members presented Conan Doyle with a silver mounted lemonade jug inscribed *To Sir Arthur Conan Doyle, Chairman of the Authors' Club from his fellow members'.* [10]

In November, Stoker addressed the club with a curious speech in favour of censorship: 'There exists a censorship of a kind, but it is crude and coarse and clumsy, and difficult of operation – the police... It is the coarseness and unscrupulousness of certain writers of fiction which has brought the evil; on their heads be it.' (Strangely, he would go on to write the bizarre, sexually hyper-charged *Lair of the White Worm*). Something of the club's former glory was recaptured in January 1908, when a well-attended dinner was addressed by a rising young Liberal MP, Winston Churchill, soon to be appointed President of the Board of Trade when Herbert Asquith succeeded Campbell Bannerman as Prime Minister in April.

None of this, however, was enough to staunch the haemorrhage of members and funds. After a disastrous attempt to organise the club's own catering, the Official Receiver was called in. In the ensuing financial panic, the club's library was sold for £60, creating a minor scandal. On Wednesday 8 April 1908, at 4 o'clock, the members gathered at Whitehall Court for the AGM. Conan Doyle was in the chair, and Lord Brabrook, Tedder and Hope were also present. The situation was so dire that they discussed whether the club should continue at all after September 1908. Francis Gribble proposed, and Robert Machray – the author of *The Mystery of Lincoln's Inn* and *The Night Side of London* – seconded, that a sub-committee be appointed to look into the matter.[11] The proposal was agreed, and the meeting adjourned until 7 May when the sub-committee, chaired by Gribble, and including Machray, Stoker, the musician Algernon Rose and Horace Wyndham,[12] would report back.[13]

When the meeting reconvened, Gribble reported that they had had no success in finding new premises at a price the club could afford, and therefore recommended that the directors issue a circular to all members, and to other persons considered eligible, asking if they were willing to take part in the reconstruction of the club, taking out at least one £5 share each. If fewer than 200 candidates were forthcoming, the directors would be authorised to wind up the club and arrange for the remaining members to be transferred to other appropriate clubs. Conan Doyle put Gribble's resolution to the vote, and the motion was carried.

An Extraordinary General Meeting on Thursday 4 June, with Tedder in the chair, voted to wind up the Authors' Club Ltd voluntarily and appoint a liquidator, Arthur Edward Green, who said he would be happy to assist with any reconstitution of the club. Tedder called a further extraordinary meeting for Monday 22 June. On the appointed afternoon, he, Hope, the Honorary Solicitor Cato Worsfold, Wyndham, Roberts and a handful of other members assembled at 4 Whitehall Court and formally wound up the Club. Beneath Tedder's signature, the remaining pages in the marble-paper bound minute book remain blank; the Authors' Club Ltd had officially ceased to exist.

At this point, Algernon Rose and Charles Garvice stepped in. If few people today have heard of Garvice, there can have been hardly anyone in the early 20th century who had not. Frank Swinnerton recalled lunching with Arnold Bennett at the club, when his host 'caught sight of a man at a neighbouring table. Jerking his head, and lowering his voice, he said "Over there is the most successful novelist in England!" I whispered, in awe, "Not *Charles Garvice?*"[14] An astoundingly prolific writer of popular fiction whose potboilers were available at every station bookstall and read on every beach in summer, Garvice had to endure much critical ridicule, but the Authors' Club had much to thank him for, and within its walls he was met with both respect and affection.

Born in 1859, Algernon Sidney Rose was first and foremost a musician. He studied piano under Ferdinand Buttschardt in Stuttgart, had founded the Westminster Orchestral Society and composed marches and waltzes; but he was also a journalist and lecturer, and the author of a 'musical novel', *A439 or the Autobiography of a Piano* (1900), and many musical handbooks.[15] 'Rose, with a clear-sighted policy, boundless energy and self-sacrifice, and inexhaustible tact, not only pulled the club out of the fire, but has made it one of the most flourishing organisations in London,' Sladen recalled.[16]

The situation was a daunting one. After the various unsuccessful attempts to put the club back on a sound financial footing, the majority of the old members had already gone to other clubs, subscriptions had been cancelled, and even those who wished the club well were understandably sceptical. After just 17 years of existence, the Authors' Club was teetering on the brink of extinction.

To preserve the copyright in the name, a company entitled The Authors' Club, Limited was registered and, on Monday 5 October 1908, a meeting was called at 4 Whitehall Court with Worsfold in the chair. Just 27 members of the original club attended. On the motion of the novelist Percy White, seconded by the civil servant C. Donald Robertson, it was unanimously resolved 'that the club be reconstructed and that the management of its social and other affairs (except those of a purely financial character) be entrusted to a committee of nine members'.

On the following day, the new committee met for the first time, with Garvice in the chair and Rose acting as Honorary Secretary. Garvice and Lacon Watson were authorised to begin negotiations with the management of Whitehall Court to secure new premises for the club. When the committee reconvened two days later, they were able to report that they had found a valuable ally in the general manager, Major F.M. Hornsby, who believed in the prospects of the Authors' Club and persuaded his fellow directors to provide the necessary premises and furnish them, with no expense spared. He estimated the cost of providing and furnishing suitable premises for the members at £1,850. The condition was that if, by 30 September 1909, the club's subscriptions amounted to less than £1,000, Whitehall Court would have the right to terminate the agreement.

While the new rooms were still in the hands of the builders and decorators, club members were able to use the facilities of the Municipal Club at Whitehall Court. The committee proceeded to canvass former members and, by 10 December, 53 of them – including Hall Caine – had re-joined. Invitations were then sent out to all those who were uncertain about re-joining to a dinner to celebrate the opening of the new rooms, giving them the opportunity to inspect the premises without incurring any obligation. This move increased the list of members to 87.

By 10 November, Rose was able to write to *The Times* that: 'The reconstruction of the AC has now been accomplished with the cordial co-operation of the former members.' The committee had also come to the conclusion that one of the main reasons why the club had languished was that there was no regular change of officers to inject new energy and ideas. The new rules therefore stated that there should be nine members of the executive committee, of which the three longest-serving should retire each year 'to provide against any similar falling off of interest or initiative in the future'.

In December, the Poet Laureate Alfred Austin joined. Austin, who has succeeded Tennyson in the office in 1896, is not remembered as one of the more distinguished Laureates; indeed, his appointment was much ridiculed at the time, as were his verses on the appendicitis of the Prince of Wales (later King Edward VII):

> Across the wires the electric message came:
> 'He is no better, he is much the same.'

Nevertheless, his membership was an enormous boost to the prestige and morale of the Authors' Club.

To support the executive committee, they decided to set up a general council to act in an advisory capacity, with a President appointed for life. George Meredith, already President of the Society of Authors, was appointed to the role. It was largely a ceremonial office; Meredith had been crippled by locomotor ataxia for some years and seldom left his home at Flint Cottage on Box Hill, but he was widely acknowledged to be Britain's foremost novelist, and was a personal friend of Hardy, Barrie and Conan Doyle. Conan Doyle, Monkswell, Brabrook and Sir Henry Bergne were elected to the general council at this time, along with Austin, Gribble, Roberts, Rider Haggard, Cutcliffe Hyne and Anthony Hope. The executive committee, headed by Garvice, consisted of the novelist C. Holmes Cautley, Thring, Machray, Lacon Watson and Wyndham as Honorary Librarian.

There was a cost to this, however. The income from subscriptions was handed over to the directors of Whitehall Court Ltd, along with control of the expenditure and general management of the Authors' Club, though the election of members and conduct of social affairs remained in the hands of the executive committee.[17]

In December, the club moved into its new suite of rooms on the first floor at No. 2 Whitehall Court. The large reception room and dining room overlooked Embankment Gardens and the Thames. There were also a conference room, dressing room and service room. The staff were employees of Whitehall Court: there were doormen, porters, waiters, kitchen staff, telephone operators, a housekeeper, a florist – a small army of some 45 people are needed to keep a building the size of Whitehall Court functioning smoothly. Food was prepared in a common kitchen that served all the proprietary clubs in the building. Each December, club members would contribute to a Christmas box for the staff, which was distributed among them according to length of service.

The housewarming dinner took place on Monday the 17th. Garvice presided, and the guest of honour was the caricaturist Francis Carruthers Gould (FCG). Some 86 writers, artists and critics, including W. Somerset Maugham, Wyndham, Roberts, Gribble and Rose, were present, including several former members who had re-joined.

After a reception in the lounge, the company moved through to the dining room. The menu card, designed by the artist Charles Ince, depicted critics as small demons setting fire to an Authors' Club, built of books, while a compositor attempts to quench the flames with printer's ink. The authors escaping from the building included one 'who bears a striking resemblance to one of the most famous modern authors'. Along the side, a mock menu included such dishes as roast critic, half calf and fine blue black. According to Victor Leuliette, a theological writer and translator who would chronicle the club dinners for the next 15 years, some members doubted the wisdom of including the critic, fearing that 'the odds were he might have the last word, and even more violently disagree with them after the banquet!'

After a toast to the King, Garvice proposed 'prosperity to the Authors' Club':

> Here, in this City of Westminster, Caxton set up his first printing press. Here, too, lived our literary father Chaucer; in the Abbey hard by rest the mortal remains of many of our greatest writers… But while paying tribute to the records of the past, let us also think of the future. Gentlemen – let us drink to the prosperity of the Authors' Club.[18]

Of the subscribers, just 158 were town members, living within a radius of 10 miles from Charing Cross. Beyond 10 miles and within 60 miles, the club had 127 subscribers; beyond 60 miles there were some 250 country members, with more than 160 overseas members living in the British colonies or abroad. Garvice attributed the club's renewed success to its Monday night dinners at the Metropole and the Trocadero, the House Dinners at the club itself, and the 'Ladies' At Homes'.

Early in 1909, buoyed up by the success of the membership drive, Garvice and *Cautley* entered into negotiations with Whitehall Court to extend the club's accommodation. This involved a further injection of capital, and an increase in the indemnity the Authors' Club would have to pay Whitehall Court if it decided to move elsewhere, but the result was to double the space available to the club. The new rooms extended to the left of the stairwell to the Whitehall Place side of the building, and included a large billiard room, a smaller card room, an office for the Secretary, which doubled as a board room, and a reference library (also known as the Silence Room), with windows overlooking the War Office, in which house dinners were held on Monday nights. Each summer, the club would close for two months for cleaning, so during July and August, members were entitled to use the facilities of one of the other clubs at Whitehall Court, usually the Golfers'.

In 1914, the artist C.R. Wylie designed a bookplate for the library and made over the copyright of the design to the club. It featured the intertwined letters AC and a crossed quill and sword illustrating the motto that Walter Bestant had chosen for his club: *Cedit Ensis Calamo* (the pen is mightier than the sword).[19] A billiard handicap was organised and won for the first time in March 1909 by Morley Roberts.

The membership drive continued. Letters went out to 'writers of distinction', including members of the Society of Authors and those listed in *The Literary Yearbook*. By the end of the year, Rose estimated that they had sent out more than 5,000 letters. Membership continued to increase: by the end of March 1909, it had risen to 300; by July it was 400; and by December, 600, despite the deletion of more than 20 names owing to deaths, non-payment of subscriptions or retirement. By February 1910, the total membership had reached 700. It was, Garvice and Rose felt able to boast, 'an achievement without parallel in the history of club resuscitation'.

To ensure that the premises did not become overcrowded, Rose limited town and suburban membership to 200 and 300 respectively, while building up as many country and overseas members as possible to maintain a steady flow of income. To ensure that out-of-town and overseas members were kept informed, the committee posted to every member, immediately after each event, the best newspaper report of the proceedings. As a result, even members in remote parts of the world were kept aware of what was going on.

Those who joined in the wake of the reconstruction included two celebrated explorers, the polar navigator Ernest Shackleton (1874–1922), and Francis Younghusband (1863–1942), who had charted the Hindu Kush and the High Pamirs to establish the extent of the Russian threat to British India; Walter Alexander Raleigh (1861–1922), the literary critic and first Chair of English Literature at Oxford; Henry de Vere Stacpoole, the Irish author of *The Blue Lagoon*; the American novelist Theodore Dreiser; and the architect and architectural historian Banister

Flight Fletcher (1886–1953), whose best known building is the 1936 Art Deco Gillette Factory that still stands on the A40 leading west out of London, while his *History of Architecture* remains a standard work of reference to this day.

Another overseas member, the African-American writer and activist Archibald Grimké (1849–1930), was the editor of the Republican newspaper *The Hub* and author of *The Life of Charles Sumner* and *The Life of William Garrison*. Born into slavery in South Carolina, he was an associate of W.E.B. Du Bois,[20] a prominent member of the National Association for the Advancement of Colored People, and president of the American Negro Academy. From 1894 to 1898, he served as US Consul to the Dominican Republic.

Edward Montague Compton Mackenzie was a prolific writer who would soon achieve literary acclaim with his novel *Sinister Street,* which was greatly admired by both Henry James and F. Scott Fitzgerald. Born into a family of actors (his sister Fay Compton had appeared in several of Barrie's plays), Monty, as his friends called him, possessed a resonant baritone voice that commanded attention; though born in West Hartlepool, he identified passionately with his Scottish ancestry and would live for many years on Barra.

The art historian Ernest Henry Short, who would later become the club's Librarian and Secretary, was born in Melbourne in 1875, the son of a journalist. Educated at Dulwich College, he had taught himself art in the galleries of France, Belgium, Holland and Italy, and established his reputation with his *History of Sculpture* (1907). Between 1922 and 1938, he worked as the London correspondent of the *Melbourne Argus*.

The club also became a family affair with the addition of the Lunn brothers, Arnold and Hugh, the sons of Henry Simpson Lunn, the founder of the travel agency Lunn Poly. Arnold was a pioneer of skiing holidays and editor of the *Alpine Ski Club Annual,* while Hugh, who wrote under the name Hugh Kingsmill, had been editor of *Isis* when at Oxford and then worked for Frank Harris on the magazine *Hearth and Home.* They were joined in 1917 by a third brother, Brian.

The Anglo-Irish poet, playwright and novelist Edward John Moreton Drax Plunkett, 18th Baron Dunsany, of Dunsany Castle, near Tara in County Meath, was proposed by Herbert Thring and seconded by Thomas Hardy. A leading donor to the Abbey Theatre in Dublin, Dunsany was well acquainted with the leading Irish literary figures of the day, including W.B. Yeats, Lady Gregory, 'AE' (George Russell), Oliver St John Gogarty and Padraic Colum, with whom he wrote a play. His poetry, now little read, was highly regarded at the time: Fitzgerald has the protagonist in *This Side of Paradise* (1920) recite one of Dunsany's verses. His enduring legacy, however, is his fantasy novels; with books such as *The King of Elfland's Daughter* and *Time and the Gods*, he single-handedly created the genre decades before Tolkein and C.S. Lewis. Yeats edited and wrote a laudatory introduction to a collection of his stories; Arthur C. Clarke corresponded with him over many years; Ursula Le Guinn has said that his book *A Dreamer's Tales* changed her life; and Neil Gaiman is also an admirer.

On 1 March 1909, Conan Doyle presided at a banquet to celebrate the centenary of the birth of Edgar Allan Poe, in the presence of the US Ambassador Whitelaw Reid, Mrs Humphry Ward, Captain Poe, the author's oldest surviving relative, many leading British authors and a large number of American residents of London. Speeches by the ambassador, Conan Doyle, Captain Poe, Garvice and Gribble were interspersed with readings of Poe's poems. Conan Doyle credited the inspiration for his own detective stories to Poe, adding that 'It is the irony of Fate that he, as he said, should have died in poverty, for if every man who wrote a story which was indirectly inspired by Poe were to pay a tithe toward a monument it would be such as would dwarf the pyramids.' The Ambassador observed that the lateness of the celebration was quite in keeping with Poe's career.

> Now, long after his unhappy death and long after the English and French literary tribunals have accepted him as one of the immortals, his countrymen still wait even beyond the century to place him with their other literary figures, some surely far smaller, in their hall of fame. Yet with all the abatements Poe's place surely is in the front rank, if not at the very head, of the world's tellers of short stories.[21]

On 18 May 1909, George Meredith died at the age of 81, at Flint Cottage on Box Hill, his home for 40 years. The Dean of Westminster Abbey, Armitage Robinson, refused to let the freethinker's ashes be interred there, despite protests from Hope, Barrie, Edmund Gosse and other distinguished writers. In the event, Barrie, Hope and Caine followed the hearse from Flint Cottage to Dorking cemetery, where they were joined by Charles Garvice for the simple burial. A simultaneous memorial service was held at Westminster Abbey, at which the Prime Minister H.H. Asquith and the US Ambassador Whitelaw Reid were joined by leading figures from the world of literature and art, including Henry James, Gosse, Burne-Jones, Holman Hunt, Violet Hunt and A.C. Benson. Among the Authors' Club members, Hardy, Austin, Kipling, Rider Haggard, Conan Doyle, Thring, Gribble and Zangwill were in attendance as Dean Robinson presided over the exequies of a writer whose dust he would not allow to desecrate his church.[22]

4

MODERN TIMES

On or about December, 1910, human character changed.
Virginia Woolf, 'Mr Bennett and Mrs Brown', 1924

On 6 May 1910, King Edward VII died at Sandringham. His funeral at St George's Chapel, Windsor on the 20th brought together the royalty of Europe, including his close relatives Kaiser Wilhelm II, Archduke Franz Ferdinand of Austria, and Prince Michael Alexandrovitch of Russia, for the last time before their nations went to war with one another in 1914.

In the autumn of 1910, rumours began to circulate that Rider Haggard had died at his home in Norfolk. On 24 October, the club sent him a telegram: 'Hope you are well. Rumours to contrary.' They were, as Mark Twain put it, greatly exaggerated.[1] In November, Haggard joined Conan Doyle, Kipling and Jerome in sending a letter of congratulation to the newly founded Authors' Lodge. Besant, Doyle and Haggard were all Masons, but there was no lodge specifically for authors. Max Montesole, an Authors' Club member since 1900, had been petitioning for some years for permission to found a Lodge specifically for members of the club, but the project was delayed by the reconstruction and then by the official mourning for King Edward, the Protector of the Craft. When the Lodge was finally consecrated on 16 November 1910, its 23 founding brothers included Max Montesole, who was elected Master, Kipling, Rose, Lucien Wolf, Milton Watkins, A.E. Aldington and the club's solicitor Cato Worsfold. The Lodge continues to this day, though it is no longer restricted to members of the Authors' Club.[2]

One consequence of Rose's determination to recruit members in all corners of the British Empire was that the walls of the club were soon festooned with big game. In 1911, the committee thanked Mr W.H. Seton-Kerr for 'a collection of beautifully mounted sporting trophies from South Africa and India' and the Hon. W.A. Deane for 'the head of a hartebeest, shot on his estate in South Africa'.[3] These were augmented the following year by more than 20 specimens donated by a Dr Dunbar-Brunton, including 'the skin of a Lioness, a very fine head of a Waterbuck shot by him in Rhodesia, besides the heads of Serval and Reed-Buck, and Wart-Hog tusks'.[4]

The ponderous colonial ambience was not to everyone's taste. One colourful and somewhat unlikely recruit was the Australian stockbroker and company promoter George Dick Meudell. Born in Bendigo in 1860, he had come to London to speculate in property, and was elected to the club as the author of *Australia for the Australians* and, in his own words, 'because of my high authorial attainments as a contributor of quips, cranks, and wanton wiles to the Sydney *Bulletin* for 40 years'.[5]

A portly bon viveur, habitually dressed in a frock-coat and top hat, Meudell was a scathing critic of British imperialism.[6] 'The English no longer is a nation of shopkeepers,' he wrote in his outspoken and very funny memoir *The Pleasant Career of a Spendthrift*. 'It can't keep shop, but, oh my, it knows how to lend money, and incidentally how to annex large areas of land, chiefly jungle and forest belonging to other people.' Nor did the Authors' Club escape his Antipodean irony:

> The Author's Club was an icy sort of cave where one trod on one's own tiptoes and suppressed both smile and laughter… The late Charles Garvice was chairman of the committee, and the most notable of the authors was Poulteney Bigelow, with whom I travelled once in the East Indies, Hall Caine, Andrew Carnegie (whose monograph on 'Steel and how to make money out of it' has never been published), Francis Gribble, Rider Haggard, Anthony Hope, Cutcliffe Hyne, Morley Roberts, Franklin Lieber, the author of a very heavy, well-bound telegraphic code, and myself.[7]

Meudell's sarcasm glosses over a serious point. Garvice and Rose had saved the club financially, but only at the cost of turning it into a bastion of the Edwardian establishment. Where once it had fearlessly championed controversial writers such as Zola, Moore and Hardy, it now found itself out of touch with, if not actively hostile to, the momentous developments then taking place in literature and the arts.

Virginia Woolf's choice of December 1910 as a watershed was prompted by the first major exhibition of Post-Impressionist painting, organised by her friend Roger Fry in collaboration with her brother-in-law Clive Bell at the Grafton Galleries in London. The exhibition, which ran from 8 November 1910 to 15 January 1911, attracted large crowds and introduced the British public to developments in the visual arts that had been under way in France for a generation. At an Authors' Club dinner the following February, the Victorian painter Sir Alfred East, President of the Royal Society of British Artists, was greeted with laughter and cheers when he told the assembled company that he would like to hear 'the chief of one of the great asylums, describe the whys and wherefores of that expression of human idiocy'.[8] The lunatics exhibited at the Grafton Galleries included Manet, Cézanne, Gauguin, Matisse, Picasso and Derain.[9]

At least three of the club's members would not have joined in the laughter. The novelist Arnold Bennett was a staunch champion of the Grafton exhibition; Wilfred Phillips was the co-founder of the Leicester Galleries, where many Post-Impressionists received their first solo shows in Britain; while Ford Madox Hueffer, one of the class of 1908, had written an introduction to the catalogue of the Grafton's 1909 exhibition of his grandfather Ford Madox Brown's paintings.

Bennett occupied an ambiguous position with regard to the Modern Movement. He was rare among his contemporaries in his enthusiasm for recent developments in the visual arts, but his writing remained firmly rooted in 19th-century naturalism. Virginia Woolf took him to task for this, classing him, with Galsworthy and Wells, as one of the 'Edwardians', as opposed to the 'Georgians' who emerged after 1910: D.H. Lawrence, E.M. Forster and, by implication, herself.[10] He also had ambivalent feelings about the club. He liked the premises, and wrote part of *Hilda Lessways* and several other novels in the Silence Room. 'I ought to be comfortable,' he confided in his diary, but 'some of the men seem to waste 3 hours in gossip every afternoon.'[11]

'A strange place!' he wrote to H.G. Wells in April 1911. 'Charles Garvice, patting me on the back, has just said to me: "The secret of your success, my boy, as of every success since Shakespere, is your universal sympathy." He then told me 6,000,000 copies of his own works had been sold, but he is very modest about them. If you are in one night after dinner I will come up. You can telephone any message: if I am not in, the august head-waiter, one Dali, will take it.' On 14 May 1911, Bennett attended an Authors' Club banquet in honour of Beerbohm Tree. It was, he thought, 'The most appalling orgy of insincere sentimentality. I left at ten, utterly disgusted and exhausted.'[12]

Hueffer was the author of numerous books, including *The Fifth Queen*, a trilogy of historical novels set at the court of Henry VIII, and *The Inheritors*, a romance co-written with Joseph Conrad. A tall, bulky man approaching 40, with a sandy moustache that drooped over a mouth that hung permanently open except when clamped around a cigarette, he cut a somewhat unprepossessing figure, though this did not deter a series of intelligent and independent-minded women from falling deeply and often disastrously in love with him. 'Fordie', as he was known to his friends, inspired affection and anger in equal measure, falling out bitterly with both Henry James and Joseph Conrad, and for much of his life was racked by his chaotic love affairs, precarious finances, and a nagging sense – with which posterity is inclined to concur – that he had not received his due as a writer.

Earlier that year, he had founded *The English Review*, which published work by Hardy, James, Conrad and Wells, from a chaotic flat over a poulterer's shop at 84 Holland Park Avenue. Among the magazine's contributors was Oswald Crawfurd's former lover Violet Hunt, now an acclaimed novelist and literary hostess whose salons at her home, South Grove in Holland Park, were attended by many leading writers of the day. In January of 1909, she was saddened to hear of Crawfurd's death at Montreux, and by the summer she and Hueffer had embarked on a tempestuous relationship that would last, on and off, for the following decade.

By 1913, Hueffer had come to regard himself as a literary anachronism. 'London at least and possibly the world appeared to be passing under the dominion of writers newer and much more vivid,' he recalled. 'Those were the passionate days of the literary Cubists, Vorticists, Imagistes and the rest of the tapageur and riotous Jeunes of that young decade… I prepared to stand aside in favour of our good friends – yours and mine – Ezra, Eliot, Wyndham Lewis, H.D., and the rest of the clamorous young writers who were then knocking at the door.'[13]

On his 40th birthday, he determined to make one last literary effort, to pour all his skill and experience into a novel that he intended to call *The Saddest Story Ever Told.* When it finally appeared in 1915, his publisher advised him that no one would buy a book of that name in the middle of a war, and suggested the title by which it has been known ever since: *The Good Soldier.* The American poet H.D. (Hilda Doolittle) took dictation for the novel, along with her husband Richard Aldington, the Imagist poet and assistant editor of the journal *The Egoist.* Aldington would not join the Authors' Club until February 1919, although he may already have been familiar with it since his father, Alfred Edward Aldington, author of *The Queen's Preferment, Geneva and Rome via Canterbury,* and numerous short stories and articles, had been a member since 1909. The elder Aldington later died of a heart attack at the club in 1921.[14]

For some, the Authors' Club's stubborn resistance to literary and artistic modernism was part of its appeal. Although still an undergraduate at Oxford when he joined in 1913, Douglas Francis Jerrold already had an air of premature fogeyism about him. Born in Scarborough in 1893, the 20-year-old editor of the *Oxford Fortnightly* was a friend of the Lunn brothers and a cousin of Laurence Jerrold, the *Daily Telegraph*'s Paris correspondent, who was also a member. The great-grandson of Douglas William Jerrold, the dramatist, *Punch* satirist and friend of Dickens, he had grown up steeped in the milieu of Victorian journalism, and it was the very qualities that irritated Bennett and Meuross that attracted him to the club:

> If it had any literary flavour, it was that of the amateur of letters, the quarterly reviewer, the civil servant guilty of an occasional volume of criticism, the business man who wrote novels for a recreation, with a sprinkling of authors whose futures, in 1914, were a little behind them – Conan Doyle, Anthony Hope, Cutcliffe Hyne and Horace Vachell, for instance. Yet even these distinguished writers had an Authors' Club touch. None of them belonged to the 'writing classes' or played much part in the literary life of their times. It was this characteristic, of course, which made the Club tolerable. A club of strictly professional authors would be only a pub.[15]

It was to this fusty sanctum beneath the turrets of Whitehall Court that the Provost of King's College, Cambridge, made his way one cold and windy Monday evening in February 1913. The distinguished scholar, antiquarian and translator of the Apocrypha was the guest of an Authors' Club dinner, at which he spoke on the subject of 'Literature in the Middle Ages' to 'middle-aged literary men'. Having handled many thousands of mediaeval books, he noted that most authors of that era 'professed to be unwilling amateurs' – a stance with which, if Jerrold was to be believed, his audience would have identified. The speaker made no allusion to his own literary efforts, but the Reverend Anthony Deane, chairing the dinner, noted that the published work of Montague Rhodes James 'was not limited to productions which the general reader would reckon dry. To read near bedtime either of Dr James's two volumes entitled *Ghost Stories of an Antiquary* was to supply oneself with a whole stud of nightmares.'

5

ZEPPELIN NIGHTS

*The plunge of civilization into this abyss of blood and darkness… is a
thing that gives away the whole long age during which we have supposed
the world to be, with whatever abatement, gradually bettering, that to
have to take it all now for what the treacherous years were all the while
really making for and meaning is too tragic for any words.*

Henry James, letter, 4 August 1914

When the Archduke Franz Ferdinand was assassinated at Sarajevo on 28
June 1914, Francis Gribble saw no reason to cancel his planned holiday
in Luxemburg. Though he had written a life of the Emperor Franz Josef
and was considered something of an expert on Austro-Hungary, he did
not suspect that 'this murder was about to be made the pretext for a
European war'. In Luxemburg when war was declared, he was arrested
by the occupying Germans as an enemy alien. In October, he was given
permission to return to England via Koblenz, but was rearrested and
interned at Ruhleben, a detention camp for enemy civilians on a race-
course 10 kilometres west of Berlin. Garvice approached the Foreign
Office and the American Embassy in an attempt to obtain his release,
providing a certificate from Gribble's doctor stating that he was unfit
for military service.[1] But it was not until 8 September 1915 that a telegram from Amsterdam was posted in the entrance hall of the Authors'
Club: 'Released, returning, Gribble'. Set free as the result of a prisoner
exchange, he returned to work in the Ministry of Information. The club
committee resolved to hold a dinner in his honour, but Gribble requested that it be postponed until after the war. [2]

Not all the club's members were taken by surprise by the outbreak
of war. As early as April 1914, from his house, Max Gate in Dorchester,
the Club's president Thomas Hardy could hear the naval exercises in the

Channel, and was filled with foreboding. In his poem 'Channel Firing', the skeletons in a country church are awakened by distant gunfire:

> Again the guns disturbed the hour,
> Roaring their readiness to avenge,
> As far inland as Stourton Tower,
> And Camelot, and starlit Stonehenge.

Conan Doyle was in Canada when the Archduke was assassinated, arriving home on 19 July. His nephew, Oscar Hornung, wrote to him in August to say that he had volunteered for Kitchener's army, asking him to use his influence to get him accepted for active service. Though now 55, Conan Doyle volunteered himself. He was turned down.[3] Barry Pain was touring the United States. Although also well over age, he returned to join the anti-aircraft section of the Royal Naval Volunteer Reserve in April 1915, and was posted to a searchlight station on Parliament Hill until eye-strain forced him to abandon the work. In 1917, he became a member of the London Appeal Tribunal, adjudicating on claims for exemption from military service.

Some 300 members of the Authors' Club saw active service. Shackleton was a commander in the Royal Navy, but most served as junior officers. Horace Wyndham proceeded to France in 1914 as a railway transport officer graded staff captain, and was seconded to the Ordnance Corps in 1917 and the Army of the Rhine in 1918; he was awarded the Mons Star, the Allies Victory Medal and the War Medal.[4] Compton Mackenzie, commissioned as a captain in the Royal Marines, fought at Gallipoli, and subsequently ran an intelligence network out of Athens.

Jerrold abandoned his studies at Oxford to enlist. He spent the early months of the war in the Authors' Club, 'where Charles Garvice retailed the gossip of the Shires, Lucien Wolf gave the English point of view on the international situation, and Morley Roberts from a point of vantage in the club which he had occupied every afternoon for as many years as any one could remember, played, with eloquent bravura, the part of the adventurer in strange lands to whom a night spent in an ordinary bed was a startling luxury.'[5]

It was a short-lived idyll. In October, Jerrold joined the Royal Naval Division as a sub-lieutenant and went for training at Crystal Palace. By the following May, he too was fighting at Gallipoli. In November 1916, advancing in the front line in the Ancre Valley, he felt a blow and realised that his left arm was hanging somewhere behind his back. Although he was relieved not to lose it altogether, the shattered limb was useless for most purposes, and would cause him pain for the rest of his life.

Alec Waugh, the brother of Evelyn and author of the controversial memoir *The Loom of Youth*, fought at Passchendaele, was captured by the Germans near Arras in March 1918, and spent the rest of the war in PoW camps.[6] Hugh Kingsmill Lunn, serving in the Royal Naval Volunteer Reserve, was also taken prisoner after blundering into a German patrol on the Somme in February 1917. After 14 months at Karlsruhe, he was transferred to Mainz citadel, where he found Waugh reading a copy of Lytton Strachey's *Eminent Victorians*.[7]

Shortly after hostilities began, some members of the club objected to the premises being used by visitors with 'pro-German sympathies'. The committee discussed the matter at two meetings and, as a result, the following notice was displayed in the vestibule:

> All Members, or guests of Members, of German or Austro-Hungarian origin, who are not naturalized British subjects, are informed that they are not eligible for admission to the Club premises during the war.

Despite such anti-German sentiment, Hueffer clung stubbornly to his Teutonic surname throughout the war, only changing it to Ford, after his maternal grandfather Ford Madox Brown, in 1919.

Within days of the declaration of war, the Prime Minister, H.H. Asquith, asked the Liberal politician Charles Masterman to develop a secret bureau to counter German propaganda and promote the British point of view abroad. To conceal its activities, he decided to run his War Propaganda Board, which was partly funded by the Secret Service, from the National Health Insurance Commission's offices at Wellington House in Victoria. On 2 September, he summoned a number of prominent writers, including Doyle, Hardy, Kipling, Galsworthy, John Masefield, Zangwill, Wells, Chesterton, Bennett and Hueffer to a secret meeting, at which many of them agreed to write books and pamphlets for the board. Bennett recorded his impressions of the meeting in his diary:

> Masterman in the chair. Zangwill talked a great deal too much. The sense was talked by Wells and Chesterton. Rather disappointed in Gilbert Murray, but I like the look of little R.H. Benson. Masterman directed pretty well, and Claude Schuster and the Foreign Office representative were not bad. Thomas Hardy was all right.[8]

All the writings, while ostensibly independent publications, were commissioned and approved by Wellington House. Bennett contributed an article entitled 'Liberty: A Statement of the British Case', which first appeared in the *Saturday Evening Post*. It was subsequently expanded and published as a pamphlet by Hodder & Stoughton.

Hueffer was already a good friend of Masterman's; they had met in 1897, playing golf, and he and Violet Hunt had holidayed with Masterman and his wife Lucy on the Rhine in 1913. In 1915, with the assistance of Richard Aldington, Hueffer wrote *When Blood Is Their Argument* and *Between St. Dennis and St. George*. Both works discussed differences between European nations, stressing that Germany had developed an authoritarian, militaristic culture while Anglo-Saxon countries prospered under more democratic forms of government.

A Committee for the Purchase and Publication of Books was established, and met daily under the direction of Anthony Hope. Masterman was acutely aware of the need to win hearts and minds in the United States, which remained neutral and had a substantial population of German descent. To this end, he set up a special department, headed by Gilbert Parker. Married to a wealthy New York heiress, Parker had travelled extensively in the United States, where he was well known to the reading public through his bestselling novels.

Parker understood the need for subtlety. 'Any attempt to have an organised British propaganda in the United States,' he told his staff, 'would be fatal. In American propaganda the only plan is to do good by stealth.' He assembled a sophisticated network to distribute Wellington House literature, using *Who's Who* to assemble a mailing list of 100,000 American 'leaders of opinion' to whom he posted books from his private address, 'With the Compliments of Sir Gilbert Parker'. Often he would send signed copies of works by eminent authors, including Doyle, Hope, Wells, Hueffer, A.J. Toynbee and G.M. Trevelyan – attractive gifts that few would refuse.

The war came to British soil in January 1915, when the first Zeppelin attack killed two people in Great Yarmouth and King's Lynn; the airships, launched from occupied Belgium, reached the capital at the end of May in a raid that killed 28 people and injured another 60. Aerial bombardment was a new and terrifying development, and Britain was woefully unprepared. The government's advice was to 'go in the cellar and take your whisky with you'. Though eclipsed by the raids of the Second World War, this 'First Blitz' created a great deal of fear, panic and resentment. By the summer of 1916, when the development of incendiary bullets enabled the anti-aircraft batteries to mount an effective defence, at least 550 British civilians had been killed.

In a letter to the poet F.S. Flint, Aldington described a raid on London in September 1915, which took 22 lives and injured 87:

> My God, we had shrapnel bursting overhead for 15 minutes, & saw the Zeppelin wondering where it would plant its next bomb! The Post Office was just missed; Wood St., Cheapside is burnt to the ground; an immense warehouse in Farringdon Road is smashed & every window for a hundred yards around broken; Queen's Square has a bomb in the middle of it, every window in the Square smashed, frames & doors broken – one window of the Poetry Book Shop smashed![9]

As these ghostly Leviathans rained bombs on London, Hueffer collaborated with Violet Hunt on a curious little book called *Zeppelin Nights*. Subtitled *A London Entertainment*, it takes the form of a series of linked stories, in the manner of Boccaccio's *Decameron*, told to a group of friends to divert them from the boredom and anxiety of waiting out the raids. While the 23 stories, which range in time from ancient Greece to the recent coronation of King George V, are mostly by Hueffer, the framing narrative is by Hunt. A group of intellectual friends attend a series of parties at the home of Mrs Candour Viola (clearly modelled on Hunt herself) where they are entertained by readings by her friend Serapion Hunter (Hueffer). As the Zeppelin nights wear on, the war intrudes into the narrative with increasing frequency. Shocked by the deaths of friends at the front, Serapion decides to enlist. His explanation reproduces Hueffer's actual words: 'Damn it all, haven't I been for forty years or so in the ruling classes of this country; haven't I enjoyed their fat privileges, and shan't I, then, pay the price?'

On 30 July 1915, Hueffer – though he was already 41 – obtained a commission as a captain in the Welch Regiment, partly to escape from his increasingly troubled relationship with Hunt. After a year training in Wales, his unit was sent to France in July 1916 as the Battle of the Somme was raging. Although not in the front line, his battalion was stationed in the first line of transport in what was called Sausage Valley, behind Bécourt Wood, under heavy German shellfire. After ten days he was concussed by an exploding shell and taken to the casualty clearing station at Corbie. For 36 hours he could not remember his own name, and did not recover his memory fully for a month.[10]

While he was in hospital, the 9th Welch was relocated to the Ypres salient, and Hueffer had to make his own way there to re-join them. On 6 September 1916, he wrote to Joseph Conrad:

> Shells falling on a church: these make a huge '*corump*' sound, followed by a noise like crockery falling off a tray – as the roof tiles fall off… Screams of women penetrate all these sounds… I saw two men and three mules killed by one shell… When I was in hospital a man three beds from me died *very* hard, blood passing thro' bandages and he himself crying perpetually, 'Faith! Faith! Faith!'[11]

After a further spell in hospital suffering from pneumonia as a result of exposure to poison gas, Hueffer was invalided home. The night he got back to London, he telephoned Flint and invited him for sherry at the Authors' Club, asking him to get a volume of his poems published 'before the war ends or I am killed'. [12]

Ford was too traumatised by his experiences to write about the war in its immediate aftermath. In the 1920s, however, he embarked on the tetralogy that has been described by Anthony Burgess as 'the finest English novel about the First World War' and by Samuel Hynes as 'the greatest war novel ever written by an Englishman'. Published between 1924 and 1928, the four novels that make up *Parade's End* recount the misadventures of Christopher Tietjens, a stolid Yorkshire squire with a wayward wife and an anachronistic sense of honour, plunged into the horrors and bureaucratic imbecilities of industrialised warfare. It is not a novel of trench fighting in the manner of *All Quiet on the Western Front*, though its descriptions of combat are all the more harrowing for their restraint, but rather a sweeping panorama of English society before, during and after the war. With an unerring feel for the spirit of the age, it shows how the old order was irreparably fractured.

Aldington, meanwhile, was conscripted in June 1916. He embarked on 21 December 1916, and fought in France and Flanders, attached to the 6th battalion of the Leicestershire regiment as a private. He returned to England to train as an officer from June to November 1917, when he was commissioned in the 9th Royal Sussex Regiment, returning to the front in April 1918. While on active service, Aldington composed two volumes of poetry, *Images of War* and *Images of Desire*. In 'Concert', he records the after-effects of battle in a spasm of self-disgust:

> Undressing with indifferent eyes each girl,
> instead of women's living bodies
> I see dead men – you understand? – dead men
> With sullen, dark red gashes
> Luminous in a foul trench.

Dunsany joined the Royal Inniskilling Fusiliers as a captain. Probably on account of his age (he was 36), he was transferred to a reserve battalion in Derry. Ironically, his first taste of active service occurred when he was home on leave at Dunsany Castle in April 1916. On receiving news of the Easter Rising, he reported to British GHQ in Dublin and was sent to relieve an outpost in Amiens Street. Driving along the Quays, his party was ambushed by Nationalists near the Four Courts; the driver was injured, though not fatally, and Dunsany was hit in the face by a ricochet bullet. 'The man that took me prisoner,' he recalled, 'looking at the hole in my face… made a remark that people often consider funny, but it was quite simply said and sincerely meant: he said, "I am sorry."'[13]

His captor was none other than the celebrated Republican leader Peadar Clancy. 'Although in different uniforms, we are all Irishmen and you are all gentlemen,' Dunsany told him. His reaction was characteristic of the complex allegiances of the Anglo-Irish. Although he was raised a Protestant, many of his relatives were Catholic, and the family name was associated with the nationalist cause. His ancestor was a first cousin

Right: Sir Walter Besant, founder of the Authors' Club. 'Had Chivalry so brave a Knight?' wrote J.M. Barrie

Below: Besant's co-founder Oswald Crawfurd, a diplomat 'of melancholy but distinguished aspect' who 'made the club go'

Below: 1904 prospectus for the Authors' Club (Borough of Richmond upon Thames Local Studies Library and Archive)

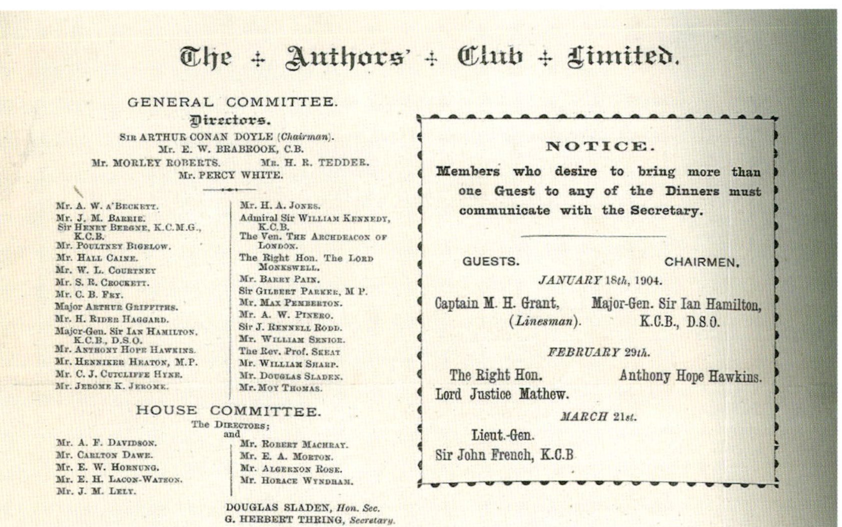

The ✢ Authors' ✢ Club ✢ Limited.

GENERAL COMMITTEE.

Directors.

SIR ARTHUR CONAN DOYLE (Chairman).
Mr. E. W. BRABROOK, C.B.
Mr. MORLEY ROBERTS.   Mr. H. R. TEDDER.
Mr. PERCY WHITE.

Mr. A. W. a'BECKETT.
Mr. J. M. BARRIE.
Sir HENRY BERGNE, K.C.M.G., K.C.B.
Mr. POULTNEY BIGELOW.
Mr. HALL CAINE.
Mr. W. L. COURTNEY
Mr. S. R. CROCKETT.
Mr. C. B. FRY.
Major ARTHUR GRIFFITHS.
Mr. H. RIDER HAGGARD.
Major-Gen. Sir IAN HAMILTON, K.C.B., D.S.O.
Mr. ANTHONY HOPE HAWKINS.
Mr. HENNIKER HEATON, M.P.
Mr. C. J. CUTCLIFFE HYNE.
Mr. JEROME K. JEROME.
Mr. H. A. JONES.
Admiral Sir WILLIAM KENNEDY, K.C.B.
The Ven. THE ARCHDEACON OF LONDON.
The Right Hon. The LORD MONKSWELL.
Mr. BARRY PAIN.
Sir GILBERT PARKER, M P.
Mr. MAX PEMBERTON.
Mr. A. W. PINERO.
Sir J. RENNELL RODD.
Mr. WILLIAM SENIOR.
The Rev. Prof. SKEAT
Mr. WILLIAM SHARP.
Mr. DOUGLAS SLADEN.
Mr. MOY THOMAS.

HOUSE COMMITTEE.

The DIRECTORS;
and

Mr. A. F. DAVIDSON.
Mr. CARLTON DAWE.
Mr. E. W. HORNUNG.
Mr. E. H. LACON-WATSON.
Mr. J. M. LELY.
Mr. ROBERT MACHRAY.
Mr. E. A. MORTON.
Mr. ALGERNON ROSE.
Mr. HORACE WYNDHAM.

DOUGLAS SLADEN, Hon. Sec.
G. HERBERT THRING, Secretary.

NOTICE.

Members who desire to bring more than one Guest to any of the Dinners must communicate with the Secretary.

GUESTS.	CHAIRMEN.
JANUARY 18th, 1904.	
Captain M. H. Grant, (Linesman).	Major-Gen. Sir Ian Hamilton, K.C.B., D.S.O.
FEBRUARY 29th.	
The Right Hon. Lord Justice Mathew.	Anthony Hope Hawkins.
MARCH 21st.	
Lieut.-Gen. Sir John French, K.C.B	

Above: menu for the inaugural dinner at 2 Whitehall Court, December 1908

Above left: floorplan of the premises at 2 Whitehall Court. Right, from top: a 1930s Authors' Club brochure shows Whitehall Court from Embankment Gardens and Whitehall Place, with the club's windows marked, and the same views in 2016

Above: the journalist C. Scott Lindsay joined the club in 1909 at the age of 21. He is pictured here in his first car, a 20hp Berliet which he drove all over Europe, writing articles on his trips for *The Car* magazine (courtesy of Michael Lindsay)

Below: Sir Arthur Conan Doyle demonstrates his enthusiasm for new technology on the cover of *Popular Wireless Weekly*

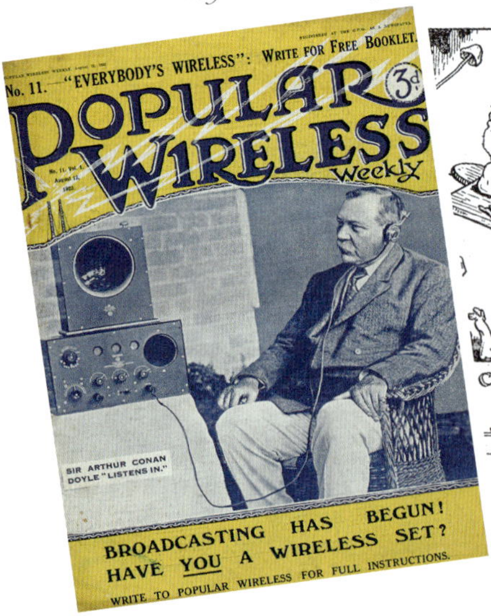

Above: Lindsay Symington sketched these comic bacteria for a 1909 dinner talk by the immunologist Almroth Wright

Right: Algernon Rose,
Secretary from 1908
to 1934. 'With a clear-
sighted policy, boundless
energy and self-sacrifice,
and inexhaustible tact,
[he] not only pulled the
club out of the fire,
but has made it one of
the most flourishing
organisations in London.'
This portrait by Arthur
David McCormick was
commissioned by the
Club after Rose's death
(Authors' Club)

Below: the Poet Laureate Alfred Austin addressed the club in 1909 on the authors
who were, in his view, England's greatest prose writer and poet respectively.
The son of Keats's painter friend Joseph Severn, who had followed his father's
profession, recalled Ruskin's kindness to him as a young artist

Left: 'I looked on Death in Flanders': Lord Dunsany, pictured in 1919 by the American portrait photographer Eugene Hutchinson (Mary Evans Picture Library)

Above: Ford Madox Ford, seen here in a sketch by Frederick Carter, was concussed and gassed while serving on the Western Front (Mary Evans Picture Library/ Grosvenor Prints)

Left: a 1909 dinner on naval gunnery sounds an ominous note of warning. 'Our most modern naval weapon,' Admiral Sir Percy Scott told the club members, 'is double the length of this long room'

Above: the club billiard room, seen in a 1930s brochure. Left: the Authors' Club billiard trophy was won by Sir Arthur Conan Doyle four times. Below: the library, or 'Silence Room', where Arnold Bennett wrote *Hilda Lessways*. Inset: the club bookplate, designed by C.R. Wylie in 1914

Above: J.M. Barrie, pictured around 1900. Above right: Morley Roberts: 'He *was* the Club.' Right: when the quill was inserted into this silver inkstand, a bell rang. Barrie used it to terminate his own speech at a dinner for Roberts in 1935

Left: a selection of books from the Authors' Club library, including Francis Gribble's 1929 memoir *Seen in Passing*, presented by the author

of Oliver Plunkett, the Archbishop of Armagh executed in 1681 for his alleged role in the Popish Plot and canonised as a Catholic martyr in 1975. Dunsany's uncle Sir Horace Plunkett was a prominent agricultural reformer and supporter of Home Rule, while his cousin Joseph Plunkett, the poet and member of the Irish Republican Brotherhood, was executed by the British for his role in the Easter Rising.

The Nationalist fighters took Dunsany to Jervis Street Hospital. After a slow recovery, which left one side of his lip permanently paralysed, he was declared fit for active service in October and posted to France. He too attempted to come to terms with the horrors he witnessed in Flanders in verse. The closing stanzas of his 'Songs from an Evil Wood', which reflect his experiences at Ploegsteert, outside Ypres, are a powerful expression of what we would now call survivor guilt:

> I met with Death in his country,
> With his scythe and his hollow eye
> Walking the roads of Belgium.
> I looked and he passed me by.
> Since he passed me by in Plug Street,
> In the wood of the evil name,
> I shall not now lie with the heroes,
> I shall not share their fame;
> I shall never be as they are,
> A name in the land of the Free,
> Since I looked on Death in Flanders
> And he did not look at me.

With too many staff on active service and many speakers unable to attend, the club dinners were discontinued. Only one was held during the war, when on 3 February 1916, Rider Haggard gave a talk on the After-War Care of Soldiers and Sailors. After pointing out that it was thanks to the efforts of Britain's servicemen that the club's members were able to assemble in relative peace and comfort that night, Haggard turned to a subject on which he would speak in the course of a lengthy tour of South Africa, Australia, New Zealand and Canada over the following months. After the war, he said, a great many men would want to embark on a different walk of life – an outdoor life. Because of the difficulty in obtaining smallholdings in Britain, he was convinced that land should be found for them to farm throughout the Empire. The project would also, he claimed, bind the Dominions more strongly to face whatever challenges might arise after the present war was over. He also alluded to the role of women in filling the places of the men who had joined the colours. 'Was it supposed that when the struggle was over all those women who had tasted the joys of independence would agree to cease their activities?' He was a great believer in the capacities of the female sex, he said, and had always been on the side of the Suffragists, so he thought the answer must be no.[14]

From the club's windows, the view of the Thames was obscured by a clutter of huts and bungalows built in Embankment Gardens to house the many new government departments brought into being by the war: the Directorate of Organisations, the Director-General of Military Railways; the Ministry of Munitions; and the Ministry of Labour.[15] Whitehall Court, meanwhile, was quietly becoming an unofficial nerve centre of the home front. In December 1916, widespread dissatisfaction with the conduct of the war resulted in the ousting of Asquith as Prime Minister and his replacement by David Lloyd George. The new premier immediately set about transforming the way the government was run. A small War Cabinet was established, with Sir Maurice Hankey as its Secretary, while Thomas Jones, first secretary of the Welsh Insurance Commission, was summoned to London to ensure things went smoothly.

With the War Cabinet installed in Whitehall Gardens and Mansfield Smith-Cumming running MI6 from an upstairs flat in Whitehall Court, the Authors' Club was a natural base for Jones's operations, particularly as the National Liberal Club next door was a bastion of Asquith's supporters and therefore off limits. W.G.S. Adams, the founder of the *Political Quarterly*, secretary to the Prime Minister, editor of the War Cabinet reports and a club member since 1916, proposed Jones for membership. Jones was what we would now call a spin-doctor, and his informal cabinet – which became known as the 'Garden Suburb' – was a controversial forerunner of Harold Wilson's 'kitchen cabinet' and Tony Blair's 'sofa government'. On 12 December 1916, he confided in his diary:

> I saw Sir Maurice Hankey and talked over the sort of work I
> might do. L.G. had spoken to him. I explained I didn't want to

touch office machinery but rather to act as a fluid person moving about among people who mattered and keeping the PM on the right path as far as possible. He quite understood.

Jones swiftly made the Authors' Club his centre of operations. On 12 January 1917, he hosted a dinner for a group of civil servants at the club, and was pleased to report that 'they have welcomed me into the inner circle of their discussions'. On 25 November, he proposed R.H. Tawney for membership.[16] The historian was a key member of the Romney Street group of Liberal intellectuals associated with *The Athenaeum* magazine, along with the social reformer James Joseph Mallon who, on Jones's recommendation, had been appointed commissioner for industrial unrest. On 9 January 1918, Tawney, Jones and Mallon dined at the club, with Sir Alfred Zimmern, then working in the Ministry of Reconstruction, Sir Hamar Greenwood and A.G. Gardiner, editor of the *Daily News*.

> The talk entirely about the War, and the relief we all felt at the speeches of the PM and [President Woodrow] Wilson… Towards the end of the evening I threw out a suggestion, which was warmly embraced. I argued that if the impending combing-out leads to strikes of a very serious character – as it probably will among the engineers – it may become necessary in the interests of national unity and for the prosecution of the War, to take every possible step to remove the prevailing mistrust of the War Cabinet in the ranks of Labour.
>
> The rank and file have no faith in Milner, Curzon, Carson, as likely to work for a democratic peace, nor do they trust the PM. But the PM is absolutely indispensable to the efficient running of the war. Therefore, I argued, it may become necessary to ask the other three to make the 'great sacrifice' of office, for the war's sake.[17]

As the war dragged on and the casualty lists lengthened, the internationalism of the pre-war years gave way to bitterness, and early in 1918 the executive committee added the following by-law to the club rules:

> That no person of German birth or nationality, whether naturalized or not, be eligible for membership of the Authors' Club, or be introduced as a visitor during the war, or until further notice.[18]

When the guns finally fell silent on 11 November 1918, Britain was left to come to terms with its bitter victory. Four great empires had fallen, and the political geography of Europe and the Middle East had changed beyond recognition. Back in 1915, Hueffer, with depressing foresight, had told Wyndham Lewis, 'When this war's over nobody is going to worry, six months afterwards, what you did or didn't do in the course of it… Within a year disbanded "heroes" will be selling matches in the gutter.' [19]

Millions were bereaved, hundreds of thousands physically or psychologically maimed, many demobilised servicemen returned to face unemployment and social unrest, and the continent was ravaged by a flu epidemic that would claim more lives than the war itself. Twenty-five members of the Authors' Club had been killed in combat. Among them was Lieutenant-Colonel Philip Blair Oliphant of the 11th Battalion, Royal Irish Rifles, who died of his wounds on 14 April 1918 at the age of 50. A member since 1913, he was, under the name Philip Laurence Oliphant, the author of *Little Red Fish*, *River of Vengeance*, *The Tramp* and *Edward VII as Sportsman*. John Stagg had also been a member since 1913; under the pseudonym John Barnett, he had published 12 novels including *The Luck of the Lanes*, *Geoffrey Cheriton* and *A Queen of Castaways*. He was serving as a lieutenant in the 16th Battalion Middlesex Regiment when he was killed, aged 35, on 24 September 1916.

The journalist Sydney Morris was killed at Suvla Bay during the Gallipoli landings, on 9 August 1915. Edgar Frere, the author of the novel *Rebels* and a light comedy *Match-Making in Mayfair*, served as a lieutenant in the 8th London Regiment, and died of his wounds in France on 22 May 1916. Lieutenant Reginald Tiddy, a lecturer in English Literature at Oxford University, was killed in France in August 1916. The theatre critic Sydney Brookfield, a captain in 17th Battalion Sherwood Foresters, was killed in action on 10 September 1916.

Many members lost sons and other close relatives. Rudyard Kipling, that staunchest of patriots, never came to terms with his bereavement after his son John was reported missing in action at Loos in 1915:

> 'Have you news of my boy Jack?'
> Not this tide.
> 'When d'you think that he'll come back?'
> Not with this wind blowing, and this tide.

Oscar Hornung, a second lieutenant in the 3rd Essex regiment, was killed on 6 July 1915 on the Yser Canal in the Ypres salient. Conan Doyle's son Kingsley survived the war, but died of flu in December 1918, his health undermined by injuries sustained in the Battle of the Somme. In the years to come, Doyle would make many attempts to communicate with the spirits of Kingsley and his nephew Oscar through séances.

Dunsany summed up the exhaustion and bitterness that greeted the end of the war, and the numbing consciousness of the legions of dead, in a bleak sonnet entitled 'A Dirge of Victory':

> Lift not thy trumpet, Victory, to the sky,
> Nor through battalions nor by batteries blow,
> But over hollows full of old wire go,
> Where among dregs of war the long-dead lie
> With wasted iron that the guns passed by
> When they went eastwards like a tide at flow;
> There blow thy trumpet that the dead may know,
> Who waited for thy coming, Victory.
>
> It is not we that have deserved thy wreath,
> They waited there among the towering weeds.
> The deep mud burned under the thermite's breath,
> And winter cracked the bones that no man heeds:
> Hundreds of nights flamed by: the seasons passed.
> And thou hast come to them at last, at last!

6

AFTERMATH

I find a good way of dating after the War is to take the General Strike,
1926, as the next milestone. I call 'post-war' between the War and the
General Strike. Then began a period of a new complexion...

Wyndham Lewis, Blasting and Bombadiering

On the signing of the Treaty of Versailles on 28 June 1919, the committee resolved to set up a tablet on the Authors' Club premises as a memorial to members who died in the conflict. The Monday night dinners were resumed though, owing to staff shortages, attendance was restricted to members for the time being. On 20 October, Garvice took the chair as Lord Leverhulme discussed the topic of 'Industrial Unrest'; on 15 December, Frederic Kenyon, Chief Librarian of the British Museum, spoke on the subject of 'Books and Libraries'; while on 26 January 1920, J.W. Fortescue, Librarian of Windsor Castle, discussed 'War History' with Anthony Hope in the chair.[1]

In June 1919, Hueffer wrote to his publisher James Pinker from the Authors' Club to inform him that he had changed his surname by deed poll to Ford, assuming the identity – Ford Madox Ford – by which he is now known. 'A Teutonic name is in these days disagreeable & though my native stubbornness would not let me do it while the war was on, I do not see why I shd. go on being subjected to the attacks of blackmailers indefinitely.'

That summer he finally broke off his relationship with Violet Hunt, and set up home with the young Australian painter Stella Bowen at a cottage, called Red Fort, in Pulborough in Sussex. To avoid giving Hunt his real address, he wrote to her from the Authors' Club, and in June of that year she turned up at the club with a bundle of his clothes, demanding to know his whereabouts.[2]

This was not the only embarrassment to beset the club in the immediate aftermath of the war. For some time, books had been disappearing from the library in substantial quantities. On 9 June 1920, a well-known journalist 'who had held a commission in the Army and done good service in the war' was detecting smuggling books out of the premises. A meeting was summoned to deal with this 'painful matter', at which the committee resolved not to prosecute him, but to expel him from the club.[3]

Despite an increase in the subscription fee, the decline in membership caused by the war was reversed in the year 1919–20, when membership reached 1438: 176 town members, 176 outer London, 413 country and 673 overseas.[4] From this high point, however, the numbers would slowly but steadily dwindle over the following decades.

On Friday 20 February 1920, Charles Garvice called at the club to check the agenda for the AGM, which he was due to chair the following Monday.[5] On the day of the meeting, however, the Secretary received a message to say that Garvice was too ill to attend. He had suffered a cerebral haemorrhage, and lay in a coma for a week before dying at his home in Richmond on 1 March. Gilbert Parker, who would succeed him as Chairman, attended the funeral, along with Francis Gribble, Herbert Thring, Douglas Sladen, Ernest Short and several other members. A wreath from the club was placed on his grave, and his portrait was hung in the dining room alongside that of Walter Besant.[6]

There was trouble brewing, however. The agreement made with Whitehall Court in 1908 had been due to run for ten years, and had thus expired in 1918. No new agreement had been made, with the lease simply being renewed from year to year. Furthermore, since 1911, instead of submitting the names of all candidates for the executive committee to a ballot of members, the officers had simply put forward those they considered most suitable. A Reform Movement of some 40 members was dissatisfied with this state of affairs, and concerned that the management of Whitehall Court was making an excessive profit from the club. Rumours were circulating that the Honorary Secretary, Algernon Rose, was on the payroll of Whitehall Court, in contravention of the rule that none of that company's employees could sit on the executive committee of the Authors' Club.

The three main instigators of the rebellion were Captain Hugh Pollard, a flamboyant intelligence officer and author of *A Busy Time in Mexico* and *The Book of the Pistol and Revolver*, David Stelling, a contributor to the *Saturday Review*, and Horace Wyndham. On 24 February 1922, a day before elections to the committee were due to close, Stelling returned his ballot paper with an angry letter to Rose saying that the procedure 'reduced the process of election to a mockery' and that he could 'only record my humble protest by declining to play a part in this farce'.

Immediately before the AGM on 27 February, the reformers submitted a memorandum demanding that an Extraordinary General Meeting be called to discuss these issues. When some 130 members assembled in the club library for the EGM at 4.30 pm on 29 March 1922, feelings were running high. Sir Gilbert Parker, in the chair, was obliged to deploy all his political experience and acumen, balancing conciliatory language and judicious concessions with fierce determination. 'I am very sorry that in my term of office as the Chairman of this club this difficulty should have occurred,' he told the meeting. 'But believe me this club is not going to die.' Behind the scenes, he and Gribble had been working hard to defuse the situation, persuading 10 of the rebels to withdraw their objection, and he knew that he had the upper hand.

Parker also understood that the Reform Movement's attack on the popular and hard-working Rose was its weakest point, and mounted an outraged defence of his integrity, pointing out that the club had asked Whitehall Court to reimburse the secretary's expenses 14 years previously, and that they amounted to no more than his lunches and telephone bills. 'There has been no more faithful friend in this club than the Honorary Secretary,' he said to cries of 'Hear, hear' and prolonged applause.

Parker then called on Major Hornsby, the managing director of Whitehall Court, to explain the financial situation and the relationship between his firm and the Authors' Club. 'I certainly cannot claim to be a literary man,' Hornsby reassured them, 'though I must confess that I have made some efforts in that direction by producing a little work which sets forth the advantages to residents in this most well-favoured building.' Although he sat on the boards of all the other proprietary clubs in Whitehall Court, 'neither I nor any of my colleagues have any desire to serve upon the executive committee of the Authors' Club... We do not think we are competent to enter into any of the abstruse matters which are discussed there.' He recalled the agreement of 1908, which saved the Authors' Club from ruin by handing over control of its finances to Whitehall Court Limited, since when 'our relations have been of a most friendly character'. He too mounted a vigorous defence of Rose who, through the allegations against him, had 'suffered a wound which will take a long time to heal'.

Beneath Hornby's self-deprecation lay a clearly implied threat. After deducting expenses such as rent, salaries and contributions to the staff welfare scheme, Whitehall Court had made a profit of no more than £148 from the Authors' Club during the previous year. This represented a poor return for its shareholders, and while 'from a purely sentimental point of view we should have feelings of regret at your departure... we are bound to consider what I might term the sordid aspect...'

On the first resolution in the memorandum, Parker insisted that the election procedure had 'worked well [as] proved by the prosperity of the club during the past eleven years', but promised to revert to the previous system in accordance with the wishes of the members. The motion was carried unanimously.

Douglas Jerrold said that he was not a signatory to the memorandum, but regretted the Chairman's suggestion that there were 'two factions' within the club. He explained that when he had served on the committee, a member had complained about the system of election; he had put the matter to the committee and had been overruled. That, he said, was as it should be; he did not want electioneering in the club.

Parker then stated that he did not wish to put the second resolution, that a joint committee be formed to consider new rules and regulations, because he believed it to be an unnecessary and unjustified attack on Rose, and he was sure it would be defeated. Ernest Short added that 'I feel and sympathise very deeply with Mr Algernon Rose with regard to this attack made upon him,' and urged that the resolution be voted on in order that it might be overwhelmingly defeated.

After thanking the Chairman for clarifying the position, and accepting that the 'gossip' about Rose being a salaried employee of Whitehall Court was incorrect, Pollard agreed to withdraw the resolution. Morley Roberts jocularly suggested 'a small alteration' – that 'all the words after the word "that" be eliminated' and replaced by an expression of the meeting's confidence in the executive committee. When Pollard agreed to second this motion, Roberts could not resist a colourful attack on the routed Reform Movement. 'We now know our Bolsheviks!' he declared, to laughter. 'The gentlemen in the background have formed a "Workmen's and Soldiers' Committee". I believe they have appointed a new Chairman who they have in their pocket... Captain Pollard may be the Trotsky or the little Trotsky; but who is Lenin?'

As for 'my friend Captain Pollard', Roberts added, 'he simply loves a row. He reminds me of the old woman who tried to get her husband to go home and he said; "No, I will not" and she said; "I want to fight you, go home..." They hoofed him out of Mexico, but he came back because there was a European War and that kept him quiet for some four or five years. He got shot. Well, sometimes I am rather sorry that he was not shot worse. But after that what, what did they do with him? Gentlemen, they put him in the Intelligence Office. I do not know why.'

The vote of confidence in the committee was passed unanimously.[7] At a Special General Meeting in December, Gribble announced that the management of Whitehall Court had agreed to renew the lease for a further seven years.[8] A curious postscript to this controversy, however, reveals that the reformers were right in their suspicions. In February 1937, two years after Rose had died, Gribble noted in a memorandum to the committee that while Rose was originally 'an Honorary Secretary in fact as well as in name', Whitehall Court had subsequently agreed to remunerate him. 'That arrangement worked smoothly as long as nobody noticed it,' Gribble noted drily, but after the revolt, 'in consideration of the services for which [the club] was indebted to him,' a compromise was reached whereby 'his stipend was described as an allowance for expenses'.[9]

In April 1922, the war huts that obstructed the view of the river were finally demolished, after questions had been asked in Parliament about the delay.[10] On 20 November, six days after the newly formed BBC had made its first official broadcast, club members witnessed a demonstration of a technology that would have a profound impact on their professional lives, when the military engineer Matthew Riall-Sankey of the Marconi Company discussed 'Wireless Discoveries' at a Monday dinner. Marconi himself was due to attend, but was prevented by illness, although he did provide a wireless set for the occasion.[11] Conan Doyle was fascinated by the new medium; that August, he had been pictured with a 'listening-in' apparatus and headphones on the cover of *Popular Wireless Weekly*.

It is possible that the dinner came about through the connections of a new member, Major John Munro, who had joined in February of that year. Born in 1883, this versatile man had worked at the Post Office until the age of 26, when he won a place to read English at Christ Church, Oxford. After taking his degree, he became assistant director of the Early English Text Society, editing Caxton's *Life of Jason* among other works. During the First World War he served as a radio engineer in the Royal Corps of Signals in Gallipoli and Palestine, and was awarded the MC. He went on to become general manager of the Egyptian Marconi Company, and in 1930 would move to Cable & Wireless Ltd.[12] In 1924, he was joined at the club by his friend and neighbour, the lexicographer Sir William Craigie, editor of the *Oxford English Dictionary*.

The film critic, poet and thriller writer Edmund George Cousins, who also joined the club in 1922, left a vivid description of its appearance and atmosphere at this period:

> On entering the door at the top of the bare stone stair one had the choice of turning right or left. On the right at the end of the passage was a good large lounge where we relaxed before and after lunch or dinner, and met for informal discussions of almost anything except literature – in those days one did not talk shop. Next to this was a small but adequate dining room, where the food, I understand, was hauled up from the main kitchen downstairs. Both these rooms overlooked the River Thames in all its glory.
>
> At the other end of the passage, if one had turned left, was a door with a tiny window and the sign 'Wait for the Stroke', which of course led into the billiards room. Having duly waited, straining to hear, and squinting, one opened the door and passed through into the reading-room, lined with a rich collection of Members' own-begotten books and general books and particularly a first-class showing of books of reference. This room overlooked Whitehall Court, where the parking was free and commodious, controlled by the four imposing commissionaires of the building in their dove-grey uniforms.

The reading-room was furnished with writing desks, at which one could write a letter to *The Times* or one's masterpiece… In a cubbyhole off this room was the office of the Secretary, dear old Algernon Rose, a Dickensian character if ever I met one; short, plump, red- faced, half-bald with a halo formed by spiky white hair. He was a Pickwick, a Fezziwig, and a Cheeryble Brother rolled into one; he ran the club most efficiently and unobtrusively, and, as I found to my advantage, was kind to new members; his influence was wide and beneficial.

On my first visit I met a number of members, each of whom confided in as that they did not really feel important enough as authors to belong to the Authors' Club, and it struck me that a club to which its members did not feel worthy to belong must be pretty good, and I summoned up the resolution to apply – and to my elation was elected, and for eight years found it extremely pleasant and useful. I lived with my wife and two young daughters at Blackheath, and every day when I came up to work (I was a wage-slave, editing film magazines) it was a welcome refuge, if only during my lunch-hour-and-a-half, and my family used it as a regular *rendez-vous* when they came to Town. In fact, it was impressed on our daughters, from the ages of eight and five, that if they were ever lost in London all they had to do was to hail a taxi and go to 2 Whitehall Court, where the doorman had been instructed to pay their fare.[13]

Cousins was a remarkable character with an eventful life and career. Born in 1893 in Tientsin, China, where his father was the representative of Jardine Matheson, he witnessed the 1900 Boxer Rebellion as a child. The family then returned to Britain, where they lived in Sidcup.[14] The young man then set out to travel around the world, until the outbreak of the First World War found him working as a farmhand in New Zealand. He signed up as a private in the Wellington Regiment, and sailed from Wellington for France on 16 October 1914. In the spring of 1917, he was back in New Zealand, where he married, before embarking for Europe again on 26 April as a second lieutenant in the 25th Reinforcements, Otago Infantry Regiment, D Company.[15] In addition to his writing for *Picturegoer Weekly*, in which he had a regular column called 'E.G. Cousins on the British Sets', he was the literary editor of the *Poetry Quarterly* and a prolific novelist.

The early 1920s saw a revival of interest in cricket, and in June 1923 several members expressed their willingness to form an eleven. A cricket sub-committee was set up, chaired by the theatre critic H.M. Walbrook, and a team of authors – including non-members – came together to play against a publishers' team. When the latter proved unable to assemble an eleven, actors were approached instead. The MCC let them play at Lord's on 14 September. During the summer of 1924, the Authors' Club XI played six matches, winning two, losing three and drawing a sixth against the Honourable Artillery Company at their ground near Finsbury Circus.[16]

In 1923, the committee ordered a billiard trophy from the firm Joseph Fray of Birmingham – a large shield of dark oak, with a copper relief in the centre, around which were small silver shields engraved with the names of all the winners of the handicap since it was started in 1910. That November, the shield was delivered and hung in the Billiard Room.[17]

In April that year, the committee heard that 240 acres of wooded parkland that surrounded the home of the club's first President, George Meredith, were under threat of development. *Country Life* magazine had already raised a large sum towards its purchase, but the acre immediately adjoining Flint Cottage was still up for sale. Major Gordon Home, the author of several books on travel and the countryside and a Fellow of the Society of Antiquaries, proposed that club members contribute to raise the £28 needed to buy the land. A notice was displayed in the club hall, illustrated with a drawing of the scene by Major Home. The sum was raised by October, and a cheque sent to the Box Hill Trust. To identify the spot, it was suggested that an oak bench, made from timber felled in the neighbourhood, should be placed there, inscribed with the name of the Authors' Club.[18]

Rider Haggard, one of the last surviving original members, could look back with satisfaction on the club's achievements. On 7 October 1924, he noted in his diary:

> Yesterday I went to town to take the chair at the Authors' Club dinner to Sir Joseph Cook, the High Commissioner for Australia. Being the first of the season it was quite a function and very crowded. I met with a warm, and I might say, almost affectionate reception, who am one of the original members of the club that is now entering its 34th year.[19]

Sir Arthur Conan Doyle was still in regular attendance, and could often be seen at the billiard table; in 1923–4, he won the billiard handicap for the fourth time. Now in his sixties, he was increasingly preoccupied with spiritualism, and spent much time and effort attempting to prove the authenticity of photographs of fairies taken by two young girls in their garden in Cottingley, Yorkshire. Essentially a Victorian, he was alienated by the social and artistic developments of the 1920s. In January 1922, he had presided over a dinner for the playwright Henry Arthur Jones. This founding member of the Authors' Club had taken a blimpish turn in old age, attacking H.G. Wells and George Bernard Shaw for their alleged lack of patriotism, and remarking that Ibsen should have ended *A Doll's House* with Torvald 'pouring himself a stiff whisky and exclaiming "Thank God, I'm well rid of her".'

Doyle, while insisting that Shaw and Wells were his personal friends, took up the cudgels on Jones's behalf. Shaw, he told the dinner guests, had 'used his great powers, unfortunately, too often not in the useful criticism which braces the nation in its strength, but the destructive criticism which in other lands gives entirely false impression of the situation here'. He went on to berate Israel Zangwill, another friend, for misrepresenting Britain in his play *The Melting Pot*, which suggested that conditions for Jews were much better in the United States. At a time when a Jew (Rufus Isaacs, the Marquess of Reading) could hold the offices of Lord Chief Justice of England and Viceroy of India, he added, 'a little recognition on the part of a prominent writer would be in good taste'.[20]

Nor were such views confined to literature. In May 1925, the Prime Minister Stanley Baldwin unveiled a monument to the writer and naturalist W.H. Hudson in Hyde Park. Jacob Epstein's *Rima*, a vigorously Modernist depiction of the heroine of Hudson's 1904 novel *Green Mansions*, provoked an outcry. 'Take this horror out of the Park,' screamed the *Daily Mail*. The row went on all summer and in to the autumn. On 5 October, the artist John Collier addressed an Authors' Club Monday night dinner, chaired by Francis Gribble, on the subject of 'Art Tendencies'. A pupil of Alma-Tadema famed for sensuous, late Pre-Raphaelite canvases such as *Lady Godiva*, *Clytemnestra* and *A Glass of Wine with Caesar Borgia*, Collier (1850–1934) was a man out of time and out of sympathy with recent artistic developments. In a diatribe reminiscent of

Alfred East's attack on the Post-Impressionists 15 years earlier, the old painter launched a vitriolic attack on modern art in general and Epstein's *Rima* in particular.

'Here you have a female figure purporting to represent an exquisitely beautiful girl,' he told his audience. 'What do we get? I have no hesitation in calling it a bestial figure, horribly misshapen, with enormous claw-like hands and withered, pendulous breasts, an enormous and distorted pelvis, and head and face of a microcephalous idiot.

'Nearly all the critics and highbrows,' he went on, 'go into ecstasies over the monstrous perversion of the female form. If they met a woman like that in the street they would flee from her shrieking, but because it is by Epstein they are almost willing to embrace her,' he added, to laughter and cheers.[21]

The day after Collier's speech, the *Morning Post* – whose editor, H.A. Gwynne, was an Authors' Club member – carried a letter demanding the removal of Epstein's 'inappropriate and even repellent' work. Among the signatories were Collier, Conan Doyle, Alfred Munnings and Hilaire Belloc.[22] Epstein, who exhibited regularly at the Leicester Galleries, replied in an interview with the *Manchester Guardian* the next day. 'Of course I feel honoured because the Hon. John has directed this violent attack against me,' he began disarmingly. 'He has what modern scientists call "feminine complex" on the brain. He is not only distressed about women in art but about women altogether… We talk in two different languages. I am concerned with sculpture and art and he is very much concerned with nudes and things of that sort.'[23]

On 23 November, the artist Muirhead Bone published a 'Reply to Advocates of Removal' in *The Times*, defending the sculpture and deploring 'any proposal to remove so completely authorised a work'. Among the many signatories were Arnold Bennett and Morley Roberts, a friend of W.H. Hudson, along with George Bernard Shaw, Hugh Walpole, the sculptor Eric Kennington and the former Prime Minister Ramsay MacDonald.[24]

Less than a year later, modern art would lose its staunchest champion at the Author's Club in mysterious and tragic circumstances. On 6 April 1926, Wilfred Phillips, the co-founder of the Leicester Galleries, was found unconscious at a firing range off Haymarket with a gunshot wound to his head. He was taken to Charing Cross Hospital but was dead on arrival.[25] Guy Doran, the proprietor of the range, told the coroner's inquest three days later that Phillips, 48, who was unknown to him, had come to the range and asked to practise with a small revolver. As there was none available, he gave him a Colt automatic. 'He handled it as if he understood it,' Doran said. 'His first shot was rather bad, but the next two were very good.' After the sixth shot, Phillips fell to the ground. Charles Phillips testified that his brother was not in financial difficulties, had never threatened suicide, and that there was no history of mental illness in the family. While noting that 'by the track of the bullet it did not seem likely it was an accident,' the coroner returned an open verdict.[26]

There was more conflict to come. On 1 May 1926, the Trades Union Congress announced a General Strike in support of coal miners in the north of England, Scotland and Wales who had been taking industrial action against an enforced cut in pay. At midnight on 3 May, the country ground to a halt. With more than four million union members called out, the iron and steel, building, engineering, shipbuilding, chemical, textile and printing industries all ceased production; there were no trains, buses or trams, and no national or local newspapers.

In a climate of fear and suspicion of the Soviet Union, the strike was widely seen as a call to Bolshevik insurrection. It was less than two years since a forged letter purporting to be from the Soviet official Grigori Zinoviev had helped to bring down Ramsay MacDonald's Labour government. What was originally an industrial dispute over pay and conditions escalated into an overt class conflict, each side pursuing its own, mutually antagonistic interests.

Baldwin's government set up an Organisation for the Maintenance of Supplies (OMS) to deploy volunteers to keep essential services running. It also produced a newspaper, the *British Gazette*, while the TUC brought out its own publication, the *British Worker*. Many young middle and upper-class men signed up gleefully, like Charles Ryder in *Brideshead Revisited* and Jon Forsyte in Galsworthy's *Swan Song*, regarding the whole thing as an enormous lark. Some writers rallied to the workers' cause – at the instigation of Tawney, Leonard Woolf circulated a petition in support of the strikers and calling for a negotiated settlement, and the young Auden (who would later join the Authors' Club) drove a truck for the TUC – but many club members were unsympathetic. Conan Doyle was appalled by the strike, regarding socialism as 'un-English'.[27] Bennett was not opposed to the idea of a strike in itself, but saw it as 'a political crime' to lead out men 'who hadn't a chance when the overdogs really set themselves to win'.[28]

The response of Compton Mackenzie was ambivalent to say the least. He was a socialist, and a friend of the Scottish poet Hugh MacDiarmid, a local organiser of the strike, which he commemorated in *The Drunk Man Looks at a Thistle*; in 1928 the pair founded the left-of-centre National Party of Scotland, the precursor of today's SNP. Yet the only mention Mackenzie makes of the strike in his autobiography is to express his worry that it would affect the sales of his latest novel: 'I suppose this will kill *Fairy Gold* dead. Only two notices so far.' A month later, travelling to Inverness, he complained that train services had not yet recovered from the effects of the action.[29]

The Authors' Club stayed open throughout the nine days of the strike: 'The Club Staff, despite exceptional difficulties, carried on their duties admirably, and while the publication of newspapers was suspended, members took advantage of a "Loud Speaker" in a reception room on the ground floor of the premises, which gave Wireless news bulletins five times daily.'[30] Because of the strike, the first cricket matches of the season had to be cancelled, but once it was over, the Authors' Club XI played Neasden, Chingford, the Hosatus C.C., Three Bridges (in pouring rain) and Broxbourne.[31] The 1927 season, however, was to be the Authors' Club XI's last. On 4 May, the team defeated the Honourable Artillery Company at Finsbury by 157 runs; on the 25th, they met Rickmansworth, a strong side that included several county players and made 248 runs for 4 wickets against the Authors' 123. Subsequent fixtures had to be cancelled, however, because of poor weather and a lack of players. As a result, the committee resolved that unless the team were made up of club members, it could not continue to call itself the Authors' Club XI.[32]

In the absence of newspapers, the General Strike offered a historic opportunity to the fledgling BBC. Established in 1922 as the British Broadcasting Company, it was financed by a licence fee of 10 shillings – payable by anyone who owned a receiver – but take-up had been slow.

To defend the interests of the newspapers, it had been restricted to broadcasting news only after 7pm; but now its general manager, John Reith, obtained permission to run news all day. Skilfully resisting Cabinet demands to make the BBC a mouthpiece of government, he avoided the inflammatory anti-strike rhetoric of the *British Gazette* while fundamentally supporting the status quo. The following December, the BBC was incorporated under Royal Charter as the British Broadcasting Corporation.[33]

Two days after the strike was defeated, on 14 May, Rider Haggard died, aged 68. The founding generation of the Authors' Club was passing away. Thomas Hardy died at his home at Max Gate in Dorchester on 11 January 1928. The furore over *Jude the Obscure* long forgotten, his widow received telegrams of sympathy for the King and Queen, hailing him as England's foremost man of letters. A delegation from the Authors' Club, including Conan Doyle, Rose and Thring, attended the funeral in Westminster Abbey. Conan Doyle said that 'Thomas Hardy came nearer to nature in his writing that any other contemporary writer, in my opinion.'

'Although he was rarely seen at the club in recent years,' said Rose, 'he was tremendously popular with everyone. When we gave dinners or ladies' nights he would never forget in his absence to send a telegram of good wishes.'[34] The vacant Presidency was first offered to Kipling, who declined,[35] and then to Barrie, who accepted. On 5 May 1928 another founding member, Barry Pain, died of heart failure at his home in Bushey, Hertfordshire.

That month the club put on a lavish dinner at the Hotel Cecil on the Strand for the Conservative politician Lord Birkenhead. Born F.E. Smith, this friend of Winston Churchill and former Lord Chancellor was now Secretary of State for India. As a young MP, Smith was accustomed to use the lavatory at the National Liberal Club on his way to the Houses of Parliament. When asked if he was a member, he is said to have replied, 'Oh, I didn't know it was a club as well.' A *Vanity Fair* cartoon of Smith adorns that facility to this day. A friend described him as 'pure 18th century', and his prodigious intake of alcohol led to his death aged only 58 just two years after the club dinner.

Addressing the mixed audience on the subject of 'Women Writers', Birkenhead seized their attention with the provocative statement that 'woman cannot hope to rival man as a creative literary artist of the first rank'. He then proceeded to disprove it. Praising Jane Austen's 'good humoured assumption of women's intellectual equality with man in everything that is of vital importance', he went on to demonstrate a nuanced and well-informed appreciation of modern literature. He dismissed the contention that there were no contemporary women writers of the calibre of George Eliot, saying, 'That sort of lament is heard in every generation, and will probably continue to be heard until the end of time...

'The modern novel,' he added, 'differs greatly from the novel of the seventies and eighties... as in another branch of art, the work of a Cubist or a Futurist, or a Post-Impressionist is different... from the meticulous inventions of a Pre-Raphaelite conviction. And it is in fiction of this modern and unrestricted type that women are beginning to hold their own.' The books of May Sinclair, Storm Jameson and Rebecca West revealed 'creative powers of a high order', he believed, while it was 'hardly possible to estimate the loss to literature entailed by the premature death of Miss Katherine Mansfield.'[36]

On 28 September, Victor Leuliette was found drowned at Ramsgate, aged 53, having left home at 5 am wearing a vest, nightshirt, overcoat and slippers. The inquest was told that his nervous system had recently 'gone to pieces', and that he had undergone psychoanalysis but found it 'a disease worse than the original one from which he had suffered'.[37] Sadly, this was not the first time that this well liked and respected member of the Authors' Club had 'gone to pieces'. Back in 1910, Leuliette had been charged with theft at Bow Street Magistrate's Court after stealing several books from Mudie's Library in New Oxford Street, despite having more than enough money on him to pay for them. His landlady told the court that he had been agitated and had not eaten for several days. 'The only explanation I can give for my momentary aberration,' he told the police, 'is that the principal of my training college has told me that I am almost certain to be dismissed from the college because I am in love with one of the students.'[38] The Ramsgate coroner returned a verdict of found drowned.[39] Algernon Rose attended Leuliette's funeral on behalf of the Authors' Club.[40]

That year, the American novelist and playwright Thornton Wilder, newly awarded the Pulitzer Prize for *The Bridge of San Luis Rey*, joined the Authors' Club. Though he would live in Connecticut from 1929 until his death in 1975, he remained a member throughout his life, keeping a room at Whitehall Court, with sweeping views over the Thames, where he would stay whenever he was in London. He was elected to the general council in 1932.

The question of censorship was raised once again in December 1928, when a club dinner was addressed by the Home Secretary William Joynson-Hicks. 'Jix', as he was known, was a stern evangelical much ridiculed for his attempts to suppress London nightclubs in the Roaring Twenties. He assured the Authors' Club that it was not within his remit to discuss what did or did not constitute indecent literature. In four years, he claimed, there had been only two books which he thought it his duty not to stop, but to put before the magistrates.[41]

The Home Secretary was being disingenuous; since his appointment in 1924, he had worked closely with the Director of Public Prosecutions Sir Archibald Bodkin to prevent the distribution of books of which he disapproved. The two titles in question were James Joyce's *Ulysses*, which he had described as 'this loathsome book' and ordered customs to impound, and Radcliffe Hall's *The Well of Loneliness*, which he forced its publisher, Jonathan Cape, to withdraw on pain of prosecution.[42] Just a month after Joynson-Hicks gave his speech to the Authors' Club, British customs, acting on direct instructions from the Home Office, began seizing copies of D.H. Lawrence's *Lady Chatterley's Lover*.[43]

On 7 July 1930, Conan Doyle died of a heart attack at his home in Sussex. Gilbert Parker, Rose, Lacon Watson and E.W. Lancaster represented the club at his funeral in Crowborough. Parker paid tribute to 'a splendid man who had always been a faithful friend to the Authors' Club'. In his will, Sir Arthur left £50 to the Authors' Club 'to be used for the greater comfort of the members'. Several members suggested that the bequest be spent on 'a wireless set… with earphones to be used in the Club rooms'. 'The Engineer of one of the foremost Electrical Companies' was sent for, but unfortunately reported that because of the number of electrical substations in the vicinity the reception would be too poor, so it was decided to spend the bequest on history books for the club library instead.[44]

A plaque in Sir Arthur's memory was set up in the club and unveiled at a dinner on 2 May 1932. Francis Gribble, Gilbert Parker, Lord Gorell and the club's Librarian, Ernest Short, all spoke in tribute to their friend. Theirs 'was not a big library, nor a perfect library,' Short declared. It 'was not like the British Museum, a stronghold of learning, nor yet the London Library, nor even the library of the National Liberal Club next door… but it was definitely better than the Golfers'.' (Laughter and cheers.)

He went on to quote a Japanese poem:

> Scatter your blossoms, cherry tree, I pray,
> To keep my friends still longer by my side.
> Quick with your drifting snow of blossoms hide,
> Oh, hide the road by which he thinks to go away.

The friend, Short explained:

> left behind him a host of fragrant memories, so that it seemed as if he were still there in the flesh. His many gifts would assure Arthur Conan Doyle the same fragrant immortality to those who worked in that Silence Room and among those who frequented that Club. Seeing his books in the Lounge, his name upon the Billiards Shield, and those shelves of modern history books, they would be assured that their friend [had joined] that Choir Invisible that George Eliot spoke of:

> > Of those immortal dead who live again
> > In minds made better by their presence…[45]

7

CLEVER HOPES EXPIRE

The decade just ended may be legitimately regarded as unusually eventful. There can seldom in ten years have been fewer days on which a chief sub-editor was embarrassed for lack of news.

Malcolm Muggeridge, *The Thirties*

In 1930, the Authors' Club acquired a dash of Hollywood glamour when Douglas Fairbanks became a member, on the strength of his achievements as a screenwriter. Appropriately, his son, Douglas Fairbanks Junior, would later star in the film of Anthony Hope's *The Prisoner of Zenda*. For many across Britain, however, the Thirties was a decade of great financial hardship, and authors were no exception. On 8 March 1937, the novelist Hugh Walpole told an Authors' Club dinner that there were 'far too many authors and far too many books'. He believed it was no longer true that 'no good book passed unnoticed. A great many books worthy of attention were scarcely seen.'[1]

For every writer who enjoyed the massive sales of an Anthony Hope, a Rider Haggard or a Conan Doyle, there were many more who struggled to make a living. The Authors' Club was active on their behalf, particularly in supporting their applications to the Royal Literary Fund (RLF). Established in 1790, and funded by bequests and donations from writers, the RLF offers grants to published authors in financial difficulties. Among its beneficiaries was James Joyce, who was awarded £75 after he was forced to leave Trieste for Zurich on the outbreak of the First World War.[2] Ford Madox Ford had also applied back in 1907, but was rejected because his 'income and debts [were] outside the scope of the Fund'.[3]

Morley Roberts, 'present means of support – his own pen', had found himself in difficulties as early as 1909 when he and his family were beset by ill health. His stepdaughter Vere died of appendicitis, and he too then contracted it, followed by thrombosis and pneumonia; his wife Alice's health also collapsed. Anthony Hope, who sat on the RLF committee, wrote in support of his application: 'He has worked hard and courageously, and only a chain of misfortune has compelled him to seek the assistance of the fund.' In July 1909, Roberts was awarded £250.[4]

Alice died in 1911 and, as a distraction from his grief, Roberts embarked on the novel *The Private Life of Henry Maitland*, based on the life of his friend George Gissing. Despite its acclaim, Roberts abandoned fiction soon after the First World War to devote himself to science, publishing titles such as *Warfare in the Human Body: Essays on Method, Malignity, Repair and Allied Subjects* (1920). Although he had no scientific training, his attempts to combine sociology and pathology to understand the causes of cancer met with the approval of a number of eminent medical men.[5] They did not, unfortunately, enjoy the commercial success of his novels, and by 1922, now 65, he was in serious financial difficulties once more. 'There is no doubt,' noted the RLF secretary John Cole Marshall, 'that his earnings powers have recently decreased.' Rather than make an award itself, the fund successfully petitioned Downing Street to award Roberts a Civil List pension.[6]

To cheer Roberts, the club invited him to address a Monday night dinner at Whitehall Court on 7 October 1935, on the subject of 'Science, Literature and Life'. The guest of honour presented a striking figure: 'He was tall, very thin without being slight, since he had broad shoulders; he had a narrow face, at once delicate and strong, the skin not so much lined as weathered, like old wood, with a fine aquiline nose and deep-set eyes under strong eyebrows: the mouth was hidden by a moustache very like those worn years later by war-time airmen.'[7]

J.M. Barrie, making a rare public appearance, presided. At the end of the dinner, after members had sung the first verse of *Auld Lang Syne*, he announced: 'I was just about to sing you the extra verse when, behold, our secretary came and put this into my hands.' Before him were the silver quill and inkwell that triggered a bell to signal the end of the speeches. Barrie dipped the pen in the well and sat down.

Horace Annesley Vachell proposed Roberts's health. In reply, Roberts recalled his early days when he was destitute in San Francisco. What a great thing it would have been if he could have had that dinner then, when he had no money, nowhere to go, and no friends.[8] Roberts now had friends and places to go but, once again, no money. Herbert Thring, who had resumed the secretaryship of the Authors' Club, was not a man to refuse to help an author in trouble, and did not fail Roberts in his hour of need. On 27 November, he wrote to Marshall about 'the case of Morley Roberts'. It is clear from the exasperated tone of his letter that even Thring was losing patience with Roberts, and coming to regard him as his own worst enemy:

> We endeavoured to get him to apply to the RLF. I am sorry to say that through some false pride on his part, he refuses to make any application or even to state that he will receive any grant that the Fund might choose to make him. I am very disappointed at the whole matter, not only because I am a close friend of Roberts, but also because I value his literary work, and know his financial position.
>
> I am afraid his plunge into the scientific world has rather upset his mind. He would gladly, I think, receive an addition to his Civil List pension if it was given to him on the ground of his scientific work, which he reckons is a thousand times more valuable than the books he has written, and has really cost him heavily in the income he might have received from his books. Well, there it is, and I am afraid there is nothing more to be said.[9]

Horace Wyndham's financial difficulties dated back to the outbreak of war. 'My income from authorship has practically ceased,' he wrote in November 1914, pointing out that he had still received no royalties on a book published in 1913 and was 'unable to collect various sums of money due to me'. Accepting a commission in the Army had compelled him to abandon his literary work, on top of which he had had to pay for his own uniform. His application – hardly helped by Barrie's lukewarm endorsement that he had 'read one or two of Mr Horace Wyndham's books, and though he considers their literary merit is mild he thinks they justify sufficiently a claim' – was refused.

Wyndham tried again in 1922, stating that his income consisted mainly of 'interest on investments (good and doubtful), authorship of books, and free-lance journalism'. The RLF attempted to get him a Civil List pension, but Downing Street rejected the application, partly on the basis of Barrie's letter, stating bluntly that 'his work is mediocre'. The RLF awarded him £75 on this occasion.[10]

Philip Walsingham Sergeant (1872–1952), who joined the Authors' Club in 1899, was an 'author and journalist all my life since the time I left Oxford', specialising in chess and popular history. 'My main line of writing, historical biography,' he wrote to the RLF on Authors' Club paper in October 1930, 'unfortunately brings me more praise than money. Few publishers take the trouble to push a book after the first four weeks.' Supported by Thring, a friend of 30 years, his application was rewarded with a grant of £75. In March 1937, however, the breakdown of his marriage left him in further difficulty. 'My wife deserted me and compelled me, against my will, to divorce her in 1935,' he explained. He was 'dependent entirely on book writing and occasional journalism'. He was awarded a grant of £100 from the fund.[11]

Perhaps the saddest case, however, was that of Herbert Morrah. The author of a volume of poems called *The Shepherd* and the romantic novels *A Serious Comedy* and *The Faithful City*, Morrah joined the Authors' Club in 1909. In February 1914, he applied to the RLF for a grant, stating that he had edited the *Literary Year Book* for four years, which 'involved me eventually in heavy financial loss, from the effects of which I have never really recovered'. He had a son at Oxford to support, and there was a bill of sale on his furniture. He was awarded £75.

During the First World War, Morrah had served as a lieutenant in naval intelligence; his son had also served in the war before resuming his studies at Oxford. By 1920, he was in difficulty once more. In support of his application, Rose wrote, on Authors' Club paper, that he 'did excellent service at the Admiralty during the war, but in consequence of matters for which he has been in no way responsible, has latterly lost nearly everything. You will see by the heading of this paper that he is a member of the executive committee of the Authors' Club. This shows that he is held in high esteem by the body of members who elected him…' He was awarded £50.

Despite a period of work as literary secretary to Lord Birkenhead in 1924–5, this was by no means the end of Morrah's troubles. In 1926, with a younger son at Westminster, he was forced to apply for help once again. 'I lost my home and all that I valued some four years ago,' he wrote, explaining that he would soon have to vacate the property he had rented in Notting Hill because the owner was returning from India. The strain proved too much for him; by the end of the following year he had been committed to the Maudsley hospital in south London. In April 1928, his wife Alice applied for another grant on his behalf, as he 'has been in a Mental Home since Nov 8th and is still <u>very</u> ill', 'incapable of carrying out his own affairs' and 'unable to carry on a lucid conversation'. A grant of £100 was awarded.[12] Morrah died in 1939, having been an 'invalid' for 12 years.[13]

Compton Mackenzie, then editor of *The Gramophone* and the writer of a weekly column in the *Daily Mail*, had troubles of a different kind. In October 1933, he published *Greek Memories*, an account of his wartime intelligence activities in Athens, where he had plotted to assist the Liberal Prime Minister Eleftherios Venizelos and oppose the pro-German King Constantine. Cassell, his publisher, was immediately forced to withdraw the book (it would not be published unexpurgated until 2011), and, on 4 November, he was prosecuted under the Official Secrets Act, charged with revealing the name of MI1(c) – later known as MI6 – the fact that it used Passport Control as a front for spying, and the identities of its then chief Mansfield Cumming and 16 agents still likely to be employed in the field. At his committal proceedings at the Guildhall, Mackenzie mounted a vigorous defence, arguing that he had revealed nothing that was not already public knowledge.

When the case came to trial before the Attorney General, Sir Thomas Inskip, at the Old Bailey on 12 December, Mackenzie's counsel, Henry Curtis-Bennett, told him he had no hope of winning; the case had been brought by MI5 and authorised at the highest level. If he were to plead guilty, he would avoid prison and be fined £500 plus £500 costs. The case was heard in camera, with the MI5 director Sir Vernon Kell watching grimly from the balcony. The prosecution was conducted with such in-eptitude – at one point Mackenzie had to inform the court that Mansfield Cumming had died in 1922 – that Inskip reduced the agreed fine to £100 plus £100 costs. MI5 would keep Mackenzie under surveillance for many years, but he had his revenge by writing a comic novel, *Water on the Brain,* about the farcical bungling of rival intelligence agencies.[14]

By now, the ranks of the old guard at the Authors' Club were thinning. In 1931, Rose told the *Manchester Guardian*; 'On the average about forty of our members die every year. This high number is because to be a member of the Authors' Club a man must have accomplished something, and this may take time. Consequently our average age is higher than in other clubs.'[15]

Arnold Bennett died on 27 March 1931 at his home in Baker Street, after contracting typhoid by drinking tap water in a Paris hotel. Hall Caine, one of the founding members, died in August. That same month, Major Hornsby, the managing director of Whitehall Court who had facilitated the club's reconstruction in 1908, died, and his son Noël was appointed in his place.[16] Anthony Hope Hawkins died on 8 July 1933, and on 6 September the club's Chairman, Sir Gilbert Parker, died suddenly at his flat in Whitehall Court. As his deputy, Francis Gribble, did not wish to stand for the position, Banister Fletcher was appointed. Rose himself died on 16 September 1934. He was succeeded as Secretary by Thring, who had last held the post in 1906, and had retired as Secretary of the Society of Authors the previous year.

Fortunately, the club was able to replenish its membership with writers of distinction. In 1932, H.G. Wells joined, despite an acrimonious row with Thring a couple of years earlier. Wells had embarked on an ambitious book he planned to call *The Science of Work and Wealth,* and as with his other non-fiction works, had employed collaborators to assist him. Unfortunately the two men, Hugh Vowles and Edward Cressy, did not get on, and after Cressy quit, Wells terminated Vowles's contract. Claiming unfair dismissal, Vowles turned to Thring at the Society of Authors to fight his case. The Society's lawyers wrote to Wells, advising him that he was in breach of contract and liable for damages. Acting on behalf of authors in contractual matters was, and remains, a fundamental remit of the Society, but Wells was so incensed that he wrote an account of the dispute entitled *The Problem of the Troublesome Collaborator,* had it privately printed at his own expense, and sent it to every member of the Society. In it, he alleged that Thring had 'jumped at once naturally and joyfully into the blackmailing attitude'. Only after Thring threatened to sue for libel did Wells apologise.

Rafael Sabatini (1875–1950) is best remembered today for tales of high adventure, sword-fighting and damsels in distress; two of his most famous works had been adapted into the classic Hollywood swashbucklers *Scaramouche* (1923) and *Captain Blood* (1924). However, these books represent a small fraction of Sabatini's output, which included 31 novels, eight collections of short novels and short stories, and six works of non-fiction. Known as Raffles or Rafe to his friends, Sabatini joined the Authors' Club in 1933. A director of Compton Mackenzie's publisher, Martin Secker, he was elected to the general council within a year of joining, and would remain a member of the club until his death in 1950.

When Albert Victor Alexander joined the club in 1935 as the author of *Parliament and the Consumer* and pamphlets on the Co-Operative Society and naval affairs, he had already served as First Lord of the Admiralty in the Labour administration of 1929 to 1931, returning to the backbenches after Ramsay MacDonald formed the National Government. A blacksmith's son from Weston-super-Mare, Alexander had begun his career as a Liberal champion of the Co-Operative movement before being elected as the Labour and Co-Operative MP for Sheffield Hillsborough in 1922. Universally known as A.V. Alexander, he was described by Beatrice Webb as 'a hard-headed administrative socialist… a singularly good-tempered, sane-minded, direct-speaking person'.[17]

Olaf Stapledon, who also joined the Authors' Club in 1935, was acclaimed as both an academic philosopher and science fiction writer. A conscientious objector during the First World War, he had driven an ambulance on the Western Front. For many years he worked as a tutor for the Workers' Educational Association (WEA) teaching philosophy, history and poetry to dockworkers, miners and railwaymen. His *A Modern Theory of Ethics* appeared in 1929, but it was the publication of *Last and First Men* that made his name. This ambitious fictional projection of human evolution over the next two billion years drew praise from both scientists and imaginative writers including J.B.S. Haldane, J.B. Priestley and H.G. Wells.[18]

Another new member that year was the Congregationalist theologian and principal of Mansfield College, Oxford, Nathaniel Micklem. Alarmed by the situation of churchmen of all denominations under the Nazis, Micklem visited Germany in 1937, becoming friends with the pastors Martin Niemöller and Dietrich Bonhoeffer and the philosopher Martin Buber, and bringing back a collection of clandestine church literature that he later donated to the Bodleian Library. His 1939 book *National Socialism and the Roman Catholic Church* warned that a 'ferocious and illimitable anti-Semitism' was central to Nazi ideology.[19]

Inevitably, the great struggles being fought out on the world stage reverberated within the walls of the Authors' Club, and often divided its members. In July 1935, the committee received a letter from the journalist Hubert Peet, who had been a member since 1933, complaining that some black friends of his had been refused admission. This was accompanied by several letters from other members supporting his protest. Peet was a man of strong principles. During the First World War he had served three terms of imprisonment, totalling 28 months, as an 'absolute' conscientious objector who refused to contribute to the war effort in any capacity. Now editor of the Quaker journal *The Friend*, he had toured the United States to assess the situation of the black population there.[20]

'The progress and culture of coloured people in America had been achieved in the face of serious obstacles,' he had written in the *Manchester Guardian*, adding that, just two generations from slavery, 'there were now over 20,000 coloured men and women in America completing their university courses.'[21]

Peet's memorandum has not been preserved in the archives, but its general tenor is clear from the minutes, and a letter of support from the colonial educator Arthur Mayhew does survive. 'A colour bar in the world of letters seems to me inconceivable,' he wrote. 'I should certainly not have applied for admission to the Club if I had been aware that it would be impossible for me to introduce as guests… the many Indian men of letters and scholars who are among my friends.'

In response, Thring argued that while there was nothing in the club rules explicitly excluding men of colour, it was 'a matter of practice' and could not be changed without the agreement of Whitehall Court. A sub-committee was set up, consisting of Thring and the novelist William Henry Williamson, to discuss the matter with Noël Hornsby. In the meantime, Thring was instructed to write to Peet and his supporters to express the committee's 'regret for the inconvenience caused to your friends who should, in accordance with the general practice of the club, have been conducted to the reception room downstairs', while explaining that 'the practice to which you take exception is common to all the clubs in Whitehall Court controlled by the proprietors. The change of practice which you desire cannot, therefore, be effected without their approval.'

At the next committee meeting in September, Thring reported that Hornsby 'considered that it would be a mistake for the Authors' Club to admit any man of colour to its membership' as 'none of the other clubs in Whitehall Court had coloured members'. He had no objection, however, 'to their admittance, or to their using, as guests, the public rooms'. Banister Fletcher, the chairman, agreed with Hornsby, and after some discussion the committee decided that coloured men should be admitted to the club and the rooms of Whitehall Court as guests when accompanied by members. Thring was instructed to write to Peet and his fellow protesters to inform them of the decision.

In March 1936, the committee decided to redraft the club rules 'as some of them were difficult of interpretation, and others did not agree with accepted practice'.[22] Most of the changes related to the role of the Secretary arising out of the dispute in 1923, and to the position of deputy chairman, which was not covered by the previous rules. By the time the new regulations were released in March 1937, however, it had also been 'deemed expedient' to amend Rule 1 to include 'a clear definition that the club was constituted for the association of gentlemen *of pure European descent* occupied or interested in any branch of literature'.[23] This was by no means the end of the matter, which would continue to be disputed over the coming years.

On 5 October 1936, a banquet was held to commemorate Walter Besant's centenary, but several of the topics discussed that season's dinners reflected the worsening international situation: 'The Balkans', 'National Defence' and 'Peace and Freedom'. On 8 February 1937, the Olympic runner Harold Abrahams addressed a club dinner. Now retired from active sport, he had been a BBC commentator at the Berlin Olympics the previous summer, and took the opportunity to warn his audience against the danger of a country's use of sport as a method of proving itself superior to other nations.

'Going into Germany,' he recalled, 'I saw an engine bearing the swastika flag, while on the tender was the Olympic flag. That was the perfect symbol of the 1936 Olympic Games,' which he characterised as 'the acme of perfect organisation, but somehow… lacking in humanity… What puzzles me,' he concluded, 'and, to a certain extent, worries me, is where this race in athletic armaments is going to end. You are a fool if you do not use a universal instrument like sport for the purposes of better international understanding.'[24]

The early months of 1937 found the committee much occupied with plans for the coronation of King George VI and Queen Elizabeth, scheduled for 12 May. The procession would pass along Victoria Embankment on its way back to Buckingham Palace, so the club's windows afforded a prime view. In the troubled international climate, and after the abdication of Edward VIII the previous December, this reassuring display of imperial pageantry was eagerly anticipated; all the bedrooms in Whitehall Court were booked months in advance. A circular was sent to members setting out the arrangements. Women would be admitted to the club that day, and the two front rooms were reserved for spectators until the procession had passed. A seating plan of 38 places was drawn up. Each seat would cost £2.2s, including lunch at 10/6, all the proceeds of which went to the Whitehall Court Company. Tickets would be limited to two per member, and any member ordering two places had to be accompanied by a lady. Because of the position of Whitehall Court, ticket holders were advised to arrive by 8.30 in the morning.

In May of the same year, Thring reported to the committee that he had written, on his own responsibility, to his old friend George Bernard Shaw, who had a flat in Whitehall Court, encouraging him to join the club. 'Is there a life subscription?' Shaw had replied, 'not that at my age life subscriptions are anything but excessive donations.' The committee decided to award him honorary life membership.[25]

Douglas Jerrold also had a flat upstairs at Whitehall Court, and was often seen in the club playing bridge and amusing or irritating other members, depending on their views, with his jeremiads on the state of the world. A fogey even in his youth, he habitually dressed in an old-fashioned black coat, striped trousers and stiff collar. 'How did he ever get out of the Forsyte Saga?' Anthony Powell once asked.

After returning from the war, Jerrold had worked for the publisher Ernest Benn with Victor Gollancz, another Authors' Club member and a friend from his Oxford days. Both men were Liberals then, but the collapse of the Liberal Party in the 1920s sent them in diametrically opposed directions. Gollancz became a communist and went on to found the Left Book Club, while Jerrold gravitated ever further to the right. Like Hilaire Belloc, whom he admired, he was a conservative Roman Catholic who loathed capitalism and communism equally, and yearned for the reestablishment of a pre-Enlightenment, Christian, monarchical society. In his view, Baldwin's Conservatives had abandoned the old High Tory principles of king, country and the landed aristocracy under God to become an unprincipled managerial party of big business.

In 1929, he became a director of the publishing house Eyre & Spottiswoode, retaining that post after he was appointed editor of the *English Review* in 1931. Since Ford Madox Ford had sold the magazine, it had mutated from a literary journal into a political review. Jerrold assembled a team of contributors that included such like-minded Catholic conservatives as Arnold Lunn and Sir Charles Petrie (who would join the Authors' Club in 1946 and become its President in 1973). These men, who saw Mussolini and Franco as the saviours of Christian civilisation from communism, went on to form the nucleus of a group called the Friends of Nationalist Spain, whose members also included Luis Bolín, the London correspondent of the Spanish monarchist newspaper *ABC* and subsequently Franco's press advisor, and the Duke of Alba. In 1933, Eyre & Spottiswoode published a book entitled *The Spanish Republic: A Survey of Two Years of Progress*, by 'Anonymous'; written by members of the group, it was a sustained attack on the Republican government.

Jerrold's support for Franco went further than propaganda. In 1936, over lunch at Simpson's in the Strand he, Bolín and the Spanish aeronautical engineer Juan de la Cierva hatched a plot to charter a light aircraft for what was ostensibly a holiday jaunt to the Canary Islands. Jerrold telephoned his old friend and fellow Authors' Club member Hugh Pollard. Now a major, Hugh Bertie Campbell Pollard, sports editor of *Country Life*, Black and Tan organiser, friend of Aleister Crowley, fascist and spy, was living in Midhurst, Sussex. He 'had a habit of letting off revolvers in any office he happened to visit', Jerrold recalled. 'When I asked him once if he had ever killed anybody he replied, "never accidentally".'

The three men were in Sussex by teatime. Pollard found a co-pilot, Captain Cecil Bebb and, to lend verisimilitude to the pretence, enlisted his daughter Diana and a friend of hers called Dorothy Watson to accompany them on the trip. Dorothy 'kept her cigarettes in her knickers', Jerrold noted approvingly after they finally tracked her down in a local pub. 'Obviously she was the type that went to Africa.'[26]

On 11 July, a de Havilland Dragon Rapide biplane took off from Croydon Airport for the Canaries. Landing at La Palma, it picked up an extra passenger: General Francisco Franco, whom the government had stationed in the islands to prevent him from staging a Nationalist coup. On 19 July, Bebb and Pollard flew Franco to Tetuán in Spanish Morocco, where he took charge of the army and invaded Spain. The Spanish Civil War had begun.

Juan de la Cierva was killed in an air crash at Croydon the following December. Jerrold motored through Nationalist-held Spain in 1937, reporting enthusiastically. On the outbreak of the Second World War, Pollard came under suspicion from MI5 as a fascist sympathiser and associate of Oswald Mosley, but they were warned off his case by MI6, which made him station chief in Madrid in 1940. Arnold Lunn's backing for Franco was rewarded in the 1950s, when the family's travel business pioneered cheap package holidays to Spain.

The Republican cause, which attracted writers such as Ernest Hemingway, George Orwell and Laurie Lee, also found support within the Authors' Club. Ford Madox Ford declared himself 'unhesitatingly for the existing Spanish Government and against Franco's attempt... The government of the Spanish, as of any other nation, should be settled and defined by the inhabitants of that nation.' Olaf Stapledon also favoured the Socialist republic. 'I support the Spanish Government,' he announced, 'because, whatever its faults, it is defending the oppressed and preserving culture.'[27]

A member since 1910, Geoffrey Theodore Garratt had resigned from the Indian Civil Service in 1921 in protest against the squandering of money on a fountain at Government House while many Indians lacked food and basic necessities, to become the Berlin correspondent of the *Westminster Gazette*. A man of radical sympathies and a strong sense of public responsibility, he served as a Labour member on Cambridgeshire county council from 1925 to 1931, and in 1936 went to Ethiopia to report on the Italian invasion for the *Manchester Guardian*. A leading member of the National Joint Committee for Spanish Relief, Garratt spent much of 1937 in Spain organising transport to and from Madrid, bringing food into the beleaguered city and evacuating children.[28] In the embattled Republican city of Valencia, he wrote *The Shadow of the Swastika*. Dedicated to 'the Englishmen in the International Brigade who died in what may well be the last fight for English freedom', the book warned of the dangers posed by Hitler and Mussolini and poured scorn on British 'Fabio-Fascists' and their literary supporters, among whom he named Petrie, Jerrold and Arnold Lunn.

Although by no stretch of the imagination a fascist, the journalist Malcolm Muggeridge was a close friend of the Lunn family and joined the Authors' Club in 1937 at the suggestion of Hugh Kingsmill. Born in 1903, he had worked as a leader writer on the *Manchester Guardian* before going to live in the Soviet Union with his wife Kitty. Expecting to find a socialist Utopia, he became disillusioned after witnessing the Ukraine famine, and was one of the first figures on the British left to warn of the dangers of Stalinism. Now freelance, he had published two novels and a biography of Samuel Butler. Ebullient, abrasive and opinionated, he later pursued a highly successful career as a broadcaster.

In June of that year, James Barrie's health deteriorated suddenly and he was taken to a London nursing home. Such was his standing in the country that *The Times* and other newspapers carried regular bulletins on his condition. After rallying briefly, he died of bronchial pneumonia on Saturday 19 June 1937, at the age of 77. The creator of *Peter Pan* was buried in his birthplace, Kirriemuir, on the 24th. The club sent a wreath to the funeral, and Banister Fletcher and Herbert Thring attended the memorial service in St Paul's Cathedral on 30 June. 'It is for his unfailing kindness, leadership, and affectionate interest in this club,' the committee wrote to Barrie's adopted son Peter Davies, 'that we shall especially remember him and deplore his loss.'

The presidency was conferred on one of the few surviving original members: James Rennell Rodd, now Baron Rennell of Rodd, a much decorated diplomat who had been British Ambassador at Stockholm and then, for the duration of the Great War, in Rome; a pillar of the Establishment whose romantic youth as a *fin de siècle* poet and friendship with Oscar Wilde were but a distant, embarrassing memory. Petrie had met him a few years earlier at a conference in Rome. 'Let me give you a word of advice as an old man to a young one,' Rodd had told him, 'when Germans talk about things that end in "*-ismus*", and Frenchmen talk about thinks that end in "*-ologie*", it is wisest for an Englishman to retire to the bar.'[29]

In October, having written to a number of European societies with a view to establishing reciprocal links, Thring received a letter from Eberhard von Thadden of the Deutsch-Englische Gesellschaft (German-English Fellowship) in Berlin. That December, when the organisation's chairman, Dr Gert Schlottmann, was in London, Thring showed him around the club premises. Schlottmann told him he would write on his return to Germany to arrange the terms of affiliation. The Gesellschaft presented itself as an innocuous organisation dedicated to fostering cultural links and Anglo-German friendship, and with Chamberlain's government committed to a policy of appeasement, it enjoyed wide support among the British establishment: Rennell Rodd was a member of its UK wing, the Anglo-German Fellowship, and Nevile Henderson, Britain's ambassador to Germany, had addressed a dinner it gave in his honour in Berlin in the summer of 1937.[30] In fact, the Gesellschaft was a front organisation funded by Germany's Foreign Minister and former Ambassador to the Court of St James, Joachim von Ribbentrop, to recruit and organise Nazi sympathisers in Britain.[31]

When Thring retired as Secretary at the end of that year, John B. Lincoln, a barrister and legal writer who had been a club member since 1908, was appointed in his place, but died suddenly the following May. In June 1938, the committee instructed Francis Gribble, then acting secretary, to write to Schlottmann informing him that affiliation with the Deutsch-Englische Gesellschaft was 'not practicable'. The minutes offer no clue to the reason for this change of heart.

Thus, as Auden wrote, expired 'the clever hopes… Of a low dishonest decade'.

8

A Nest of Spies

*The great advantage of being a writer is that you can spy on
people. You're there, listening to every word, but part of you is
observing. Everything is useful to a writer, you see – every scrap,
even the longest and most boring of luncheon parties.*

Graham Greene[1]

At 11.15 am on a bright, clear Sunday morning in September, a thin, reedy voice crackled over the radio: 'This morning the British Ambassador in Berlin handed the German Government a final note stating that unless we heard from them by 11 o'clock that they were prepared at once to withdraw their troops from Poland a state of war would exist between us. I have to tell you now that no such undertaking has been received, and that consequently this country is at war with Germany.'

There was a long pause, and then, 'You can imagine what a bitter blow it is to me that all my long struggle to win peace has failed. Yet I cannot believe that there is anything more or anything different that I could have done and that would have been more successful.'

The injured tones of Neville Chamberlain had scarcely faded when the air-raid sirens sounded and the white, ghostly shapes of barrage balloons floated up into the London sky. Sandbags and gas masks had already been distributed and air-raid shelters designated in cellars and basements; two days earlier, as soon as German troops had crossed the Polish border, a blackout had been imposed and children began to be evacuated from Britain's towns and cities.

The next day, carrying a small suitcase of necessities, Malcolm Muggeridge set out from his home outside Hastings to the nearest re-cruiting office. The atmosphere, he noted, could not have been more different from that of August 1914. There were no bands playing, no flags flying, no king's shilling or white feathers; 'Just the eternal question-naire – name, age, address, married or single, educational qualifications, religion, any record of VD...?' Told that at his age (he was 36) he could better help the war effort with his typewriter, Muggeridge returned home feeling foolish.[2]

With many members drafted into the forces, the committee received a spate of resignations, and decided to suspend their subscriptions for the duration of the war. Among them was Edmund Cousins. 'Suddenly', he recalled:

> BANG! Adolf Hitler blew the foundations out of my pleasant life – and that of hundreds of thousands of others. In my case, within a fortnight of Neville Chamberlain's fateful announce-ment, the magazine I was editing and two others to which I was contributing weekly came to a sudden sad end, and soon the five prosperous film companies to which I had entrusted my modest capital folded also, and I was left flat broke with a wife and two healthy children to support. The first thing I had to do was to cut down expenses, beginning with membership of a London club, so I went along to see Algernon Rose's very worthy successor.
>
> He was ready for me. 'I'm quite sure,' he said, 'the committee won't accept your resignation. Your membership can be suspend-ed until after the War. I expect you'll be going back to the Army?'
>
> He was right about that, and I spent the next seven years on active service overseas, and when I returned my wife had moved into Town ('where I can cope better with the Blitz!') and I felt no need of a club...[3]

A committee meeting on 16 October also agreed to offer temporary honorary membership to 'authors, who are now Officers in the Services: such membership being limited to two months from election'. During the first weeks of the war, the club remained open in the evenings, but by October it was almost deserted after dark. The committee decided to close the club at 10 instead of at midnight, and the restaurant at 6.30, so that staff could leave earlier. In December, the committee agreed that under wartime conditions they would meet once every two months instead of every month. Since the closure of the dining room in the evenings had put a stop to the Monday night dinners, in March 1940 the committee decided to hold a series of fortnightly 'Wartime Literary Luncheons' with invited speakers. The formality of the club was relaxed and a snack bar set up, despite the objections of some members.

Rationing of bacon, butter, and sugar was introduced in January 1940, and later extended to almost all foodstuffs except for bread and vegetables. At first the restrictions applied only to food for domestic consumption, but the fact that the better off could supplement their rations by eating out aroused widespread resentment and so, in the interest of national solidarity, rationing was extended to clubs and restaurants in 1942. Such wartime inconveniences offered a rich vein of humour for satirists. Cecil Hunt had made his name with several collections of amusing errors made by schoolchildren. *Howlers* (1928) *Fresh Howlers* (1930) and *Latest Howlers* (1934) were packed with gems such as 'Lourdes is a cricket ground in London' and 'People go about Venice in gorgonzolas'. In 1940, he teamed up with the illustrator William Heath Robinson to produce three books, *How to Make the Best of Things*, *How to Build a New World* and *How to Run a Communal Home*, that made gentle fun of air-raid precautions, shortages, and the communitarian spirit encouraged by the government.

On 9 April 1940, the Nazis invaded Denmark and Norway, bringing the Phoney War to an end. Britain sent an expeditionary force to Norway to repel the German invasion, but by the end of the month it had been forced to withdraw. The failure of the campaign led to the resignation of Neville Chamberlain and his replacement as Prime Minister by Winston Churchill, who summoned A.V. Alexander to Downing Street to take up his former post as First Lord of the Admiralty in the new National Government. The committee wrote to Alexander congratulating him on his appointment, and a signed photograph – which the club still possesses – was hung in the dining room.

Even as Churchill was assembling his War Cabinet, German troops were crossing into France, Belgium and Holland; on 26 May, the evacuation of Allied troops from Dunkirk began, and by 14 June, Paris had fallen. After the onset of the Blitz in September 1940, bombs exploded in Whitehall Place and Embankment Gardens, shattering some of the club's windows, although the building escaped serious damage. Whitehall Court, the members were assured, had good air raid shelters where they could take refuge.[4]

At 2 am on 25 September 1940, the home in Inner Temple of the 67-year-old Horace Wyndham was hit by a high explosive bomb. While he was unhurt, the building was declared unsafe, and he was ordered to evacuate. To assist him in finding alternative lodgings, and to compensate for the loss of his clothes, books and typewriter – 'in fact my whole stock in trade' – he was awarded £75 by the Royal Literary Fund.[5] Other members whose homes had been bombed were encouraged to use the club's bed and breakfast facilities.

On the night of 7 October 1940, an incendiary bomb fell on the roof of the National Liberal Club, but was extinguished by a Home Guard officer stationed there. Despite the Blitz, the literary lunches continued. On 26 November, Olaf Stapledon spoke on the future of democracy, and on 17 December Malcolm Muggeridge, whose book *The Thirties* had recently been published to great acclaim, addressed a lunch on the subject 'The Press in the Thirties'. By this time Muggeridge had joined the Field Security Police and was posted to GHQ Home Forces, then based at Kneller Hall in Richmond upon Thames. In 1941 he was recruited into MI6 and sent to Lourenço Marques in Mozambique to spy on German naval activity; engaged in the same work at the same time in Sierra Leone, on the opposite coast of Africa, was his friend Graham Greene.[6]

Muggeridge was not the only Authors' Club member engaged in military intelligence. During the First World War, the archaeologist Stanley Casson had fought with the East Lancashire Regiment in Flanders, where he was wounded in 1915. He then served on the General Staff in Salonika, and was mentioned in dispatches and awarded the Greek Order of the Saviour. After the war, he became Assistant Director of the British School at Athens, and in 1920 took up a Fellowship at New College, Oxford.[7] On his arrival in the quadrangle, the Warden, William Archibald Spooner (who contributed an -ism to the language), invited him to lunch 'to welcome Stanley Casson, our new archaeology Fellow'. 'But Mr Warden,' he said, 'I *am* Stanley Casson.' 'Never mind,' Spooner replied. 'Come all the same.'[8]

Casson's primary interest was sculpture, but his tastes were eclectic. His many publications ranged from *The Technique Of Early Greek Sculpture* (1933) through 'Byzantium and Anglo-Saxon Sculpture'[9] to *Some Modern Sculptors*, a 1929 survey of the art from Rodin to Epstein – whom he, unlike some of his Authors' Club colleagues, admired. One of his students at Oxford was Max Mallowan, the archaeologist who went on to marry Agatha Christie, and in 1938 Casson even published his own detective story, *Murder by Burial*.

An Authors' Club member since 1938, Casson joined the Intelligence Corps with the rank of Lieutenant Colonel as soon as war was declared, and became an instructor at the Intelligence Training Centre in Matlock, Derbyshire. Among his pupils there was a young second lieutenant who shared his passion for Hellenic culture, and with whom he always conversed in Greek. His name was Patrick Leigh Fermor. Casson was setting up a military mission to his beloved Greece, to which he recruited Fermor, who would subsequently capture the commander of the German forces on Crete, General Heinrich Kreipe.[10]

The domestic counter-intelligence service, MI5, was also represented at the club. During the war, M15 was based at Wormwood Scrubs, from which the prisoners had been evacuated, but the Authors' Club member and spymaster Maxwell Knight thought security there was too lax, and so operated out of a flat in Dolphin Square, about 10 minutes' walk from Whitehall Court. Knight had joined the club in 1937 as the author of two thrillers, *Crime Cargo* and *Gunman's Holiday*; his proposer, Grierson Dickson, was another thriller writer who doubled as an M15 agent. Knight, whose greatest success had been the penetration of a Communist spy ring at Woolwich Arsenal in 1938, would recruit agents over dinner at the Authors' Club; among his protégés was Ian Fleming, who based the character M in his James Bond novels on Knight. Although gay, Knight carefully cultivated an image of assertive heterosexuality, and was married three times; unsurprisingly, none of these marriages was happy, and his first wife committed suicide. A lifelong jazz lover, he chose Jelly Roll Morton, the Original Dixieland Jazz Band, Sidney Bechet and Jack Teagarden when he appeared on *Desert Island Discs* in 1965.

With the outbreak of the war he turned his attention to the activities of Mosley's British Union of Fascists and other potential Nazi sympathisers. In the spring of 1940, one of his agents, Joan Miller, succeeded in infiltrating the Right Club, an organisation led by a Captain Archibald Maule Ramsay, which aimed to keep the United States out of the war, oust Churchill as Prime Minister and negotiate peace with Germany.

Knight raided the flat of Tyler Kent, a cipher clerk at the US embassy, and found evidence that he had been intercepting secret communications between Churchill and Roosevelt. Ramsay was interned under Regulation 18B, while Kent and his contact, a fanatical White Russian named Anna Wolkoff, received seven and ten-year jail sentences respectively. Less successful was his operation against Ben Greene, a cousin of the novelist, whom he suspected of spying for the Germans and had interned under Section 18B. Greene, a Quaker and a pacifist, was easily able to refute the charges against him, and was released and exonerated.

By 1941, Knight had become convinced that MI6 had been penetrated by Soviet agents, and filed a memorandum entitled 'The Comintern is not Dead' outlining his suspicions. As we now know, he was right; but with his position undermined by the departure of his mentor Vernon Kell and his reputation tarnished by the Ben Greene case, his warnings were not taken seriously, and the 'Cambridge Five' continued to operate unhampered for another decade. At the end of the war, increasingly sidelined within MI5, Knight launched a new and highly successful career as the TV naturalist 'Uncle Max'. Two of his nature books, *Talking Birds* (1961) and *Animals and Ourselves* (1962), were illustrated by a young man he met at MI5 towards the end of his intelligence career: David Cornwell, better known today as John le Carré.

In the club, as in the country at large, there was considerably less anti-German hysteria than during the First World War, but after Norway and Dunkirk many German and Austrian citizens were interned as enemy aliens. Among them was Dr Hans Frisch, a Viennese scientist who had been a member of the Authors' Club since 1928. In February 1939, the club had supported his successful application to become domiciled in Guernsey; though neither politically active nor a Jew, he was strongly opposed to the Nazi regime and hoped to apply for citizenship after five years. Now, having fled to the mainland before the Germans invaded the Channel Islands, he was interned, and the committee agreed to suspend his payments until he regained his liberty.

Throughout the war, Nathaniel Micklem broadcast on the BBC's Home Service on Sunday afternoons, reporting on the state of the church in occupied Europe, religious resistance to the Nazi regime, and the ever-worsening persecution of the Jews. Many of these talks were printed in *The Listener*. In 'One Reich, One Fuehrer, One Church', broadcast in 1940, he warned that

> In a totalitarian state the state lays claim to the whole of the national life; it can tolerate no department of the national life organised beyond its control; it must dominate the minds as well as the bodies of men; education, music, the Press, religion – all must be departments of State and subject to the control of the Party. Least of all can an international society like the Christian Church be tolerated.[11]

At 1.15 am on Sunday 11 May 1941, the National Liberal Club suffered a direct hit by a bomb, which completely destroyed the main spiral staircase and caused considerable damage elsewhere. The dining-room superintendent, H. Moyse, who was also a member of the Home Guard, was killed by bomb fragments.

On 26 July 1941, Rennell Rodd died, aged 82. He had been President for just four years, and was succeeded by Banister Fletcher, who had been Chairman since 1933. Fletcher's deputy, Major Munro, stepped in as acting chairman, to be confirmed in the post the following year under a new rule that stipulated that no chairman should serve more than three years. Munro – ably assisted by a new Secretary, Ernest Short, who had taken over from St Barbe Sladen the previous summer – proved a briskly efficient Chairman and a popular figure in the club. 'By a single interjection,' Petrie recalled, he 'killed long-winded speeches…' On one occasion,

> One of our leading bores was proposing my health in a wearisome discourse mainly consisting of extracts from *Who's Who*, and when he reached the sentence 'For several years Sir Charles and Mr Douglas Jerrold collaborated in the publication of the *English Review*', John Munro shouted out, 'And serve them both bloody well right.' It was some minutes before the laughter subsided, and we never had a vote of thanks again.[12]

The wartime lunches continued into 1942. On 23 January, T.S. Eliot gave a talk on 'Poetry and Drama'. It was a subject that preoccupied him at the time; he had already written three verse dramas, *The Rock*

(1934), *Murder in the Cathedral* (1935) and *The Family Reunion* (1939), and his talk was an early exploration of ideas that he would develop in a lecture at Harvard in 1950.

On 5 February, Geoffrey Faber, chairman of Faber & Faber and of the Publishers' Association, addressed a lunch on the subject of the wartime tax on books, and warned his listeners that authors and publishers would face a struggle obtaining adequate supplies of paper and other publishing necessities.[13] Paper rationing was a serious problem; by 1942, only 37½ percent of the pre-war supply was available. The Ministry of Supply had agreed to provide another 250 tons, on condition that the Publishers' Association could demonstrate that is was being used for 'essential' books. Jerrold and his old friend Victor Gollancz, whom professional rivalry and political disagreement had driven apart, joined forces that March to oppose the scheme; both, albeit from diametrically opposed ideological standpoints, objected strongly to the government deciding which books got printed. Their campaign failed, but revived their friendship, and they would continue to meet for lunch until Jerrold's death in 1964.[14]

The difficulties of publishing in wartime were again the subject of discussion at the April lunch, when Jock Brebner, director of the News Division at the Ministry of Information, paid tribute to the reporters and photographers risking their lives to cover the conflict. He also praised the printers and editors for continuing to bring out the papers throughout the Blitz. 'In spite of the failure of gas and electricity during the great attack on London,' he observed, 'the national papers made their appearance next morning', adding that when offices of the *Coventry Telegraph* were wrecked during the raid of 14 November 1940, the paper had been printed in Birmingham.[15]

The Authors' Club did not suffer casualties on the scale that it did in the First World War; by this time, few of its members were of military age. But there were losses. In April 1942, J.R. West, the Director of Education in Dorset who had been a member since 1937, was one of 25 spectators killed during a dive-bombing demonstration on Salisbury Plain after a Hurricane pilot mistook them for target dummies in poor visibility. The same month, Geoffrey Garratt was killed along with 18 other officers and men at Pembroke Dock when a mine accidentally exploded during a military lecture.[16]

Melville Stewart Banner, a contributor to the *Straits Times* and res-ident in Hong Kong, joined the Authors' Club in 1934. In February 1940, he received an emergency commission as a lieutenant in the 44th Light Anti-Aircraft Regiment of the Royal Artillery. His battalion was stationed in Burma during the Japanese invasion, and he was killed on 22 March 1942. The club did not learn of his death until 1946, when he was mentioned in dispatches. He is commemorated on the Kanji War Memorial in Singapore.

The Reverend Joseph Edward Gough Quinn, chaplain to the 5th Battalion Northamptonshire Regiment, was awarded the Military Cross for his coolness and courage tending the injured during the evacuation of Belgium in 1940. He was killed at the age of 29 in September 1943 during the Allied invasion of mainland Italy, and is buried in the Salerno War Cemetery. His diaries, which record his service in France, Syria and Italy from 1940 to 1943, are held in the Imperial War Museum.[17]

Theodore Hume, a young American Congregationalist churchman and friend of Nathaniel Micklem, was killed on 22 October 1943 when the airliner on which he was travelling to an ecumenical conference in Stockholm was shot down by the Germans. He had joined the Authors' Club on arriving in Britain just a few weeks earlier.[18]

With the passing of Barrie and Rennell Rodd, there were few mem-bers left who remembered the Victorian twilight when the Authors' Club resounded to the wit of Oscar Wilde and Jerome K. Jerome. In the dark-est days of the war, on 26 March 1943, the club organised a lunch for the handful of surviving members who had joined before 1900. It came too late for Herbert Thring and Morley Roberts, who died in November 1941 and June 1942 respectively, but Francis Gribble, Douglas Sladen, C.J. Cutcliffe Hyne, Poulteney Bigelow, Horace Annesley Vachell and Lacon Watson were among the Victorians who gathered, under the chairman-ship of Henry de Vere Stacpoole, to reflect on those distant days. It was to be one of the last of the wartime lunches; by the end of the year, they had to be curtailed on account of staff and fuel shortages.

At the AGM on 26 March 1943, Percy Scholes, author of *The Oxford Companion to Music*, and the travel writer Gordon Home circulated an el-oquent four-page memorandum, which Scholes read out to the meeting, condemning the clause in Rule 1 that stated that the club was 'constituted for the association of gentlemen *of pure European descent'*. After observing that the rule, taken literally, would exclude Jewish authors – 'though it has, happily, not been so applied' – they stated that it did, and was clearly intended to, exclude African and Asian authors, 'even those who are citizens of the Empire in whose capital the club is situated'. This 'narrow view', they argued, posed an 'actual danger to the peace of the Empire'. The unrest taking place in India was, they believed, in part due to the fact that Gandhi, 'in early manhood, as a member of the legal profession in South Africa, [had] been treated with the contempt there frequently shown to men and women of colour'.

Scholes and Home went on to point out that the Athenaeum – 'the most distinguished club in the world for men of cultural achievement' – operated no such bar, and that an Indian, Sir Atul Chandra Chatterjee, was then on its committee. Yet one of London's smaller clubs, while admitting European and American authors 'of relatively small achievement', would exclude such eminent writers as the Nobel Prize winner Rabindranath Tagore; the great Basotho novelist Thomas Mafolo, whose book *Chaka* had recently been published by the Oxford University Press; the 'very able author' Lin Yutang; and even the Aga Khan ('who, by the way, could buy Whitehall Court and not notice that he had spent any money'). The rule, they said, was 'based on racial discrimination strikingly similar to that which the Nazis have introduced against what they call Non-Aryans', and constituted 'an offense against Empire feeling and the general dignity of humanity... The time has come,' they concluded:

> when many members would look on it as a pleasure and a privilege to meet their fellow authors of whatever race – from contact with whom they may learn much that is interesting and valuable... to help to create that wide-spreading friendship between men of letters of all countries and races which is capable of becoming an important element in the reconstruction of the shattered world...[19]

The meeting resolved that the committee should consider the desirability of calling a Special General Meeting with a view to altering the rule. It was agreed that any change would have to be discussed with Whitehall Court. At the next committee meeting, held on 6 May, Munro reported that he had discussed the matter with the general manager of Whitehall Court, who had informed him that 'obvious difficulties presented themselves' in terms of the relationship between the club and the company that owned the building. The committee therefore resolved that 'in view of the conditions of tenure of the club's premises in Whitehall Court and of the club's relations with other clubs in the building, they have decided not to recommend any change in the present wording of the Rule.' Scholes resigned from the club the following year.

Graham Greene returned from Sierra Leone in March 1943 to work at Section Five headquarters in St Albans under Kim Philby. As the officer in charge of Portugal and its colonies, he was thus the contact for Muggeridge in Lourenço Marques. In the summer of 1943, the section moved to Ryder Street in St James's, where he and Philby would regularly drink together in the King's Arms. Greene joined the Authors' Club, and soon persuaded Philby to become a member. Their friend and fellow agent Malcolm Muggeridge returned to England in 1944, moving into a flat in Buckingham Street, a stone's throw from the club, and joining the staff of the *Daily Telegraph* as a leader writer.

In February 1944, Greene and Casson were invited to join the committee. Before the next meeting, however, the club was shocked to learn that Casson had been killed in a plane crash off the coast of Cornwall while on active service. The committee commissioned his wife to compile a memorial bibliography of his works, and once the war was over, on 29 November 1945, held a reception with the Anglo-Hellenic League at the Dorchester, at which tributes were paid to his life and work, and a collection was raised to fund a library of English books in Greece.

In June 1944, Philby offered Greene a promotion at MI6. Rather than accept it, he resigned from the service. The reason for his decision has never been adequately explained; his biographer Norman Sherry has speculated that he may have suspected Philby of being a Soviet agent, and did not wish to be forced to choose between betraying a friend and betraying his country. In July, after a brief spell at the Political Intelligence Department (PID) of the Foreign Office, where he edited an anthology to be airdropped into occupied France, Greene accepted a directorship at Eyre & Spottiswoode at Jerrold's invitation.

By the spring of 1945, the committee was beginning to look forward to the post-war renovation of the premises, and discussed bringing the staffing back to its pre-war level. To accomplish this, Jerrold, who succeeded Munro as chairman in June, recommended increasing the subscription, which had stayed at 6 guineas since 1908 – to 7 guineas for existing members and 9 guineas for new ones. This was approved at an EGM in March 1946, and came into force on 1 July that year. The Monday night dinners were eventually resumed in February 1947; the first guest was the sailor and naturalist Peter Scott, who gave an account of his experiences in the Navy during the war under the title 'Small Ships'.

Despite the improvements, the Authors' Club remained a dowdy enclave decorated with William Morris tiles and framed letters from Kipling, Barrie, Haggard, Shaw and Wells. Over the fireplace in the writing room hung a portrait in oils of Algernon Rose, which is still in the club's possession. The novelist Anthony Powell, who joined the Club in 1945, found it 'an odd little backwater… dominated by Edwardian literary memories and a gargantuan black cat'. Most of its policies, he observed, were 'settled by Jerrold, the most prominent member of its committee and in general guardian angel'.[20]

On New Year's Day 1946, Kingsmill arrived at the club before lunch in an ebullient mood and found Greene at the bar. 'Everyone I've passed in the street looks happy,' he told him. 'I suppose because the most unpleasant year in our lifetimes is over – Belsen, bombs, peace with Germany followed almost immediately by peace with Japan, and life on our hands again, a prospect which only a convinced believer in personal immortality can stomach. Are you with me, Graham? Oh, I forgot – you're a Catholic.'

'Are you *well?*' Greene replied.[21]

In *The End of the Affair,* Graham Greene offers a lugubriously funny picture of the Authors' Club at this period. His narrator, Maurice Bendrix, entertains Henry Miles, the man he is cuckolding, at a 'seedy club' to which he belongs 'because there is so little likelihood of meeting a fellow writer'. Though the club is unnamed, the 'staghead presented by Sir Walter Besant in 1898' and the portraits of Conan Doyle and Garvice on the wall leave little doubt as to its identity. The meal is 'hideous', while the club secretary is 'a man with a long grey beard and a soup-stained waistcoat, who looked like a Victorian poet but in fact wrote little sad reminiscences of the dogs he had once known'.

Greene's withering portrayal belies his affection for a club steeped in memories of Anthony Hope, Rider Haggard and Conan Doyle, the writers who had shaped his childhood imagination.[22] He was actively involved in the club's affairs: he served on the executive committee from 1943 to 1946, attended its meetings regularly, and was elected to the general council in 1951. But it was his habit of mind to relish failure and unhappiness. As Jerrold observed, 'No man has a greater reluctance to enjoy himself simply, than Graham Greene. His club must be what he calls "the seedy club"; if he goes to a party it must be "simply appalling" or "perfectly ghastly"; even a quiet cocktail with two or three friends becomes, on leaving, "a dreary little drink".'[23]

Despite their shared Catholic faith, Greene and Jerrold were diametrically opposed in their political opinions. Muggeridge considered their ability to work successfully together at Eyre & Spottiswoode, where they shared an office in Bedford Street, 'a tribute to both their characters'. Greene's fame as a novelist has somewhat eclipsed his flair as a publisher; among his inspired signings were R.K. Narayan, Mervyn Peake and François Mauriac. He also initiated the Century Library, a series of reprints of neglected 20th-century classics, each with an introduction by a prominent writer. They included *The Wings of the Dove* by Henry James, with an introduction by Herbert Read; H.G. Wells's *The History of Mr Polly*, introduced by V.S. Pritchett; and *Frost in May*, by Antonia White, with whom Greene had worked at the PID, and for which he commissioned another friend, Elizabeth Bowen, to provide an introduction.

Almost half the list consisted of titles by Authors' Club members: Conan Doyle's *The Lost World* and *The Poison Belt*; Hornung's *Raffles*; Eden Phillpotts's *Widecombe Fair*; Anthony Hope's *The King's Mirror* (for which Jerrold furnished an introduction); and Ford Madox Ford's *Fifth Queen* trilogy. Greene was a great admirer of Ford, and wanted to publish a complete edition of his work – a plan that would not come to fruition until 20 years later, when he was a director at the Bodley Head.

Much of the business of Eyre & Spottiswoode and the *New English Review* (which Jerrold founded in 1945 as a successor to the defunct *English Review*) was conducted from the smoking-room of the Authors' Club.

Hugh Kingsmill was the magazine's literary editor, and Powell a contributor. 'If consultation about some book was necessary – or talk about literature, love, marriage, the meaning of life, anything but politics – Kingsmill was always to be found asleep every afternoon in one of the upright chairs; a coma from which he would emerge for tea at about four o'clock.'[24] Alternatively, he might be found on one of the Club's battered leather sofas, his white hair floating and his face crimson with benevolence, holding court to Malcolm Muggeridge and Hesketh Pearson. [25]

Charles Petrie vividly recalled Kingsmill as 'as an outstanding spontaneous wit'.

> I remember an American professor arguing in his presence that Marlowe had written Shakespeare; asked to prove his point he maintained that the man killed at Wapping was not Marlowe at all, but that the whole affair was a deliberate hoax to create the impression that Marlowe was dead, before, as a member of Walsingham's secret service, he was sent to the Continent to unravel one of the numerous conspiracies against Elizabeth I. 'When that assignment was ended, what could Marlowe do as he was officially dead?' asked the professor. 'I'll tell you,' he went on, 'He wrote plays under the name of William Shakespeare. What do you say to that, Mr Kingsmill?' Like a flash came the crushing reply, 'Damned annoyed Bacon must have been.'[26]

A former actor with Herbert Beerbohm Tree's company and erstwhile protégé of Frank Harris, Hesketh Pearson was a prolific and popular biographer whose subjects included Dr Johnson, Tom Paine, Hazlitt and Shaw. 'His technique,' Michael Holroyd has observed, 'derived in part from his early years as a stage actor. To some extent he acted his subjects' lives on the page.'[27] He now turned his attention to two great figures from the Authors' Club's past. *Conan Doyle: His Life and Art* was published by Methuen in 1943; it was much admired by Graham Greene, who wrote an introduction to the book when it was reissued in 1977.

While working on this biography, Pearson gained a foretaste of a problem that was to bedevil his next project, a life of Oscar Wilde. Among Conan Doyle's papers, he found a letter from Lord Alfred Douglas – Wilde's lover Bosie – threatening to horsewhip Doyle for his 'blasphemous ravings' about spiritualism. 'I was relieved to get your letter,'

Doyle replied. 'It is only your approval which could in any way annoy me.' Obsessively litigious, Douglas had scuppered every previous attempt to write a biography of Wilde. Pearson visited him twice, and found the unpleasant old egotist uninformative on any subject other than himself. Douglas died soon afterwards, in March 1945, too late to help the book; it was only in the second edition, published in 1954, that Pearson was able to write frankly about Bosie's role in Wilde's downfall.[28]

Pearson had collaborated with Kingsmill on two books, *Skye High* (1937) and *This Blessed Plot* (1942), in which travelogue was interspersed, in the tradition of Boswell and Johnson, with conversation about literature and life. In 1945, at the urging of Jerrold and Greene, they embarked on a third. This time, constrained by 'eld and increasing indolence', they would not venture as far afield as the Scottish islands or even the pubs of Sussex, the setting for *This Blessed Plot*. Their new venture, *Talking of Dick Whittington*, would take them no further than London and its environs. Discussing Shakespeare, Tolstoy and Dickens, they visited Dr Johnson's house in Gough Square, Poet's Corner in Westminster Abbey, and those living literary monuments, George Bernard Shaw and G.K. Chesterton. Many of their jaunts started at the Authors' Club. When it was raining, they got no further.

In September 1948, at a lunch where Muggeridge and Kingsmill were also present, Greene had a blazing row with Anthony Powell over his refusal to publish his *John Aubrey and his Friends*, describing it as 'a bloody boring book'. By the end of the lunch, Greene had offered to re-lease Powell from his contract with Eyre & Spottiswoode. Jerrold was in the United States at the time, and on his return, hit the roof. Whatever he may have thought about Powell's biographical study of the 17th-century antiquary, he did not want to lose him as a novelist. The upshot was that Greene – whose novels were now selling more than well enough for him to manage without the day job – resigned from the publishing house.[29]

The post-war years saw the arrival of a number of members who would go on to play key roles in the affairs of the club. In 1946, Jerrold's friend Sir Charles Petrie became a member. In 1947, they were joined by Laurence Meynell, the prolific crime novelist and editor at the Bodley Head and *Time and Tide*, and in 1948 by Kenneth Garside, a former in-telligence officer and assistant librarian at Leeds University, who was then deputy librarian at University College, London. Another member who joined in 1947 was a rising star of the Labour Party called Harold Wilson, soon to be appointed President of the Board of Trade and, at 31, the youngest cabinet minister in 20th-century history.

In 1948, Jerrold was succeeded as Chairman by Thomas Smith Sterling, a former professor of English Literature at the University of Calcutta, the Egyptian University in Cairo and, more recently, at the School of Oriental and African Studies in London. At a special meeting that November, a new set of rules was adopted. Strangely, there are no minutes of this meeting, so we do not know what deliberations took place, but it appears that the clause restricting membership to men 'of pure European descent' was, as Scholes had recommended, 'quietly re-scinded and forgotten'. Noël Hornsby, the manager of Whitehall Court, had clearly changed his mind on the subject; when consulted later by the Authors' Club Secretary about the election of a West African member, he said he had 'no objection whatever'.[30]

In the autumn of 1949, W.H. Auden joined the Authors' Club. A US citizen since 1946, he lived in New York, returning to Europe each year to spend the summer in Ischia. His 'Baroque Eclogue' *The Age of Anxiety* had won the Pulitzer Prize in 1948.

The decade ended sadly with the loss of a vivid presence. While working on *Talking of Dick Whittington*, Hugh Kingsmill, suffering from an undiagnosed stomach ulcer, had the first of a series of gastric haem-orrhages. On 23 February 1949, having recovered from another bout of internal bleeding, he was well enough to have lunch with Pearson at the club. In April, however, he was admitted to the Royal Sussex Hospital in Brighton, where he died on 15 May 1949, six months short of his 70th birthday. 'My one regret,' he said on his deathbed, 'is that I have used too many commas. On the question of semi-colons, I have nothing to reproach myself.'[31]

The committee directed the Secretary, Ernest Short, to make ar-rangements for a memorial service,[32] which was held at St Paul's, Covent Garden – the Actors' Church. Pearson and Muggeridge read the lessons.[33]

9

'A Pleasant but Impoverished Institution'

Don't clap too hard – it's a very old building.

John Osborne, *The Entertainer*

The new decade found the nation struggling to shake off the austerity of the war years, and the Authors' Club was no exception. 'No London club is finding it easy to hold its own in these difficult times,' Sterling told the AGM on 4 April 1950. 'The Authors' Club is in no immediate trouble but its financial position is deteriorating and, unless the situation can be steadily improved, may before long become precarious.'[1]

To recruit new members, it was decided to suspend the admission fee of 7 guineas which, charged in addition to the annual 9-guinea subscription, was seen as a deterrent. Since the club's own income consisted largely of the quarter of the entrance fee that was remitted to it by Whitehall Court Ltd, a new arrangement was agreed whereby Whitehall Court would pay the Authors' Club a percentage of the subscription income, rising with the number of new subscriptions. Sterling predicted that if the club could recruit another 150 members, it would achieve a measure of financial independence it had not enjoyed before, while securing a reasonable profit for Whitehall Court. A sub-committee was appointed to investigate ways of increasing recruitment, including a new brochure aimed at the universities, the BBC and the civil service; supplementing the monthly dinners with 'cocktail hour' meetings; and instituting annual literary prizes.

Malcolm Muggeridge joined the committee in 1950, but retired the following year. Midway through his life's journey from hard-drinking, womanising hack to pontifical Catholic curmudgeon, 'Saint Mugg' was by no means universally liked. When he resigned his membership on 31 December 1953, Thomas Kirkwood, who had recently succeeded Short as Secretary, noted drily in the margin of the membership book, '*Laus Deo!*'

108

In 1951, Laurence Meynell was elected on to the committee, and Thomas Sterling's three years as Chairman came to an end. He was succeeded by Sir Charles Petrie and, on 26 September, Graham Greene chaired an inaugural dinner in his honour. Other dinner speakers that year included Colin Coote, editor of the *Daily Telegraph*, Frank Swinnerton, Sir Banister Fletcher, the Irish Ambassador Frederick Boland, and the broadcaster Wynford Vaughan-Thomas, who had joined the club in 1950. At the informal cocktail hours, Julian Amery discussed Joseph Chamberlain, H. Montgomery Hyde discussed his forthcoming biography of Lord Carson, and Hugh Ross Williamson spoke about the Gunpowder Plot.

The Reverend Edwin H. Robertson (1912–2007), the broadcaster, theologian, minister of Heath Street Baptist Church in Hampstead and biographer of Dietrich Bonhoeffer, who joined in 1951, recalled the atmosphere of the club at the time.

> The dining room was still its heart, especially at lunch, with good conversation at the 'long table' between authors of many persuasions: Charles Petrie talking about Spain; Laurence Meynell, expert on Dr Johnson and an excellent story-teller; John Davenport, the critic; Harold Brockman, the architect; Leonard Clark, the poet; and even an up-and-coming Catholic priest, called Heenan, might be found joining in the discussion. Graham Greene too.[2]

By the spring of 1952, despite the efforts of the committee, the financial situation had become desperate. The club's income from subscriptions and catering in 1951 was £4698 while its expenses, mostly staff wages and rent, came to £5601, leaving a deficit of £923.[3] The Micawberish conclusion was unavoidable. In June, a letter was sent out to members:

> The Executive Committee has to announce with regret that after nearly fifty years residence at Whitehall Court, the Authors' Club is faced with a serious financial crisis which may force it into dissolution unless all members are prepared to subscribe to an Emergency Trust Fund without delay. It will also be necessary to raise subscriptions to the level of other equivalent West End Clubs. Although the average subscription to most West End Clubs is from 18 to 20 guineas, the Authors' Club has attempted to continue its existence with a maximum subscription of less than half this average. This policy has failed, and in the last three

years expenditure has approached and now exceeds income, resulting finally in a net loss.

Whitehall Court Limited have, in fact, informed the Committee of the Club that they cannot carry on the Club after the end of the current year, on the existing basis.

The Executive Committee has carefully examined the whole position. It is satisfied that the rent of the premises, now in arrear, is extremely reasonable and that no comparable premises and amenities could be secured at a similar figure elsewhere. It is also satisfied that if the Club is to continue in existence certain administrative changes must be adopted at once.

A special meeting of members was convened at the club for 24 June, at 5 p.m., immediately before the AGM. Members were asked to contribute to an Emergency Trust Fund, to which Banister Fletcher donated £100. The Club's Honorary Solicitor, H. Sutton Syrett, undertook lengthy negotiations with Whitehall Court *pro bono*, and eventually hammered out a new agreement. The most important change was that the Authors' Club ceased to be a proprietary club of Whitehall Court, but was now owned by its members and governed by the Authors' Club Ltd., the company set up in 1908 to protect the name. The club would receive its subscriptions directly from its members, and pay an annual rent of £1500 to Whitehall Court, which remained responsible for catering. Subscriptions were raised to 14 guineas, and although this led to many resignations, the increased revenue more than compensated.

Lynton Fletcher, the broadcaster and former director of recorded programmes at the BBC, succeeded Sir Charles Petrie as chairman in 1953. At his inaugural dinner, he played a series of archive recordings to illustrate changing fashions in public oratory, contrasting the voices of Beerbohm Tree and John Gielgud, and that of Gladstone with that of Winston Churchill.[4] Fletcher had been one of the principal architects of the club's revival and, if not quite on the scale of the reconstruction of 1908, it was a notable achievement. 'I am glad to learn from Lynton Fletcher,' wrote the *Sketch*'s correspondent that August, 'that the Authors' Club — that pleasant but impoverished institution which has been in financial low water for so long — has for the first time for years made a profit and not a loss. It would have been a pity if the Authors' had to close, if only for the excellent oratory at its dinners.'[5]

At the AGM on 15 June 1954, Fletcher was able to report that despite the decrease in membership, subscription income was probably the highest in the history of the club. He paid tribute to the work of the finance committee, and to the efforts of the deputy chairman and the Secretary, Tom Kirkwood, thanks to whose efforts many ex-members who had left after the price increase in 1952 had now rejoined. He felt that 'cautious mutual congratulations' were in order.

The club's renewed confidence was reinforced by a strong programme of distinguished speakers at its dinners. Bertrand Russell spoke in February 1953 on the publication of his first venture into fiction, *Satan in the Suburbs and Other Stories*. 'Fiction,' he told his audience, 'liberates man from the tyranny of contemporary fact. It releases the imagination, the potent force which has brought marking forward from age to age, from unpleasant facts in the past to what we hope will be more pleasant ones in the future.' Alluding to the club's motto, he said, 'I should like to modernise and correct it. It should be "Authors' Royalties are larger than Army Pay".'

During the coronation of Queen Elizabeth II on 2 June 1953, as at that of her father in 1937, the route passed down Northumberland Avenue and along the Embankment, before turning back into Whitehall, so once again the club's windows offered a grandstand view of the procession. For the first time, the coronation would be televised, so the club bought a Decca large-screen projector so that members and their guests could view the actual ceremony as it took place in Westminster Abbey.

Banister Fletcher died on 17 August 1953, aged 87. At his funeral, which was held at the Savoy Chapel on the 21st, the Authors' Club was represented by Lynton Fletcher, Robin Goodfellow, Ernest Short and Thomas Kirkwood. The committee then offered the vacant Presidency to Lord Dunsany. One of the club's longest-standing members, the septuagenarian baron now sported a white goatee that lent him the air of a wizard from one of his own fantasy tales. His great-niece Antonia Fraser spent childhood holidays at Dunsany Castle and remembers her great-uncle Eddie with affection as 'deeply, gloriously, heroically eccentric'.[6] The Authors' Club got a taste of the puckish, mercurial humour of its new President the following January when, at a dinner on the 24th, Dunsany read a 'poem' to great applause, before revealing that it was made up of the first lines of a number of modern poems. 'Poetry,' he concluded, 'should ring like a bell – modern poetry clunks like lead.'[7]

In April 1954, the Archbishop of York, Cyril Garbett, discussed the threat of nuclear weapons. 'It is childish to speak as if the hydrogen bomb were on a par with the discovery of gunpowder or dynamite.' The Church, he warned, 'must protest with all its might against the use of weapons for indiscriminate mass destruction'.[8]

In March 1955, John Betjeman addressed a club dinner on a subject dear to his heart, the architecture of London. The qualities to look for, he said, were texture, skyline and movability. He recommended a lunchtime walk in St James's Park for a view of the domes and towers of Whitehall, and railed against 'the great impersonal cliffs of modern office buildings which are planned by committees which are careless of the setting and have no soul'.[9]

Given Dunsany's views on modern poetry, it was perhaps surprising that T.S. Eliot (a particular bugbear of his) should return to the club the following month, to discuss the topic 'Author and Critic'. At a dinner chaired by Douglas Jerrold, Eliot began by making a distinction between criticism and reviewing. An article, he thought, was a review when the reader was presumed not to have read the book under discussion; and criticism when the reader was assumed to have read it. Yet if a review of a new book 'contains enough learning or wisdom over and above what is called for by the book reviewed, or if it is a statement of enduring value, then it qualifies as criticism'.

Having spent the previous two decades writing largely for the theatre, Eliot went on to make a sharp distinction between theatre reviewers and critics discussing the printed text of a play. 'For dramatic critic,' he said, 'I have the same admiration that l have for Alpine climbers, channel swimmers, novelists and all those people who can do marvellous feats which I cannot even imagine myself attempting... For what I want from the dramatic critic... is to know the immediate, one might almost say instantaneous, mark that the play makes on a sensitive plate, on the mind of a man who loves the theatre, and who is so experienced that he can form an opinion simultaneously of the play itself, its construction and its language and the verisimilitude of the personages, and of the merits and defects of producer, cast and designer (and perhaps *couturier* as well), without having any more previous knowledge of play or production than the rest of the first-night audience.'[10]

Shaken by crisis of 1952, the committee had begun to investigate a new venture that might raise the public profile of the club: the awarding of literary prizes. This became a reality when it was found that Sir Banister Fletcher had left £1500 to the Authors' Club in his will, 'in recognition of the pleasure I have derived from membership of that club'. The money was to be held in trust so that the income generated could fund an award for the best book on architecture or fine art.

The prize took several years to set up. In May 1954, Kirkwood reported that the £1500 capital, invested in 4 percent consols, would yield an investment income of around £63 per annum. It was not yet clear whether this would be subject to tax, however, the prize was subsequently registered as a charity to make it exempt. In February the following year, Harold Brockman, the architectural correspondent for the *Financial Times* who had joined the club in 1954, agreed to seek the advice of the Royal Institute of British Architects in selecting the prize if it were decided to limit the field (at least for the first award) to books on architecture. It was not until February 1956, however, that a date was set for the first award: the best book on architecture published in the UK in 1955 or 1956 would be announced early in 1957.

In the meantime, Laurence Meynell – who would succeed Lynton Fletcher as Chairman in June 1955 – had set up a second book award, for the Best First Novel. Because there was no cash prize – winners would receive a silver quill pen and a year's free membership of the club – no terms of a will to negotiate, and no shortage of qualified judges among the members, the award got off to a flying start, and was presented three times before the Banister Fletcher finally materialised. Publishers in the UK were invited to submit a maximum of three first novels published in 1954. Women authors were ineligible because club membership and dinners were still restricted to men – 'a poor excuse', the *Evening Standard* protested.[11] A reading panel consisting of Meynell, Goodfellow and Waveney Girvan made a preliminary selection, from which Compton Mackenzie chose the first winner. The result was announced at a dinner at the club on 18 May 1955, where Mackenzie presented David Unwin with a silver quill for his debut *The Governor's Wife* (Michael Joseph).[12]

The Authors' Club lost its last link with its Victorian past in January 1955, when Horace Annesley Vachell died at his home near Bath at the age of 93, having recently published his hundredth book. This 'splendid old man', Compton Mackenzie wrote, 'died as he had lived – with a glass of vintage port by his side. In the typewriter on his study desk was a sheet of paper and an incomplete essay.'[13]

Another stalwart of the club, Major John Munro, died suddenly at his London home in October 1956, aged 73. Since his retirement, he had been working on a scholarly edition of Shakespeare's plays, which was almost complete bar the introduction; this was provided by the Shakespearian scholar Glynne Wickham. On its publication by Eyre & Spottiswoode in 1958, *The London Shakespeare* was hailed in the *Guardian* as 'the purest text that a fine intelligence with remarkably few prejudices and eccentricities could deduce from the latest Shakespearian studies'.[14]

Fortunately, the mid-Fifties also saw a strong intake of new members who were to make a significant contribution to the life of the club. The scion of a great Liberal dynasty, Victor Bonham-Carter was an Exmoor farmer and the author of *The English Village* (1952). He would later become secretary of both the Society of Authors and the Royal Literary Fund.[15] Paul Baker QC, who joined in 1954, was a judge of great distinction and editor of the *Law Quarterly Review.* Gavin Thurston trained as a doctor and a barrister, and had served in the Royal Army Medical Corps in India and northwest Europe during the Second World War. Since the end of hostilities, he had been deputy coroner in various jurisdictions in London and the Home Counties, and written articles on a range of medico-legal subjects.[16]

Idries Shah, who joined in 1952, was born Sayed Idries el-Hashimi in Simla, India, in 1924, and grew up mostly in England. An eloquent and tireless exponent of Sufism, which he sought to liberate from 'cultish accretions, weirdness and oriental quaintness',[17] he is best known for *The Sufis* (Doubleday, 1964) and *The Exploits of the Incomparable Mulla Nasrudin* (Octagon, 1966), a retelling of the adventures of the wise fool of Eastern folklore. Among his disciples were Robert Graves and Doris Lessing, who wrote his obituary in the *Daily Telegraph*. Although he spent much time in India and the United States, he remained a member of the Authors' Club until his death in 1996.

Langley Russell, better known as Lord Russell of Liverpool (he had inherited the baronetcy conferred upon his father, the long-serving editor of the *Liverpool Daily Post*), was a military judge responsible for war crimes trials in the British-occupied zone of Germany. He joined the club in 1954, the year he published *The Scourge of the Swastika*, which set out in chilling detail the atrocities he had uncovered.[18] In 1959, he and Bertrand Russell wrote a joint letter to *The Times:*

> Sir,— In order to discourage confusions which have been constantly occurring, we beg herewith to state that neither of us is the other.
>
> Yours &c.,
>
> RUSSELL (Bertrand, Earl Russell)
> RUSSELL of LIVERPOOL (Lord Russell of Liverpool)[19]

C.S. Forester, the creator of Captain Horatio Hornblower, also joined in 1954, and Bruce Montgomery – better known as the crime novelist Edmund Crispin – in April 1955. Under his real name, he was also a prolific composer, writing the scores for the *Carry On* and *Doctor in the House* films. The old green Penguin editions of his novels list his recreations as 'swimming, excessive smoking, Shakespeare, the operas of Wagner and Strauss, idleness, and cats'. W. Somerset Maugham was awarded honorary membership in October of that year, and he and Forester were soon elected to the general council. The historian G.M. Trevelyan became a member in 1956, proposed by Laurence Meynell, and the influential American architect and systems designer Buckminster Fuller joined in March 1957.

In 1956, Forester presented the Best First Novel Award to Brian Moore for *Judith Hearne* (Andre Deutsch). The novel, republished the following year as *The Lonely Passion of Judith Hearne,* was not in fact Moore's first – he had already published several thrillers under the pseudonym Bernard Mara – but it launched the career of this celebrated Irish writer, whom Graham Greene described as one of his favourite novelists. In 1957 the adjudicator was Somerset Maugham, who awarded the prize to the South African barrister and author Harold Bloom for *An Episode in the Transvaal.* The novel was fiercely critical of apartheid; the South African government denied Bloom an exit permit to travel to England to receive the prize, and subsequently banned his novel. The following November, a club dinner was held in Maugham's honour, at which Dunsany presided and Jerrold, Brockman, Sterling, Short and Kirkwood were all present.[20]

Despite the improvement in the club's financial situation since the crisis of 1952, its position was by no means secure. In 1955, the Authors' Club Ltd issued 5 percent debentures to its members, raising a total of £2000. The following year, to provide additional income, the club agreed to share premises with the struggling Chemical Club, which had previously occupied a separate suite in Whitehall Court. This, it was estimated, would bring in a further £1000 per annum. The 275 members of the Chemical Club, mostly industrial chemists, would be entitled to use the Authors' Club facilities and attend its functions, a combination that gave rise to the humorous epithet 'Thinkers and Stinkers'.[21]

On 25 October 1957, Dunsany, after enjoying dinner with friends in Dublin, was seized with appendicitis and taken to hospital, where he died, aged 79. At his funeral at Shoreham parish church in Kent, the club was represented by Robin Goodfellow and the aeronautical engineer Albert Thurston, a member since 1913. A wreath was sent 'in affectionate remembrance from the Chairman, Committee and members of the Authors' Club'. He was succeeded as President by Compton Mackenzie.[22]

The first Banister Fletcher prize was eventually presented by Sir William Holford, the architect and town planner, to H.M. Colvin for his *Biographical Dictionary of English Architects (1660–1840)* at a dinner at the club on 27 November 1957. What emerged only after the first award had been decided was a plan to offer the prize in alternate years to the best book on architecture and the best on the fine arts published in the previous two years. 'Fine arts,' the committee specified, 'should be defined as in its generally accepted sense, including specifically drawing, painting, sculpture, lithography, pottery and tapestry, and excluding music, theatre and dancing.' The second award was to be made early in 1958, for the best book on the fine arts, with the assistance of the V&A, the Courtauld Institute and the National Book League. After those institutions declined, the committee asked the Barber Institute of Fine Arts in Birmingham to draw up the shortlist.

In November 1958, Sir John Rothenstein, the art historian and director of the Tate Gallery, presented the award to Kenneth Clark for *The Nude: A Study of Ideal Art*. Clark, who had been appointed the youngest ever director of the National Gallery in 1933 when he was just 30, was then Chairman of the Arts Council and one of the most respected art historians in Britain; he would subsequently achieve worldwide fame as a broadcaster with his 1969 BBC TV series *Civilisation*. Nathaniel Micklem, who had succeeded Meynell as Chairman that year, presided over the dinner.

The 1959 selection was made by the architectural historian and curator of Sir John Soane's Museum, Sir John Summerson, who presented the award to Nikolaus Pevsner for the tenth book of his monumental series 'The Buildings of England', *London, Volume I: Cities of London and Westminster*, at a dinner on 10 December, presided over once again by Nathaniel Micklem. Pevsner dedicated his book to the wartime nights he had spent firewatching from Birkbeck College. His publisher, Allen Lane, the founder of Penguin Books, was present at the prize giving.

In 1960, the Barber Institute's director, Professor Thomas Bodkin, presented the Banister Fletcher Award to another German émigré who had enriched the life of this nation, Professor Rudolf Wittkower, for his book *Art and Architecture in Italy, 1600–1750*. Educated at the Humboldt University in Berlin, Wittkower had fled the Nazis with his wife in 1933 to teach at the Warburg Institute in London before moving to Columbia University in New York in 1956. Banister Fletcher, in his *History of Architecture*, had been less than enthusiastic about the Baroque, reflecting the sensibilities of his times; Wittkower's mighty survey marked a significant turning point in critical opinion.

The latter half of the 1950s saw a significant shift in literary taste. John Osborne's *Look Back in Anger* brought what was soon dubbed 'kitchen-sink drama' to the London stage, in striking contrast to the verse dramas of T.S. Eliot and Christopher Fry and the 'well-made plays' of Terence Rattigan. Along with the novels *Lucky Jim* (1954) by Kingsley Amis and *Room at the Top* (1957) by John Braine, Osborne's play was seen as a key text in a movement that became known as the 'Angry Young Men'. Amis and Braine both joined the Authors' Club in

February 1959, and in May, Laurence Meynell presented the Best First Novel Award to another writer identified with the group, Alan Sillitoe, for *Saturday Night and Sunday Morning*. Sillitoe followed up this gritty depiction of working-class Nottingham life with the short-story collection *The Loneliness of the Long-Distance Runner*, launching a career that spanned five decades and produced 30 works of fiction. Both books were made into successful films that had a massive influence on the cultural landscape of Sixties Britain.

Nor was the older generation of writers neglected: in 1959, E.M. Forster was awarded honorary membership 'in recognition of his distinguished services to English letters'.

In the course of the 1950s, there were a number of alterations to the physical arrangement of the club rooms. Michael Lindsay, who joined in 1959 and, at the time of writing, is the Club's Honorary Treasurer, recalled:

> Before I became a member the club had obviously changed quite a lot. The Conference Room and Dressing Room no longer existed, as the Dining Room had been extended to take over the space. The Billiards Room had become the Library and the Reference Library had become the Billiards Room although there were still some bookshelves. The Card Room was now the Secretary's office and the old office and boardroom had become a very cosy bar presided over by Willie our Belgian barman (of uncertain age!).

One of the Authors' Club's most stalwart members, Ernest Short, died on 29 August 1959 at the age of 83. He had been a member for 49 years, and served as Secretary for 12. He had continued to write well into his old age, and since the end of the Second World War had published two books on the theatre, a history of British painting and a survey of economic crisis.[23] Douglas Jerrold, Robin Goodfellow and J.T.C. Clarke represented the club at his funeral.

As the decade drew to a close, a discussion took place in committee that illustrated how far attitudes had changed over the previous two decades. At a meeting on 28 November 1959, the Secretary, Robin Goodfellow, tabled letters from two members, Waveney Girvan and Henry Fearon, resigning from the club because of the election of a

West Indian. Girvan was a publisher specialising in books about the West Country and literary executor to Eden Phillpotts; he was also involved in various far-right organisations including the National Front, and had a keen interest in flying saucers. Fearon, under the pseudonym Fieldfare, was the author of numerous popular hiking guides.

Goodfellow stated firmly that it had been club policy for many years to admit members regardless of race, and pointed out that at least five candidates who were 'not of European descent' had been elected recently. The committee resolved unanimously that this was indeed club policy, and that in acknowledging the letters of resignation it 'should be made quite clear' to Girvan and Fearon that the policy of the club was 'to elect to membership properly qualified gentlemen irrespective of race, colour or creed'.

With the lease on the rooms in Whitehall Court due for renewal in 1960, a rent rise was anticipated. Many members were dissatisfied with the quality and price of the food provided by Whitehall Court, so the committee began to make discreet investigations into alternative premises. In July 1959, they renewed a tentative approach made to the Arts Club in Mayfair three years earlier, and also discussed the possibility of sharing part of the National Liberal Club's premises. They do not appear to have been seriously contemplating relocating; the fact that Goodfellow was instructed to draw up an account detailing the profits generated by the Authors' Club for the Whitehall Court company over the previous five years suggests that these manoeuvres were intended to strengthen the club's bargaining position with its landlord. But the two clubs chosen as potential hosts pointed the way towards the future of the Authors' Club in the decades to come.

10

THE LIBERAL ARTS

Another factor which has done a great deal to modify the old traditions of club life as it was lived in Victorian times has been the change on the position of women… The days are gone when a man went down to his club for a few hours while his wife remained at home engaged either in looking after the children or servants, or in sewing a fine seam.

Sir Charles Petrie, *A Historian Looks at his World*

By the end of the 1950s, Whitehall Court had been running at a loss for years, and the board of directors was considering selling the building. At the beginning of 1960, Murrayfield Real Estate, a subsidiary of Jack Cotton and Charles Clore's City Centre Properties, put in a bid of £1 million. Noel Hornsby, the chairman of Whitehall Court Ltd, advised shareholders that the offer was a good one in the circumstances, and it was accepted.[1] Finding themselves now in the position of a 'caretaker government', the Whitehall Court management told the Authors' Club that they did not feel authorised to renew its lease on the premises.

Murrayfield's managing director, Walter Flack, was an bullish former Army sergeant who had made his fortune in the post-war property boom and was often photographed with a large cigar and a pint of ale. Sharing the contempt for Victorian architecture that was then widespread, Flack announced the company's intention to demolish 'one of the most hideous buildings in the world' when the remaining leases expired, and replace it with 'efficient' modern offices and flats.[2]

The search for a new home was no longer a bargaining ploy but an urgent necessity. The committee authorised Robin Goodfellow to enter into negotiations with the Constitutional Club around the corner on Northumberland Avenue with a view to sharing premises. The Constitutional Club, however, was planning to rebuild, and was unable to

Above: Graham Greene (standing) at work with Douglas Jerrold in the Bedford Square offices of Eyre & Spottiswoode (National Portrait Gallery). Below: many of the literary rambles in Pearson and Kingsmill's *Talking of Dick Whittington* started at the Authors' Club

Above: Major Hugh Bertie Campbell Pollard. According to Jerrold, he 'had a habit of letting off revolvers in any office he happened to visit'

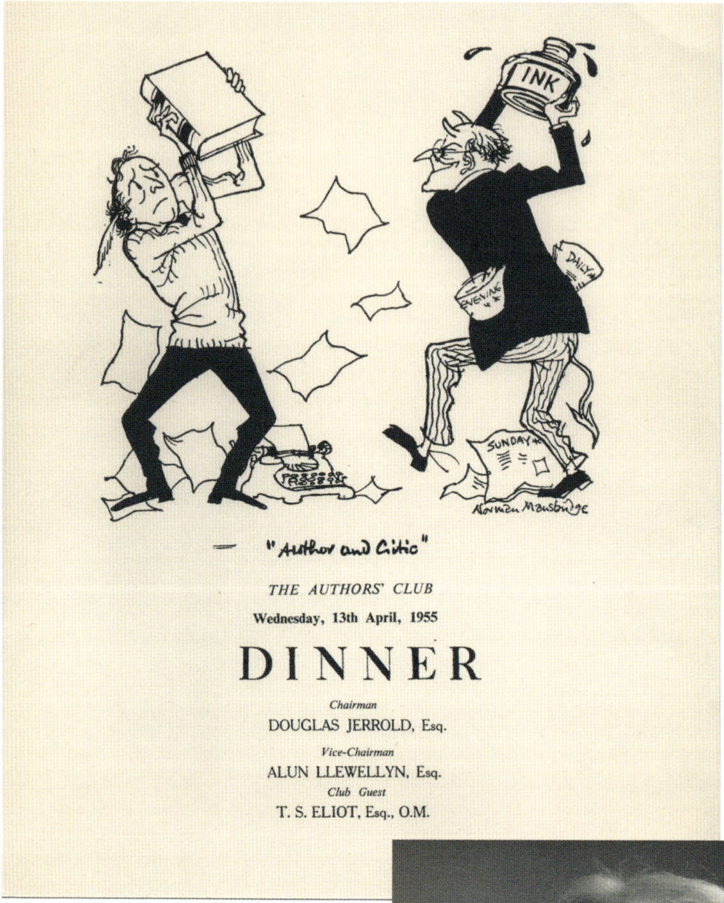
INK
EVENING
SUNDAY
Norman Mansbridge
"Author and Critic"
THE AUTHORS' CLUB
Wednesday, 13th April, 1955
DINNER
Chairman
DOUGLAS JERROLD, Esq.
Vice-Chairman
ALUN LLEWELLYN, Esq.
Club Guest
T. S. ELIOT, Esq., O.M.

Above: menu card for a 1955 dinner at which T.S. Eliot addressed the club on the topic of 'Author and Critic' (Authors' Club)

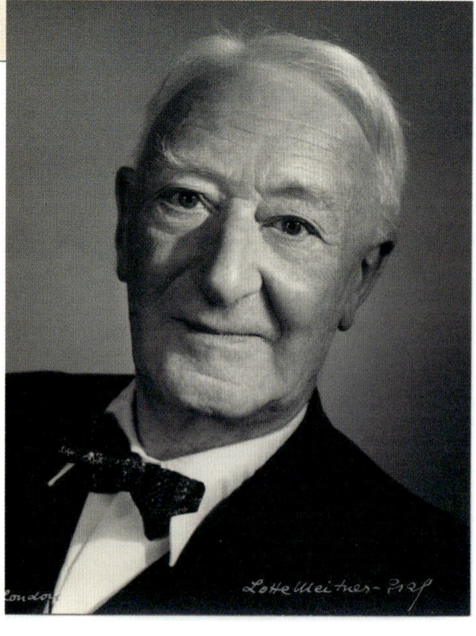

Right: the Rev. Nathaniel Micklem, theologian, broadcaster and Chairman of the Authors' Club from 1958 to 1961, photographed by Lotte Meisner (Authors' Club)

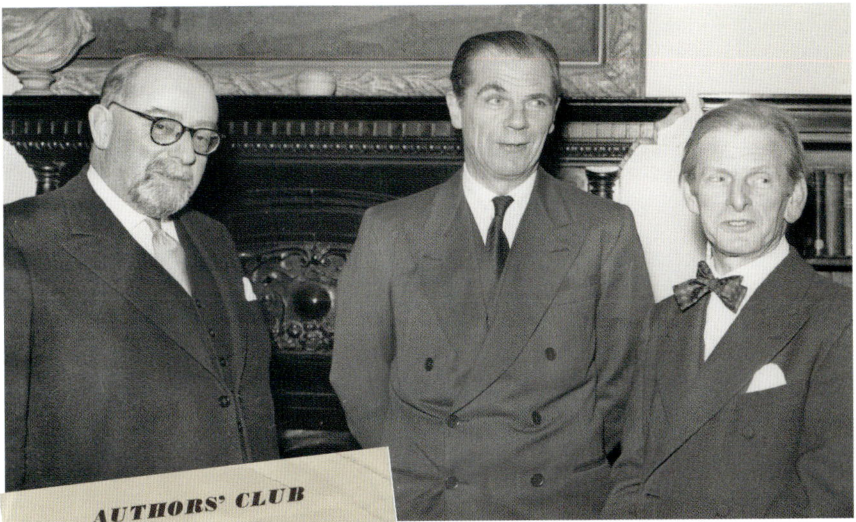

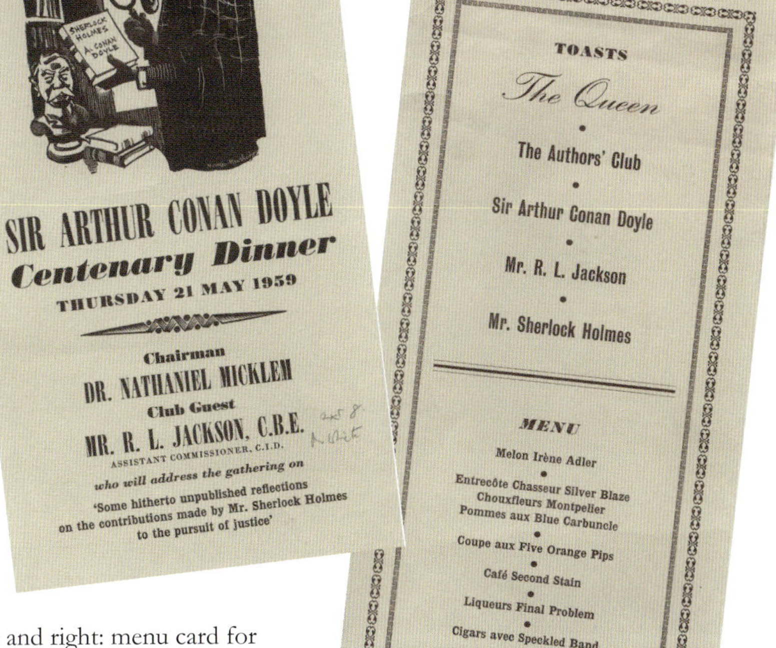

Above: Sir Charles Petrie, Laurence Meynell and an unidentified man at the Authors' Club (Authors' Club)

AUTHORS' CLUB

SIR ARTHUR CONAN DOYLE
Centenary Dinner
THURSDAY 21 MAY 1959

Chairman
DR. NATHANIEL MICKLEM
Club Guest
MR. R. L. JACKSON, C.B.E.
ASSISTANT COMMISSIONER, C.I.D.
who will address the gathering on
'Some hitherto unpublished reflections on the contributions made by Mr. Sherlock Holmes to the pursuit of justice'

TOASTS
The Queen
•
The Authors' Club
•
Sir Arthur Conan Doyle
•
Mr. R. L. Jackson
•
Mr. Sherlock Holmes

MENU
Melon Irène Adler
•
Entrecôte Chasseur Silver Blaze
Chouxfleurs Montpelier
Pommes aux Blue Carbuncle
•
Coupe aux Five Orange Pips
•
Café Second Stain
•
Liqueurs Final Problem
•
Cigars avec Speckled Band

BENHAM

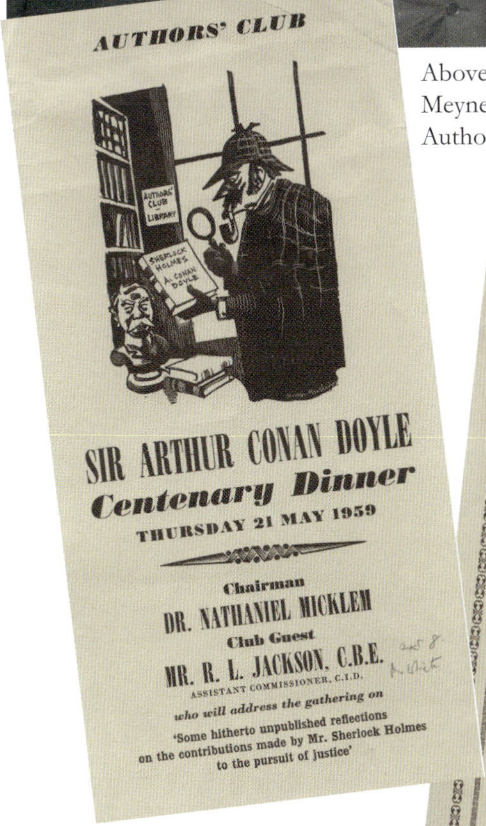

Above and right: menu card for the club's Arthur Conan Doyle centenary dinner, 21 May 1959 (Authors' Club)

Left: Compton Mackenzie, President of the Authors' Club from 1957 to 1972. The portrait is signed by Mackenzie, 'To the members of the Authors' Club from Compton Mackenzie, *amicus amicis*, April 16 1958' (Authors' Club)

Below: Lesley Macdonald Weissenborn, the first woman to chair the Authors' Club, around the time she joined in 1972, and the bookplate that her artist husband Hellmuth engraved for the club (Authors' Club)

Left: the prolific writer E.G. Cousins, pictured at the age of 100, rejoined the Authors' Club in 1984 after a 40-year absence. Below: Cousins's 1951 novel *To Comfort the Signora* was banned in Ireland on the grounds of immorality

Right: the main staircase of the Arts Club in Dover Street at the period when the Authors' Club was in residence (Arts Club)

Above: Authors' Club brochure, circa 2007. Left: flyer for the Authors' Club lunch to celebrate the publication of Mark Crick's collection of literary pastiches, *Kafka's Soup*

Right: the 2013 Dolman Prize was awarded jointly to Kathleen Jamie and Robert Macfarlane at Hatchard's bookshop in Piccadilly. The judging panel, from left, were Amy Sohanpaul, Peter Hughes, Mary Novakovich, Sarah Spankie and Barnaby Rogerson. Bill Dolman stands centre, with Jamie; to their right is David Quentin, who accepted the award on Macfarlane's behalf (Victoria Carew-Hunt)

Above: Authors' Club President John Walsh (right) in conversation with Cardinal Cormac Murphy O'Connor at a lunch in May 2016 (Sunny Singh)

Right: Sunny Singh, who became Chair of the Authors' Club in 2015, pictured with Professor Liz Kelly (left) and the Egyptian writer and activist Mona Eltahawy at the club in December of that year

Above: the Smoking Room at the National Liberal Club. Below: the NLC's grand staircase (both photographs reproduced by kind permission of the Trustees of the National Liberal Club)

make any such commitment. (The magnificent Victorian terracotta pile was torn down in 1962.) Then, in June, the new owners of Whitehall Court unexpectedly agreed to renew the Authors' Club's lease for five years, subject to a rent increase after three. That November, Flack lunched at the Authors' Club and met a number of members. Goodfellow thought he displayed 'a sympathetic interest' in the club and its affairs.[3]

With the threat to the club averted for the time being, its social events continued. On 15 February 1961, Nathaniel Micklem presided at a house dinner for E.M. Forster.[4] Now 82 years old, Forster had given evidence at the Lady Chatterley trial the previous November and, having started the year 'in abysmal depression' was looking forward to the opening of Santha Rama Rau's 'splendid' dramatization of *A Passage to India* at the Oxford Playhouse a few days later.[5] Among those present was Henry Williamson,[6] then in the process of revising *The Innocent Moon*, the ninth volume in his semi-autobiographical *roman fleuve*, *A Chronicle of Ancient Sunlight*. It may seem surprising that an author whose love of nature had curdled into a hatred of modern civilization that led him to unqualified approval of Hitler should have attended a dinner for the most urbane of Bloomsbury liberals, but Forster had done much to promote *Tarka the Otter* on its publication in 1928. And while Williamson's fascism has left an indelible stain on his reputation (to the extent that the Henry Williamson Society feels obliged to disclaim his views on its website), writers engaged with nature, from Ted Hughes to Robert Macfarlane, have held his work in high esteem.

That May, Nathaniel Micklem's term as Chairman came to an end; Langley Russell was elected in his place, and Micklem was elevated to the general council. In December, Kingsley Amis presented the Best First Novel Award to Lionel Davidson for his crime novel *Night of Wenceslas*. Laurence Meynell presided at the dinner.[7] Russell did not stand for re-election at the next AGM in July 1962, 'due to pressure of his other commitments', so Charles Petrie took up the chair for the second time. On 2 August 1962, the motoring journalist Michael Lindsay was elected Honorary Librarian, and set about 'weeding out surplus books' in the library to ensure that the collection was of more practical use to members.

At his inaugural dinner the following October, with Micklem presiding, Sir Charles addressed the members (those present included Russell,

Thurston and Goodfellow) on the topic of 'The London Club Today'.[8] We have no record of what he said on that occasion, but when he revisited the subject in his memoirs, he took a nostalgic view. 'Talleyrand once said that only those who had lived before the French Revolution knew what living was,' he wrote. 'I would adapt his adage to modern times by saying that only members of a West End club before the Second World War know what club life is really like.'[9]

To restore that lost glory, one of his first acts as Chairman was to institute an Annual Reception, and he used his extensive social and political connections to ensure that it was a glittering event. On 10 December 1962, some 150 members and guests gathered in the club rooms at Whitehall Place. The guests of honour were John Profumo, then Minister for War, and his wife, the actress Valerie Hobson. Also present were the Liberal leader Jo Grimond and his wife Laura, along with her mother, Lady Violet Bonham-Carter; George Brown, then Deputy Leader of the Labour Party; the Italian and Mexican ambassadors and their wives; the Marquess and Marchioness of Bristol; and the Earl and Countess of Kilmuir. Among the club members present were Meynell, Micklem, Gavin and Ione Thurston, Michael and Diana Lindsay, and Robin and Mrs Goodfellow.[10]

Diana Lindsay recalls that John Profumo was charming, while Valerie Hobson 'sparkled with gaiety and glamour'. The *Tatler* ran a column of photographs under the headline 'Party for Authors'. There was Sir Charles, bearded, genial, clinking champagne glasses with the Marchioness of Bristol; Laura Grimond, in earnest conversation with the Italian Ambassador, Pietro Quaroni; the novelist and historian Carola Oman and, in elegant profile, Valerie Profumo, unaware of the scandal that, within weeks, would engulf her husband and end the premiership of Harold Macmillan.[11]

Meanwhile, the threat of demolition still hung over Whitehall Court. The National Liberal Club, which had a separate lease on the eastern end of the block, remained an obstacle to the developers' plans, but in July 1962, an Extraordinary General Meeting of the NLC voted to accept an offer of £460,000 from City Centre Properties for their part of the building. Subject to planning permission, this would enable the developers to demolish the whole of Whitehall Court to make way for a new building, in which the NLC was promised leasehold premises at a peppercorn rent. There would, the members were told, be no disturbance for some years and, when complete, the new, modern premises would be more economical to run.[12]

In March 1963, however, Walter Flack was found unconscious in the bath at his flat in Whitehall Court by his chauffeur, Charles Turner, and taken to Westminster Hospital, where he died. He was 46. By a twist of fate, the inquest was conducted by an Authors' Club member, Gavin Thurston, then HM Coroner for Inner West London. A pathologist told the court that Flack had taken about 12 grains of barbiturate – not an excessive dose – and that the hot bath would also have predisposed him to sleep. Charles Turner said that his employer had told him he could think better in the bath, and that he had found his pipe, tobacco and matches on the edge of the tub. Thurston found that Flack had drowned while under the influence of barbiturates, and recorded a verdict of accidental death.[13] Although Flack was no longer a director of City Centre Properties, he still retained substantial holdings, and his death caused the company's shares to plummet on the stock exchange.[14]

In April 1963, Goodfellow began discussions with Elizabeth Barber, the Secretary of the Society of Authors, about letting male members of the Society use the club's facilities after 5pm. The following month he reported back that negotiations had run into difficulties; the Society had from its inception been open to men and women, and its committee had raised objections, though he believed the problem might be overcome by allowing women members to use the ladies' annexe at Whitehall Court. Meanwhile, parallel negotiations with the Teachers' Club had run aground on the same issue. The following November 1963, Goodfellow resigned as Secretary on the grounds of ill health. Michael Lindsay was taken on in his place, initially for a trial period of three months.

The second annual reception was held at the club on 9 December 1963 to coincide with a major exhibition of Goya's work at the Royal Academy. The guests of honour were the Academy's president, Sir Charles Wheeler, and his wife and fellow artist Muriel Bourne. Conspicuous among the guests was the Armenian businessman Nubar Gulbenkian, a larger-than-life figure with a luxuriant beard, monocle and green orchid in his buttonhole. Diana Lindsay remembers being asked to greet and make conversation with him, which she found a daunting experience. She recalls his arrival in one of the two Austin FX4 taxicabs he had adapted for his own use. Three ambassadors were present: Cornelius Cremmin of Ireland, Leon Melas of Greece, and Ardeshir Zahedi of Iran, along with representatives of the Mexican and Spanish embassies. The three main political parties were represented by Philip Rea, Liberal leader in the House of Lords, and his wife Lorna; Philip Inman, Lord Privy Seal in Attlee's government, with Lady Inman; and the Conservative Paymaster General John Boyd-Carpenter and his wife Peggy. The historian Stephen Runciman and the celebrated portrait painter James Gunn were also guests. Among the club members and their wives were Sir Charles and Lady Petrie, Nathaniel Micklem, Gavin and Ione Thurston, Kenneth and Anne Garside, Michael and Diana Lindsay, Harold Brockman, and Guy and Ellen Schofield.[15]

Schofield was one the most prominent figures in the club at this time. A former editor of the *Yorkshire Evening Post* and the *Daily Mail*, he had served as Director of Publicity for the Conservative Party from 1955 to 1957; Petrie described him as 'one of the ablest editors the *Daily Mail* ever had, and the kindest of men'. Another leading light of the club was Arthur Maiden, a doctor, medical writer and deputy chairman of the British Medical Association's representative body. 'A craggy Scot who came to London on a regular basis for meetings of the BMA,' Michael Lindsay recalls, 'he found the club suited his needs admirably. He was a GP in Lincolnshire, and I remember visiting his home in Saxilby and was amazed to find his hall decorated with framed Authors' Club dinner menus.'

Another member who was often to be found in the club at this time was Joseph Yahuda, a barrister who practiced at the Old Bailey and other criminal courts in London. Born in Jerusalem in 1900, he was also a teacher of Hebrew at the Judaic school of Tangiers, and the author of *Law and Life, This Democracy* and *Bio-Economics* (Pitman, 1938), a pioneering environmental tract that called for the introduction of a planned ecosystem throughout the British Empire. A small, bald man, Joe – as he was known to his friends – was a popular figure on account of 'his engaging personality, his arresting comments on all manner of topics, his generosity of spirit and his general friendliness. He would attend meetings of the club, raise all manner of points with a disarming and mischievous twinkle.'[16]

In 1964 this sociable group was joined by the writer Eric Whelpton. Born and brought up in France at the turn of the century, Whelpton cut an elegant figure, and proved an eloquent raconteur at the Tuesday lunches presided over by Sir Charles Petrie.[17] As an undergraduate at Oxford, he had befriended Dorothy L. Sayers, who is believed to have modelled Lord Peter Wimsey on him. After serving in the First World War, he worked as a teacher in France and an estate agent in Italy before returning to England. When war broke out again, his linguistic skills secured his deployment in intelligence in North Africa and Italy. Now 70, Whelpton could already look back on a long career as a prolific author of travel guides, mostly to destinations in the Mediterranean. Several of these books were co-authored with his wife, the artist Barbara Crocker. Many years later, she became only the second woman to chair the Authors' Club.

A link with the club's past was broken when, on 8 June 1964, Douglas Jerrold died at the age of 70. In poor health for several years, he had not been seen at the club for some time. Laurence Meynell represented the club at his Requiem Mass at Corpus Christi church in Covent Garden. In addition to Jerrold's widow Eleanor, the mourners included his old friend and sparring partner Victor Gollancz, Arnold and Lady Lunn, Charles Friend of Eyre & Spottiswoode, and a representative of the Spanish Embassy.[18] Sir Charles Petrie told the *Guardian* that Jerrold, like his great-grandfather and namesake, was 'one of nature's rebels, with a very cutting and cruel pen' but – he was quick to add – 'a kind heart'.[19]

On 7 July 1964, Micklem presided at an informal lunch for Harold Wilson, at which Petrie, Thurston, Victor Bonham-Carter, Paul Baker, Harold Brockman, Guy Schofield, Kenneth Garside and Michael Lindsay were all present.[20] Wilson had been elected Leader of the Labour Party the previous year; just three months after this lunch, following the general election of 15 October, he was Prime Minister.

That month, Michael Lindsay revived the idea of admitting women members of the Society of Authors. In a memorandum to Petrie and Thurston, he drew attention to the club's precarious financial position, and suggested three possible solutions: to move to smaller premises in Whitehall Court; to move elsewhere; or to increase the club's income by admitting Associate Members, including women, from the Society.

This, he asserted, should not be seen 'only as a money grabbing idea' – it would also reinvigorate the life of the club. While it might not be popular with some members, there were enough who believed it represented the only real future for the Authors' Club.

The committee agreed that Lindsay and Bonham-Carter should approach the Society of Authors. At the next committee meeting, in September, the two reported that that following their discussions with the Society, the 'matter should not be rushed but there should be a gradual increase of contact', starting with the Annual Reception on 20 January the following year. In the event, the reception was postponed because of the serious illness of Winston Churchill. The wartime leader died on 24 January 1965; his state funeral on the 30th was an occasion of national mourning, during which all shops, places of entertainment and public institutions were closed as a mark of respect.

When the reception was finally held on 25 February 1965, several prominent members of the Society of Authors were among the guests welcomed by Sir Charles and Lady Petrie: Elizabeth Barber,; Frank Williams (Lord Francis-Williams), a member of the Society's Management Committee; Geoffrey Trease, chairman of the Society's Children's Writers' Group; Geoffrey Household, the author of *Rogue Male*, and his wife Ilona; and the historian Cecil Woodham-Smith and her husband George Woodham-Smith.

Otherwise, the guest list followed the established formula. Nubar Gulbenkian was again a conspicuous presence, while the diplomatic service was represented by the Swiss and Greek ambassadors, Béat von Fischer and Demetrios Nicolareisis, accompanied by their wives. Balancing Francis-Williams, who was a Labour peer and former minister in Attlee's government, was the Conservative transport spokesman Enoch Powell, who attended with his wife Margaret. The club members present included Victor Bonham-Carter, Harold Brockman, Kenneth and Anne Garside, Michael and Diana Lindsay, Dr and Mrs Arthur Maiden, Laurence and Joan Meynell, Nathaniel Micklem, Guy and Ellen Schofield, and Gavin and Ione Thurston.[21]

In the spring of 1965, Victor Bonham-Carter succeeded Sir Charles Petrie as Chairman, and on 26 May, he presided as Norman Reid, the Director of the Tate Gallery, presented the eighth Banister Fletcher

Award to John Pope Hennessey for his *Italian High Renaissance and Baroque Sculpture*.[22] One of Bonham-Carter's first acts was to lend the club £1500 to refurbish the premises. Josephine Street, a fashionable Knightsbridge interior designer, was commissioned to install a new, larger bar in the old Silence Room; the former bar was renamed the Meredith Room, which could be rented out for meetings and private dinners; the Billiard Room became a library with new shelving, and the rest of the club was redecorated throughout. There was even a proposal to install a fruit machine, but nothing came of this. The conversion did not dispel the presence that was said to appear in the former Silence Room, clutching a sheaf of papers. 'A modern novelist, and member of the club,' Petrie reported, 'has suggested that it may be the ghost of Charles Garvice gloating over his royalties, for he is alleged to have written some of his books there.'[23]

Bonham-Carter was determined to modernise the club in other ways too. A new logo was designed and brochure printed to assist with a membership drive. In June, Kenneth Garside suggested that women should be admitted on four out of five weekday evenings, and it was decided to hold a ballot of club members on the question. When the papers came in, the result was 60 to 25 in favour. Balancing the majority vote against the small number of papers returned and known opposition among certain regulars, however, the committee voted not to take the matter any further at that time.

Bonham-Carter was furious. In a note to himself, typed on the back of a Society of Authors circular, he admitted that he was 'frustrated and annoyed over sniping re Admission of women' and would 'not conceal the fact I am strongly in favour of the idea'. The club needed to attract younger members, 'who no longer are in sympathy with the point of view that a man's club should be totally exclusive of female company'. The result of the ballot was 'a democratic decision freely arrived at, and must be loyally upheld… All I ask is that committee members and ordinary members acknowledge this development and support it, and also give it a fair trial in the light of the long-distance possibilities of having women in the club – or not – on a more permanent basis.' In the margin, in ballpoint pen, he added darkly: *'Otherwise VBC cannot carry on.*[24]

In November, he expanded on his ideas in a memo to Garside and Lindsay. Noting that the club was poorly used in the evenings, he recommended introducing pre-theatre buffet suppers and mixed receptions as a 'conditioner of opinion' to prepare the way for full admission of women. While noting that the lavatories would require major alterations, he stressed that 'Habits are changing and men do *not* go to the club for the evening as they used to… Behind it all, I think that sheer economics will force us to adopt this course.'

At a dinner on 11 January 1967, the novelist Brigid Brophy addressed the club on 'Being a Woman Writer'.[25] Victor Bonham-Carter, who had invited her, took the chair. Reading from handwritten notes on long slips of pink paper, she delivered a witty and trenchant critique of the club's policy of not admitting women. As a woman, she began, she was only there as a guest. If other clubs such as the Athenaeum wished to exclude women, that was entirely their own business, 'but your own case is not so simple: because… the name of your club makes free with the name of what is, after all, *my* profession. In SW10 [where the Society of Authors was located] I am recognised as an author… But when I cross London it seems I am overtaken by an invisible change. When I arrive here in SW1, I am no longer an author. I have a dreadful suspicion that I know what you think I am. You think I am an authoress.'

Disposing of the objection that the title was considered good enough for Jane Austen with the observation that Austen 'had to put up with a good many things' such as not having a vote or the right to a university education, she pointed out that the *Shorter Oxford English Dictionary* considered the term obsolete. 'You are exploiting one of those quirky inconsistencies that are part of the glory of the English language. If you were called the Writers' Club you couldn't possibly keep me out on the grounds that I'm a writeress.' Riffing playfully on these linguistic oddities, she asked, 'Why authoress and bus conductress but not writeress and driveress?… Suppose we all belonged to a slightly different profession…' Conductor, she observed, took the feminine form when a woman was in charge of a bus, but not when she was in charge of an orchestra. 'If I had the talent to be it, I'd be conductor not conductress of the Halle.'

To exclude women without changing the club's name, she concluded, was therefore a sin against the English language, which writers should never commit; but to change the name to justify the exclusion would be a sin against the imagination, which was even worse. Having delivered this *coup de grace,* she ended on an emollient note, expressing gratitude for the patience with which the members had listened to her, before observing that they had brought it on themselves, not only for their sins, 'which I've gone on about quite enough', but also by being so charming that she would now have to tell all her woman writer friends how much they would enjoy being members of the Authors' Club.[26]

By now, City Centre Properties had abandoned its plans to demolish Whitehall Court. Since the controversial destruction of the Euston Arch in 1961, the tide of public opinion had begun to turn in favour of Victorian architecture, encouraged by the tireless campaigning of the Victorian Society, founded in 1958 by Nikolaus Pevsner and John Betjeman. Among the beneficiaries was Whitehall Court, which was finally given a Grade II* listing in February 1970. Although the fabric of the building had been saved, the Authors' Club itself was in decline, as were London clubs in general. Edward Walsh, the Secretary, reminisced:

> A club like the Authors' attracted like-minded men of a literary bent who saw each other almost daily and who regarded the Club as a second home. It is a tribute to the openness of the Club that the only qualifications were literary… Not surprising then that Morley Roberts and his friends thrived in the lively (despite the regular contretemps), friendly atmosphere… But since the war, indeed perhaps before then but unobserved, there had been changes in the way of life of the men of Mr Roberts's social class. The telephone, the television, a more domesticated home life, and a more demanding business environment have destroyed the club life that Morley Roberts knew. People do not come to evening functions, members do not join the Authors' (or any other club) to enjoy the stimulating society of other writers…[27]

Subscription income from members was no longer keeping pace with expenditure, and other sources were insufficient to bridge the gap. The accounts for 1966–67 showed a deficit of £3924, and the excess of expenditure over income was £1332, nearly £500 more than in the previous year. At a committee meeting held before the AGM on 7 June 1967, Victor Bonham-Carter announced that he would not be standing as Chairman for a third year because of the demands of his work for the Society of Authors and the Royal Literary Fund. His successor, Gavin

Thurston, acknowledged that the club would have to decide whether or not it could carry on, either in Whitehall Court – which would require an immediate injection of at least £1000 a year – or elsewhere.

The committee agreed to approach some of the other clubs in the building to see if they would be interested in sharing premises. This would allay the management of Whitehall Court's concern that there were too many clubs in the building, used by too few people. Because each club naturally wanted its own dining room, the basement had become a rabbit warren issuing small quantities of food from a central kitchen to 16 different distribution points throughout the building. The arrangement was inefficient and unprofitable, and the management was threatening a general reduction in facilities.

At the AGM later that evening, the committee outlined the proposal to the members, who endorsed it. In the midst of this crisis, the Chairman, Gavin Thurston, suffered a devastating personal loss when his wife, Ione Witham, was run over and killed while they were returning from a holiday in Devon.[28] By the autumn, the plan to share premises had come to nothing, and in November, after much heart-searching, the committee was forced to conclude that the only solution was to leave Whitehall Court altogether. This was not an easy decision; the Authors' Club had been in Whitehall Court for 60 years, and much of its history and traditions were bound up in the premises.

'Then,' as Sir Charles Petrie observed, 'began that weary quest for amalgamation with some other institution which those responsible for the management of West End clubs in modern times know only too well.'[29] The Chairman and Secretary were invited to a preliminary discussion with the United Service Club in Pall Mall (known as the Senior). On 6 March 1968, Thurston wrote to members that, subject to the approval of the Annual General Meeting, the Authors' and Chemical Clubs would be welcome at the Senior. The deal would stem the club's financial losses while providing alternative facilities for its members. As there would be no separate club room, however, there was a real risk that the separate identity of the Authors' Club could be lost.

At the very last moment, just days before the AGM, scheduled for 9 April, was due to approve the move, the committee received an alternative offer from the National Liberal Club next door at 1 Whitehall

Place. It had major advantages over the deal with the Senior. Firstly, the NLC would provide the club with its own room and bar on the second floor, with easy access by lift. Secondly, the financial arrangement would enable the club to discharge its debts far more quickly. Thirdly, the club would remain in the building with which it had such strong historical associations.

Because there was not enough time to circulate the details of the NLC offer, the AGM was adjourned until 2 May. The reconvened meeting voted conclusively to move to the National Liberal Club, and on 4 June 1968, the Authors' and Chemical Clubs opened for business in their new home. They were allocated a room of their own on the top floor of the building and their own table in the NLC dining room, though much of the Authors' Club's library had to be dispersed. After a few weeks of camping out at trestle tables, a permanent bar was installed, and by mid-August things had begun to settle down. 'That the Authors' did not have to put up its shutters then and there,' Petrie recalled, 'is due to two of its members, Gavin Thurston and Kenneth Garside, and to the Secretary, Michael Lindsay, for whom no praise could be too great.'[30]

The wisdom of the move was confirmed by the news that City Centre Properties had sold Whitehall Court to another property company, Claborn Developments. While there were no plans for demolition,[31] the new owners had little intention of allowing the clubs to remain or maintaining any dining room service.[32] On 12 February 1969, the Authors' Club held its first annual reception for two years, and its first at the NLC. In the absence of Gavin Thurston, Kenneth Garside and his wife Anne welcomed the guests, including Enoch Powell, the apostolic delegate Archbishop Cardinale, the NLC Chairman Sidney Hope and the formidable *Panorama* reporter James Mossman.[33]

On 22 April 1969, Laurence Meynell chaired a dinner at which John Trevelyan, Secretary of the British Board of Film Censors, spoke on 'Censorship – Helpful or Harmful?' With his bald head fringed by black hair, thick-rimmed spectacles and cigarette clamped perpetually between his lips, Trevelyan was a familiar figure on the arts scene, and his signature appeared on the certificate screened at the beginning of every film shown in the UK. He was also a genuine cineaste who was able to admire the artistry with which a film was made while critical of its contents. He steered the Board through the most challenging period in its history, when film-makers and audiences were demanding greater expressive freedom while campaigners such as Lord Longford, Mary Whitehouse and the Festival of Light were denouncing obscenity and calling for tighter restrictions. Among the films on which he was called to adjudicate were Sam Peckinpah's *Straw Dogs*, Ken Russell's *Women in Love* and, perhaps most controversially, Andy Warhol's *Flesh*.[34]

That February, both John Betjeman and Osbert Lancaster were given honorary membership and co-opted on to the general council. Trevelyan was among the guests at the next Annual Reception, which was held on 18 March 1970. Kenneth and Anne Garside welcomed the guests, among whom were the ill-fated Turkish Ambassador Zeki Kuneralp and his wife Necla. A cultured man with a deep interest in literature, Kuneralp was subsequently transferred to Madrid where, in 1978, he was the target of an assassination attempt by Armenian separatists that killed his wife, her brother and their driver; Kuneralp himself survived, but retired from the diplomatic service to devote himself to writing. The historian Dame Veronica Wedgwood was also there, along with Laurence Meynell, Nathaniel Micklem and Gavin Thurston, who introduced his new wife, the distinguished medical statistician Janet Hazell, whom he had married the previous year.[35]

Now that the matter of premises had been resolved, the question of women members could be postponed no longer. In the changing social climate of the 1960s, the club's refusal to admit women looked increasingly indefensible. How could a club that was pleased to admit 'properly qualified gentlemen irrespective of race, colour or creed' continue to deny membership to women? 'We used to have occasional bursts of shame,' Edwin Robertson confessed, 'at the thought that Jane Austen and George Eliot could not have been admitted to the company of authors, except as guests at lunch.'[36]

In 1968, the Best First Novel Award had been awarded to Paul Bailey for his unsparing and unsentimental study of old age, *At the Jerusalem*. Not only did it launch the career of one of Britain's finest novelists, it also harked back to an earlier winner: Bailey later said he was 'haunted' by Brian Moore's *Judith Hearn*.[37] The following year, the award was opened to women writers for the first time; since the prize included a year's honorary membership alongside the silver-mounted quill, the admission of women as members became inevitable. As it happened, the prize was won that year by Barry England for *Figures in a Landscape,* and in 1970 by Peter Tinniswood – who went on to forge a distinguished career as a radio playwright – for *A Touch of Daniel.* But in 1971, the award went to Rachel Ingalls for her powerful debut *Theft*, and after that, the next five awards were all won by women: Rosemary Hawley Jarman for *We Speak No Treason* in 1972; Jennifer Johnstone for *The Captains and the Kings* in 1974; Sasha Moorsom for *A Lavender Trip* in 1976; Barbara Benson for *The Underlings* in 1978; and Katherine Gordon *The Emerald* in 1979.[38]

In the event, the long-overdue reform was achieved with little fuss. 'I think everyone saw it as inevitable,' Michael Lindsay recalls. 'Kenneth Garside and Victor Bonham-Carter were very pro having women members, and I don't think that generally it caused any undue ructions.' The 80th AGM of the Authors' Club was due to be held on 16 June 1971, but had to be adjourned, as the accounts were not ready. When it reconvened on Wednesday 8 September, the executive committee urged the members to vote in favour of a motion 'that ladies who are concerned with literature and/or members of the learned professions be admitted to membership of the Club'. The motion was passed and the rules amended accordingly. Because the National Liberal Club did not yet admit women to all its facilities, their subscription was reduced proportionately. The Authors' Club thus became the first major London club to admit women; the NLC followed five years later in 1976, the Reform in 1981, and the Athenaeum not until 2002. At the time of writing, the Garrick still does not admit women.

Among the first women to join the Authors' Club was Lynda King Taylor, whose first book *Not for Bread Alone* was a study of industrial relations as seen after a year at Volvo, and who still lectures on industrial relations and employment issues. Michael Lindsay remembers her as 'a very lively person' who often visited the club. Another early woman member, and one who would make an outstanding contribution to the club's affairs, was Lesley Macdonald Weissenborn, who joined in February 1972. A descendant of the Scottish poet and fantasy writer George MacDonald, she was married to the German émigré artist and wood engraver Hellmuth Weissenborn, whom she had met in 1943 when she was working for the Baynard Press. They married in 1946 and began publishing children's books together under the imprint of the Acorn Press. In 1952, Hellmuth provided the illustrations for Victor Bonham-Carter's *The English Village*. The couple's most ambitious collaboration, the first full English translation of Grimmelshausen's 1668 picaresque novel *Simplicius Simplicissimus* took them seven years, and was published in 1964 with 45 of Hellmuth's woodcuts.[39]

As a committed member of the Liberal Party, this diminutive, outgoing and indefatigably sociable woman rapidly became a driving force within the Authors' Club, as she did in every other area of her busy life, and in 1975 was the first woman to join the executive committee.

At the AGM in 1972, Kenneth Garside was succeeded as Chairman by the film critic and historian Roger Manvell. The aviation historian Richard Gardner, who joined the Club around this time at the suggestion of his friend David Wragg, the author of many books on railway and military history, recalls its friendly atmosphere. 'We had a cosy environment within the NLC in our little private room upstairs, and a very loyal lady, Emily, who acted as our barmaid and general club Mrs Fix-it.' At the time, Gardner was working as a public relations officer at the Ministry of Defence just a few yards away in Whitehall, so he found the club conveniently located. 'It was possible to pop in and have a quick snack at lunchtime, with a chance to share the hour or so with fellow members.' Among those he remembers being there almost every day were John Betjeman, Victor Bonham-Carter, Edwin Robertson, Lesley Weissenborn and Harold Brockman.

The club's President, Sir Compton Mackenzie, however, was seldom seen on its premises by now; age and failing eyesight confined him to his home in Edinburgh for much of the time. Despite his frailty, he remained active, publishing the final 'octave' of his 10-volume autobiography in 1971. The following year he was the subject of a Scottish Television documentary, *A Game of Islands*, in which he reflected on his experiences in two world wars, Scottish nationalism, his Catholic faith, his trial at the Old Bailey, and his life on the islands of Jersey, Capri and Barra. In March, he told *The Times* diary that he had abandoned a novel, *The Very Devil*, because of his deteriorating sight (he did not feel comfortable dictating), but still hoped to add a coda to his memoir that would cover the past 'destructive' decade. 'My only hope is that the Common Market will help to restore manners to the British and abolish Stormont.'[40]

Compton Mackenzie died in Edinburgh on 30 November 1972, just six weeks short of his 90th birthday, and was succeeded as President by Sir Charles Petrie. Mackenzie had chosen to be buried on the island of Barra, where he had lived between 1936 and 1946, and his funeral on 4 December proved as dramatic as any scene from his novels. The light aircraft carrying his body touched down on the beach that served as the island's airstrip 40 minutes late because of high winds and poor visibility. As the coffin was carried from the plane, the kilted figure of Calum Johnston, a celebrated piper, folklorist and old friend of Mackenzie's, played a lament. As the mourners marched uphill to Eoligarry cemetery in the driving rain, the 82-year-old Johnston took up his pipes again, only to collapse during the service and die shortly afterwards in the car sent to take him home.[41]

11

DOVER STREET

*As a drinker will always find a bar and a poker playe always
finds a game, writers will always find each other.*

Jane Gardam[1]

In 1976 Jeremy Thorpe, then leader of the Liberal Party, handed the management of the National Liberal Club to a Canadian property developer called George de Chabris, who claimed to hold the Papal title 'His Serene Holiness the Prince de Chabris'. This charismatic chancer promised to invest his own money to turn around the Club's fortunes; instead, he spent the next nine months pillaging its assets, selling its wine cellar at Christies and its priceless Gladstone Library to Bristol University for a derisory £40,000, running several fraudulent businesses from the premises, installing his family rent free, and paying his children's school fees from its accounts. Then, in March 1977, having emptied the till of the day's takings, he drove off in his powder-blue Rolls Royce owing the club £60,000. After a creditor filed a bankruptcy petition and Scotland Yard launched an investigation into his affairs, De Chabris – real name George Marks – fled the UK for Miami on 'health grounds'.[2]

It was clear that the Authors' Club needed to find a new home, and a sub-committee consisting of Edwin Robertson, Paul Baker and Lesley Weissenborn began searching for one. Richard Gardner, who was familiar with the Arts Club at 40 Dover Street in Mayfair, suggested that they visit the place. Founded in 1863 by Charles Dickens, Anthony Trollope and Lord Leighton, the club was located a stone's throw from the Ritz and a short walk from the Royal Academy. Though badly bombed in the war, the late Georgian townhouse still retained its grand marble staircase, dominated by Solomon J. Solomon's huge portrait of Mrs Patrick

136

Campbell, and had a large restaurant, elegant first-floor drawing room and comfortable bar. It soon became apparent that it was the most promising of the alternatives on offer.

On 14 June, having negotiated terms with Tom Kenny of the Arts Club, Robertson reported his findings to Paul Baker and the Authors' Club Secretary, Edward Walsh, and together they drafted a letter to the members recommending the move. Shortly afterwards, Robertson, Baker, Walsh and Weissenborn joined Kenny for dinner at the Arts Club, where they also met Brian Bevan and Andre Edington, the Arts Club Secretary. 'It was a lovely summer's evening and the patio looked splendid,' Robertson recalled. 'The food and company were wonderful, and there was a spirit of liveliness we had not known for a long time. In our minds the matter was clinched when we saw, adorning the left side of the bar, Dickens's cheque for his £5 membership subscription.'

On 22 June, Robertson had a meeting with Sir Charles Petrie, Laurence Meynell and Brian Bevan. A committee meeting was called to prepare a resolution for the AGM, which was well attended. After a lively discussion, the members voted unanimously in favour of the move. Twenty-five stayed on to dinner, to which Tom Kenny and Andre Edington had also been invited. 'They saw at once why we wanted to move,' Robertson remembered. 'As Tom drove me home, we had a long discussion about the naturalness of our two clubs getting together.'

The Authors' Club moved into the Arts Club on 1 July 1976, and held its first lunch there on the 8th. The first dinner in the new premises took place five days later, on the 13th, and was attended by 40 guests. On 28 July the Club held its first Committee meeting at Dover Street.[3] Sadly, Sir Charles Petrie would never see the new premises; he became seriously ill in the summer of 1976, and died on 13 December 1977. He was 82. At his memorial service at the Guards Chapel, Wellington Barracks, the following January, the Authors' Club was represented by Gavin Thurston, Kenneth Garside, Lesley Weissenborn and Edward Walsh.[4] He was succeeded as President by Laurence Meynell, an Authors' Club member of 30 years' standing. Having successfully led the Authors' Club into its new home, Edwin Robertson completed his term as chairman in the summer of 1978, and was succeeded by Paul Baker.

Robertson was hopeful about the move:

Already there is a touch of the old world back again. The monthly club lunch is an event, and the house dinners are being revived. We mean to rebuild our library; and we shall throw parties when members publish new books of note. We would like to re-forge the link with the Society of Authors. Finally, we gain enormously by uniting with other artists – painters, sculptors and architects – who have had a corporate existence longer than ourselves. Besant, I feel sure, would have approved.[5]

Not everyone took such a sanguine view, however. Visiting the Club in 1978 while researching the career of Morley Roberts, the American scholar Theophilus M. Boll struck an elegiac note:

> The minutes gave me an exciting view of the activities of this informal academy of great creative minds in the arts and sciences of the free world that gave no warning of the cultural chaos into which it was to fall. By 1978 the Authors' Club had been dissolved as an entity, its library sold, and its title absorbed into the Arts Club of Dover Street, which had become largely a luncheon club for businessmen.[6]

If Robertson was understandably optimistic about the Authors' Club's prospects, Boll was considerably too dismal. For some members, the Arts Club was a natural home. Lesley Weissenborn introduced her artist husband as a 'spouse member' in 1976; together, 'They made the monthly lunch an event not to be missed,' Robertson remembered.

> And outside Club premises she was the perfect host. Some of the most interesting and enjoyable social events in London were held in Lesley's home in Harley Gardens. She never failed to gather interesting people, always with some members of the Author' Club and usually a display of musical talent. They were wonderful evenings. Then, each year, on the first Sunday in December – a few days before Lesley's birthday – many of us would visit the annual display of books from Acorn Press at their home in Harley Gardens, with Hellmuth's engravings and paintings. They were wonderful evenings. Then, each year, on the first Sunday in December – a few days before Lesley's birthday – many of us would visit the annual display of books from Acorn Press at their home in Harley Gardens, with Hellmuth's engravings and paintings.[7]

Russell Foreman, who moved to Dover Street with the Authors' Club, was both a writer and a painter. Born in Melbourne in 1921, he enjoyed enormous success with the first of many novels, *Long Pig* (Heinemann, 1959), a historical adventure set in the South Pacific. In Fiji, he met his future wife, Mary; the couple settled in Florence, where he taught a writing course at an American girls' school and set up the Russell Foreman School of Painting. He returned to Australia each year, where he was an ardent champion for the rights of the Aboriginal people. A dapper, sociable man, he numbered the novelists Alec Waugh and Nevil Shute and the tennis player Evonne Goolagong among his many friends, and was a popular figure in both the Authors' and the Arts Clubs.[8]

In 1977, they were joined by Elwyn Evans, a senior BBC producer for the Welsh region, former director of programmes for the Nigerian Broadcasting Corporation, and the author of *Radio: A Guide to Broadcasting Techniques*, which was published by Barrie & Jenkins that year. Lesley Weissenborn became Honorary Secretary in January 1979, sharing the work with Huldine Ridgeway, a member of the Arts Club staff. Later that year Hellmuth created a new bookplate for the Club, using the technique of engraving on Perspex that he had pioneered himself. In April 1981, Lesley succeeded Paul Baker as Chairman (she did not favour the title chairperson), becoming the first woman to hold that office. Although she was heartbroken when Hellmuth died the following year, she remained a powerhouse. 'She moved us along and allowed no dawdling at committee meetings,' Robertson recalled. 'Some called her a tornado, but she was never destructive.'[9]

In 1980, Kingsley Amis judged Best First Novel Award again, presenting it to the travel journalist Martin Page for his Biblical alternative history *The Pilate Plot* at a dinner on 28 February. That summer, two longstanding members, Gavin Thurston and Harold Brockman died; Eric Whelpton died the following February. But the club continued to recruit new members including, in 1981, Norman Marsh, a human rights lawyer and founding member of the Law Commission, and Constance Babington-Smith. After a wartime career in the Women's Auxiliary Air Force, during which her analysis of aerial photographs alerted the Allies to the threat posed by doodlebugs, she became a journalist for *Life* magazine in the United States and an author.[10] Her first book, *Evidence in*

Camera (1958), an account of her work in aerial reconnaissance, was followed by biographies of Amy Johnson (1967), Rose Macaulay (1972) and John Masefield (1976). At the time of joining the Authors' Club, she was writing a life of the Russian emigré Iulia de Beausobre, which appeared in 1983.[11]

The 1981 Best First Novel Award, adjudicated by Thomas Hinde, was won by Dawn Lowe-Watson for *The Good Morrow*, a sensitive study of a troubled mother-daughter relationship that takes its title from a poem by John Donne. Although this was her debut as a novelist, Lowe-Watson was far from an inexperienced writer. After a career as a journalist and writer of stories for women's magazines, she had branched out into radio plays in the late Seventies. She enjoyed a long and fruitful collaboration with the BBC producer Cherry Cookson, and her plays attracted distinguished casts: *Short Madness* starred John le Mesurier and Elizabeth Bell, while *The Haven* featured Charlotte Mitchell and Paul Copley. Two further novels, *A Sound of Water* (1982) and *Black Piano* (1986), were to follow. After her year's honorary membership expired, she remained with the Authors' Club, and was much admired for her resourceful and enthusiastic contribution to its affairs and her support and encouragement of other writers.

That year, at the suggestion of Laurence Meynell, Lesley Weissenborn applied to the Arts Council for funding to increase the Best First Novel Award and the Banister Fletcher and help to fund their administration. She succeeded in obtaining a grant of £500, which was divided equally between the two awards, with £100 to be used as prize money, £100 as payment to the judge and £50 toward administration costs.[12] The next award, adjudicated by the *Daily Telegraph*'s literary editor David Holloway, went to Anne Smith, editor of the *Literary Review*, for her semi-autobiographical account of her Scottish upbringing, *The Magic Glass* (Michael Joseph).

On 2 March 1982, Edwin Robertson chaired a dinner for the Archbishop of Canterbury, Robert Runcie. The Archbishop, a former soldier who was among the first British troops to enter Belsen, was about to be engulfed in controversy. On 2 April, Argentinian forces invaded the Falkland Islands, a British outpost in the South Atlantic to which that country laid claim. After a short but ferocious war, in which 649

Argentinian and 255 British servicemen were killed, the Argentinians surrendered on 14 June. The conflict aroused passionate feelings in both countries, and exposed deep divisions in British society. A month after the end of the fighting, a service of thanksgiving was held in St Paul's Cathedral. Warning against triumphalism, Runcie preached penitence and reconciliation, and called for remembrance of the Argentinian as well as the British dead. The Prime Minister, Margaret Thatcher, and the tabloid press were furious.

In October, just four months after the end of the war, Richard Gardner was invited to visit the islands to see how the military were settling in and how the conflict had affected the lives of the islanders. Flying from RAF Brize Norton on a VC10 and then, from Ascension Island, a Hercules transport plane, he took his sketchbook, artists' materials and camera to record what he saw. In May 1983, he gave a slide talk to a supper party at the Club about his visit before returning to Port Stanley to serve as Joint Services Public Relations Officer for five months.[13]

Meanwhile, Lowe-Watson, Evans and Garside were busily reading the submissions for the Best First Novel Award. 'If you have over 30 novels to read between October and February,' Lowe-Watson recalled, 'you take a chapter where you can… Walking down Bond Street or up Piccadilly to 40 Dover Street, with a bag of books over my shoulder and one open in my hand…' In early March 1983, she drove to Stratford-upon-Avon in her bright blue Citroën to present the eight shortlisted books to the adjudicator, Jacquetta Hawkes, the archaeologist, poet, novelist and widow of J.B. Priestley.[14]

At the prize dinner on 28 April, Hawkes presented the award to Frances Vernon for *Privileged Children* (Michael Joseph). Written when the author was just eighteen, this saga of a dysfunctional artistic family in the Bloomsbury era was a work of precocious talent. Hawkes praised Vernon's natural, unaffected prose, and her ability to create a large cast of convincing characters, each of whom was capable of growth and change. It only remained to be seen whether she would develop the ability to tell a strong story. 'She has plenty of time to discover whether she has that gift also,'[15] Hawkes added, tragically unaware that time was not on Vernon's side. *Privileged Children* was the sparkling debut of a brilliant but tragically brief career; already struggling with severe depression, Vernon managed to complete five more acclaimed novels before her death from an overdose of tranquillisers in 1991 at the age of 27. Her last book, *The Fall of Doctor Onslow*, was published posthumously in 1994.[16]

In September 1983, the Banister Fletcher Prize, adjudicated by David Dean of the Architectural Library and augmented by £100 from the Arts Council, was presented to Stefan Muthesius, Professor of Art History at the University of East Anglia, for his book *The English Terraced House* (Yale University Press). He was the grand-nephew of the German architect and author Hermann Muthesius, whose massively influential book *Das englische Haus* (1904) – written while he was a cultural attaché in London – did much to promote the ideals of the Arts and Crafts Movement in his native land. In October Malcolm Muggeridge returned to the Authors' Club as guest of honour at a dinner. Now 80 and recently received into the Roman Catholic Church after meeting Mother Teresa of Calcutta, he had become a well-known television personality, famed for his diatribes against the degeneracy of modern society. On 1 December, Kenneth Garside died suddenly at his home in Surrey. He was 70. His cremation took place a week later at Randall's Park, Leatherhead,[17] and a service of remembrance was held in the chapel of King's College, London the following January.[18]

When Lesley Weissenborn's term as Chairman ended in 1984, Edwin Robertson took up the role once again, although Lesley continued to serve on the committee as Vice-Chairman and subsequently as Treasurer. Despite the success of the awards and a rich programme of social events, membership had now dwindled to less than 90. Robertson told the committee that it would be his 'special care' to persuade publishers to take out membership on behalf of their authors. Weissenborn reminded him drily that she had tried this and received 'only dusty answers'. The only way to recruit new members, she believed, was through personal acquaintance.[19]

That year, however, the Authors' Club did regain one long-lost member after more than 40 years' absence: Edmund Cousins. Now 91, Cousins had not renewed his membership after the war, though he had gone on to publish many popular thrillers and romances. After his wife died, he recalled,

I felt a hankering for the old camaraderie, so like an Officers' Mess. I inquired whither the Authors' Club had flitted, and came to look see, and was staggered to find the shabby old flat exchanged for a stately mansion in Ritz country. I was received with great warmth and quickly reinstated, and for seven years have enjoyed the kindness and consideration that appear to be warranted by extreme old age. Particularly I have been struck by the friendly manner in which We of the Authors' have been received and almost absorbed them of the Arts, to the extent of becoming a happy single Community.

And yet... And yet...

Perhaps I may be forgiven if, in this glance back, I feel a small twinge of nostalgia for the shabby, cosy refuge above Whitehall.[20]

Then living in Devon, Cousins still travelled to New Zealand to visit relatives, where he was interviewed by New Zealand Radio about his experiences as a boy in China. He was awarded honorary life membership of the Authors' Club in 1992, and died in 1996, in Exeter, at the age of 103.

In the spring of 1985, the Authors' Club President, Laurence Meynell, presented the Best First Novel Award to Frederick Hyde-Chambers for *Lama: A Novel of Tibet* (Souvenir Press), which overcame strong competition from Iain Banks's *The Wasp Factory* and Sebastian Faulks's debut *A Trick of the Light*. Riki Hyde-Chambers, as he was known to friends, remained a member of the club for long after his honorary year had ended. A staunch champion of Tibet, he went on to publish several other books rooted in the traditions and culture of that nation, and is now a council member of the Buddhist Society and Chairman of the Tibet Society of the UK. 'Having been associated with Tibetans for three quarters of my life,' he said in his acceptance speech, 'it really is part of the very marrow of my being... We live at an extraordinary time. The end of a civilisation is at present unique to Tibet, but then having to come to terms with a swiftly changing, confusing and often alien society... is happening about us.'

After Elwyn Evans succeeded Edwin Robertson as Chairman in 1987, he found that relations between the Authors' and the Arts Club had become strained over the question of membership. When the clubs had merged in 1976, it was agreed that the Authors' should continue to elect its own members, who would then become members of the Arts Club as of right. With the passage of time, however, it became apparent that the Arts Club secretariat no longer understood the position. One longstanding and much-valued member of the Authors' Club, having dropped out for a year, applied to rejoin and was presented with a long and in her view intrusive questionnaire by the Arts Club secretary. Victor Bonham-Carter, meanwhile, reported that he had seen in the *Writers' & Artists' Yearbook* that applications for membership should be made to the Arts Club. Evans and Weissenborn arranged a meeting with the secretary and, with the support of two senior Arts Club members who remembered the initial negotiations, were able to reach an amicable confirmation of the original agreement.[21]

In 1987, after several years on the reading panel for the Best First Novel Award, Dawn Lowe-Watson was entrusted with the final choice. At a well-attended dinner on 27 July, she presented the prize to the promising young writer Helen Harris for her debut *Playing Fields in Winter* (Century Hutchinson). The Banister Fletcher was awarded to Sir Michael Levey at a dinner on 5 October for his book *Giambattista Tiepolo* (Yale). The adjudicator, as in previous years, was Francis Goodall from the professional literature committee of RIBA.

That year also saw the inauguration of a new prize. Brian Marsh, a partner in the insurance brokers Nelson, Hurst & Marsh, expressed the wish to sponsor an award for the best biography, to be presented every two years. At a dinner on 16 October, the adjudicator, the controversial Conservative politician and author Enoch Powell, revealed in a characteristically polished speech that the winner of the first award was Roland Huntford for *Shackleton* (Hodder & Stoughton). Unfortunately the hurricane that had devastated southern England the previous night prevented the author from attending, so Ion Trewin, editorial director of Hodder, received the award on his behalf.

The 1988 Best First Novel Award was adjudicated by Jane Gardam, who presented the prize to Peter Benson for *The Levels* (Constable). A dark coming-of-age love story set on the Somerset levels that was also shortlisted for the Whitbread Prize, it was the first of several 'West Country Gothic' novels from a writer who had worked as John Fowles's gardener and received encouragement from the older writer. Gardam, author of the Booker-nominated *God on the Rocks* (Hamish Hamilton), became a regular and enthusiastic member of the club.

Elwyn Evans, who had made clear that he would only serve as Chairman for one year, was succeeded by Richard Gardner in 1988. The following spring, Laurence Meynell died, just three months short of his ninetieth birthday. Though old age had prevented him from attending many of the Club's functions for some time, he had maintained a lively interest in its affairs, keeping in touch through Edwin Robertson. The Presidency was then offered to Sir Steven Runciman, who replied that he was honoured by the invitation but that 'in view of his advanced age, were he to accept, it would in all probability mean that we would very shortly be looking for another President'. In the event, he lived until 2000, but the Presidency remained vacant for several years.

In January 1990, Dawn Lowe-Watson persuaded Kenneth Branagh to accept honorary membership, and arranged a dinner to welcome him. That year, Simon Brett – again thanks to Lowe-Watson – adjudicated Best First Novel Award, which he presented to Lindsey Davis for *The Silver Pigs*, the first of her highly successful historical mysteries featuring Marcus Didius Falco, an imperial agent in 1st-century Rome.

Victor Bonham-Carter resigned from the Club in March 1991, after 36 years of membership. Now 77, he had just completed *The Essence of Exmoor*, and was living in semi-retirement with his wife Cynthia in Milverton, Devon, and rarely visited London. Dawn Lowe-Watson was elected to the committee of the Arts Club, giving the Authors a voice in their discussions. In June, Barbara Whelpton succeeded Gardner in the chair on the understanding that she would serve for just one year. There was much to be done in that time. The committee set about winding up the Authors' Club Limited, which had outlived its purpose and was now effectively moribund. (The company was finally dissolved in 1994.) Although the Authors' Club library had been mostly dispersed during two moves, a small core remained, augmented by books submitted for the awards, along with a selection of beautiful Acorn Press editions donated by Hellmuth and Lesley Weissenborn. Many of these books, however, along with those belonging to the Arts Club, had been stored in the cellars of 40 Dover Street, where they were damaged by water from a leaking pipe. Lowe-Watson took on the job of rescuing them, reassembling the library and having it catalogued, while Norman Marsh cleaned and pressed the damaged volumes.

The Authors' Club's centenary, which fell in November 1991, was celebrated with a buffet supper in the Bronze Room of the Arts Club, attended by many members of both clubs and their guests. E.G. Cousins, the club's longest-standing member, recalled the Whitehall Court days before the war. In a speech typed up on a 1917 portable Corona (similar to the one on the cover of this book), the playwright Christopher Fry delivered a whimsical account of how he had purchased a revolving summer house that had once stood in Jerome K. Jerome's garden at Selsey. Recalling her wartime exploits and her subsequent career as a biographer, Constance Babington-Smith said that 'perhaps I can be best described as an interpreter, first of aerial photographs and latterly of famous contemporaries.' In a powerful address, Jane Gardam, who had just won the Whitbread Novel Prize for *The Queen of the Tambourine,* noted how privileged they all were to be there when, in many countries, merely 'to admit to being a member of an authors' club is to risk a sentence of death'. She went on to describe her work with PEN, and drew attention to the cases of persecuted and imprisoned writers around the world, including the Burmese poet Min Lu, who had disappeared after writing a poem critical of the military regime in his country.[22]

The spectre of political repression was also present at the 1992 Best First Novel Award. After delivering a thoughtful appreciation of all the shortlisted books, Nina Bawden, who had flown back from Greece for the occasion, awarded the prize to Zina Rohan for *The Book of Wishes and Complaints* (Hutchinson), a bittersweet exploration of a young girl's coming of age in Communist Czechoslovakia. Rohan, a documentary maker with the BBC World Service, had married a Czech colleague, and described her experiences of life in that country in her speech of thanks.

By May 1992, membership had dwindled to as few as 50. In July, Barbara Whelpton had an exploratory talk with the Arts Club chairman, Ian Jackson, about the future of the Club. Not for the first time in its history, the Authors' Club was teetering on the brink of extinction. To make matters worse, the team that had done so much to sustain it through the Dover Street years was succumbing to age and fatigue. In July, Lesley Weissenborn, in failing health, announced that she was unable to continue as Treasurer. Huldine Ridgeway, who had provided the Club with such reliable secretarial backup, was due to retire from the Arts Club at the end of the year. When Barbara Whelpton was elected Chairman, she had indicated that she would only be able to hold the position for a year. Now, after breaking three ribs in a fall, she confirmed her wish to stand down, but informed the Club that Brian Marsh had agreed to be her successor.

Marsh, who took office in January 1993, believed that the best prospect for the Authors' Club was to 'link and fuse wherever possible' with the Arts Club:

> We are moving in this direction in the knowledge that there is strength in numbers and that, in the depths of a recession, only tough, realistic measures will ensure survival. Ultimately, a lively, economically sound Authors' Club as a 'Department' of the Arts Club may well prove to be preferable to any continued solo existence for the Authors' Club itself.[23]

If Marsh brought new energy and direction, he also brought significant financial resources. From 1992 until 1997, his charity the Marsh Christian Trust subsidised the Authors' Club, enabling Ann Carter (now Ann de la Grange) to work a three-day week as club secretary, organiser of talks and dinners, and administrator of the Best First Novel and Banister Fletcher Awards, as well as two new literary prizes, the Marsh Biography and Children's Literature in Translation awards. The Trust also contributed the prize money and adjudicator's fee for all except the Banister Fletcher. The 1994 Best First Novel Award was presented by A.N. Wilson to Nadeem Aslam for his debut *Season of the Rainbirds* (Andre Deutsch), an exquisitely wrought story of the effect on a village in Pakistan of the delivery, 19 years late, of a sack of letters; in 1995 John Mortimer would award the prize to Andrew Cowan for *Pig* (Michael Joseph); while in 1996 Penelope Lively presented the first Marsh Award for Children's Literature in Translation to Anthea Bell for her translation of Christine Nöstlinger's *A Dog's Life*.

Meanwhile, Riki Hyde-Chambers and Lesley Weissenborn had put together a new brochure to attract prospective members, and listing the members of the general council, which now consisted of the publisher Carmen Callil and the novelists David Benedictus, Winston Graham and Elizabeth Jane Howard. The committee agreed to print 500 copies, which were sent out to authors, dramatists, publishers, journalists and academics in Britain and abroad. Temporary membership was offered to members of the Society of Authors and the Royal Society of Literature. By the following year, the club had recruited 20 new members, and several distinguished writers soon followed, including Fay Weldon, Auberon Waugh and Erin Pizzey. Dermot Englefied, who joined in 1993, had just retired as Librarian of the House of Commons, while Mary Medawar was a prolific and successful writer of romantic historical fiction. Reay Tannahill, having worked as a probation officer, advertising copywriter and journalist, had forged a career as a historian with *Regency England* (1964) and *Paris in the Revolution* (1966). After the groundbreaking *Food in History* (1973), which practically invented the subject, she turned to fiction with an 800-page family saga, *A Dark and Distant Shore* (1983). It was a massive bestseller, and many more historical novels followed. A fierce, chain-smoking Scot, she soon established herself as a central figure in the Authors' Club.

In June 1995, the writer and broadcaster Godfrey Howard, whose *Macmillan Good English Handbook* would appear in 1997, gave a talk on 'Whose Language is it Anyway?', which was attended by 100 people; he joined the club shortly afterwards, and was soon elected to the committee. Kevin Laffan, who joined in 1996 with his wife, the actress Jeanne Thompson, was the creator of *Emmerdale Farm* (now simply *Emmerdale*), the longest-running British television soap after *Coronation Street*, and scriptwriter of its first 262 episodes. Another temporary member recruited from the Society of Authors was the coroner, writer and broadcaster Bill Dolman. The author of *Can I Speak to the Doctor?* (Cassell, 1981), *Doctor on Call* (Virgin Books, 1987) and the volume of *Atkin's Court Forms* devoted to coroners, he was one of two regular radio doctors on the *Jimmy Young Show* for 25 years, and also worked on classical music and educational programmes. By 1997 he was a member of the committee, and the following year became deputy chairman.

While the Marsh Christian Trust continued to subsidise the Authors' Club and its literary awards and to pay the salary of its secretary, the funding was never intended to be permanent, but to provide a breathing space while the Club sought ways to become financially self-sufficient. The existing arrangement with the Arts Club made this virtually impossible, so the Authors' Club was faced with three options: to renegotiate the agreement, to find another home, or to amalgamate completely. In March 1996, Brian Marsh asked the committee for their authority to investigate other premises. The principal contenders were the English Speaking Union, a few blocks away on Charles Street, and PEN, then based in a small terrace house in Chelsea. A questionnaire was sent out to members to ascertain their views on the matter. In November, Dermot Englefield told the AGM that of the 63 who returned their slips, 33 indicated that they would move, 27 said they might possibly move, seven said they would remain at the Arts Club, while 14 said they would resign if the Authors' Club were amalgamated with the Arts Club. Several members considered that it was extremely important that the Authors' Club should have its own secretary.

A meeting was scheduled with the Arts Club committee to discuss the relationship between the two clubs. Reay Tannahill insisted that the Authors' Club should receive a percentage of the membership fees and profit from catering to secure its financial independence. The Arts Club would not agree to this, but it did agree to pay Ann de la Grange for one day a week's work on Authors' Club business when the MCT subsidy came to an end – an important concession that meant that the Authors' Club would remain at Dover Street for the time being.

The Club and its members, meanwhile, were having to come adapt to a new medium that would transform the environment in which writers worked as fundamentally as radio and television had done. On 11 November 1996, in an Authors' Club talk under titled 'How Will Art and Text Survive in the Electronic Age?', Jane Dorner, a director of the Authors' Licensing and Collecting Society, warned of the dangers of plagiarism posed by the new technology. Using live online examples, she demonstrated the ease with which text could be copied and pasted. Changing cultural attitudes, she added, lent respectability to such practices, while national laws offered little protection in a global electronic environment.[24] Before long, the club had it own website and email account – electronic media without which it is impossible to imaging it functioning today.

When Brian Marsh ended his term as Chairman in 1997, he was elected to the Presidency, which had been vacant since the death of Laurence Meynell. Despite the significant improvements Marsh had made to the club's situation, his successor, Reay Tannahill, faced the same fundamental problems that had bedevilled the Authors' Club since its days at Whitehall Court: declining membership, the relationship with the host club, the preservation if a distinct identity, and securing an independent income. The subsidy from the Marsh Christian Trust had finally come to an end, and the Biography and Children's Literature in Translation Awards had reverted to the MCT. Furthermore, in exchange for the Arts Club providing secretarial assistance and postal and telephone services, the arrangement by which the Authors' Club retained 5 percent of each subscription had been abandoned. The cumulative effect of these changes was to blur the independent identity of the Authors' Club and lead to its increasing absorption into the Arts Club, whose management by this time regarded the Authors as primarily members of the Arts Club who happened to have a special interest in books.

12

Back to the Future

Everything comes in circles… The old wheel turns, and the same
spoke comes up. It's all been done before, and will be again.

Arthur Conan Doyle, *The Valley of Fear*

In March 2004 my old college held its media group reception at the Arts Club, through the good offices of an alumnus and Authors' Club member, Godfrey Howard. Charmed by the elegant staircase, Georgian drawing room, and a cheque signed by Dickens displayed in a glass case by the bar, I picked up a membership form. I was working for the *Independent*, which was then being transformed from a broadsheet to a tabloid, involving long, demanding shifts, so a place to relax with fellow writers and like-minded friends in central London was a welcome proposition. In view of my occupation, the secretary, Lucy Jane Tetlow, directed me towards the Authors' Club, which I joined.

The Chairman at the time was Bill Dolman, who had succeeded Reay Tannahill in 2000. His main challenge, he told me recently, was finding a sponsor for the Best First Novel Award. Since 1999, the prize had been sponsored by the Folio Society. That year, Alan Sillitoe, who had won the award himself four decades earlier, had returned to the club to give the prize to Jackie Kay – now Scotland's Makar – for *The Trumpet*, her novel based on the life of the transgender American jazz musician Billy Tipton, which also won the Guardian Fiction Prize. Now, however, that sponsorship had come to an end. Unknown to me, moreover, Bill and Lucy Jane were visiting other clubs with a view to finding an alternative venue, so all was not as well at Dover Street as it appeared on its glittering surface.

Also on the committee was Edwin Robertson, then in his nineties but still a vital force within the club, Dawn Lowe-Watson, and Jeanne Laffan. Other regulars I remember vividly from this period were Alan Beecham,

151

who ran the Arts' Club film society, the writer Frank McGillion and his wife Eve, and David Mitton, the TV scriptwriter and director responsible for more than 180 episodes of the Reverend W. Awdry's children's favourite *Thomas the Tank Engine*. Lunches were held in the Bronze Room, an area that could be partitioned off from the main restaurant, although this was rarely necessary for the evening events, which always attracted a large number of Arts Club members. The members of the two clubs mixed freely, and I often encountered artists such as Peter Blake (the Arts Club's President), Maurice Cockrill, then President of the Royal Academy, and the terrific Abstract Expressionist painter John Hoyland at the bar.

At the AGM that summer, Bill Dolman's term as Chairman came to an end, and he was succeeded by the literary agent Dinah Wiener. She had first been introduced to the Authors' Club when her client T.J. Armstrong won the Best First Novel Award in 1996 for *Walter and the Resurrection of G* (Headline), and subsequently joined in order to have a base in central London at which to meet authors and publishers. Soon Ann de la Grange asked her to become Chair.

'I thought the club was fuddy-duddy,' she recalls, 'and made a few changes, introducing evening events in the Garden Room with speakers such as Fergal Keane and the tenor – and author – Robert Tear. We had a marvellous evening with Jim Burge, who had just published his book on Heloïse and Abelard.'[1] Among the guest speakers she brought to the club lunches at this time were Joanne Harris, Gyles Brandreth, Sandra Howard and the flamboyant publisher Naim Atallah, who entertained a packed audience with tales of his youthful career as a steeplejack.

Wiener also joined the board of the Arts Club, which was then chaired by Michael Godbee. She soon discovered that the parent club had been running at a loss for 20 years, and that its directors were on the verge of selling the business. She regards her greatest challenge and achievement in this context to be the sale and leaseback arrangement that allowed the Arts Club to continue. 'We did not want to be the directors who sold out,' she insisted, adding that the same was true of the Authors' Club. She also found that the submissions procedure for the Best First Novel Award was hampered by a lack of inside knowledge of the publishing industry. 'We were getting novels published by people's landladies,' she commented. With the help of Lucy Jane Tetlow, she set about putting the process on a more professional footing. By October, they had enlisted me as a reader for the following year's award.

In November, one of Dinah's clients, the cultural historian Daniel Snowman gave a talk at the Authors' Club on a subject of particular interest to me: the influence of exiles from Nazi Germany on British cultural life. At a dinner that month, Robert Tear presented the Banister Fletcher Award to Marco Livingstone and Kay Heymer for *Hockney's Portraits and People* (Thames & Hudson), in the presence of the artist himself. The following spring, Deborah Moggach – by now a longstanding friend of the club – adjudicated the Best First Novel Award, choosing joint winners, Neill Griffiths for *Betrayal in Naples* (Viking) and Susan Fletcher for *Eve Green* (4th Estate).

In 2005, Bill Dolman decided to sponsor a new literary award. Initially, given his profession as a coroner, he intended to set up a prize for crime fiction, but Dinah Wiener advised him that there were already several such awards: 'Gold daggers, silver daggers – as many daggers as you can stick in someone's back.' When the Thomas Cook Award was abandoned by the tour operator after 20 years, Dolman realised that there was now no award for travel writing, and decided to establish one. The £2500 prize would be open to any first-time travel writer published in Britain, and recognise works of literary merit that showed excellence in the tradition of great travel writing; they should combine a personal journey with the discovery or recovery of places, landscapes or peoples, and instill a sense of excitement and wonder in the reader. The award would be presented each July, after the club's AGM and immediately before the garden party.

In September 2005, Lucy Jane Tetlow was succeeded as secretary by the literary agent Stella Kane, and she and Dinah Wiener instituted a popular annual reception for literary agents and scouts attending the London Book Fair. By March 2006 I had joined the committee. That spring, Vikram Seth presented the Best First Novel Award, gracefully complimenting all the shortlisted authors on their achievement before presenting the prize to the poet Henry Shukman for his fictional debut *Sandstorm*, in which a war-weary photo-journalist attempts to come to terms with his traumatic past. The following September, the Authors' Club marked 30 years at Dover Street with a lunch for members of both clubs, at which a Seventies-themed menu was served. Brian Marsh addressed the gathering, and Edwin Robertson spoke amusingly about the early days of the Authors' Club and the move to Dover Street. The Banister Fletcher Prize was also held that November, when Desmond Shawe-Taylor, Surveyor of the Queen's Pictures, presented the award to Julian Spalding for *The Art of Wonder: A History of Seeing* (Prestel).

The first Dolman Prize had been won by Nick Jubber for *Prester Quest* (Doubleday) the previous July. While this engaging account of the author's pursuit of the mythical African king was a worthy winner, the overall level of submissions was disappointing. In 2007 Stella Kane had lunch with the travel writer Michael Jacobs and enlisted him to chair the judging panel. Dividing his time between London and Frailes, the Andalucian village that was the subject of his 2003 book *Factory of Light*, Michael was a fearless and indefatigable adventurer, Hispanophile, and brilliant, convivial companion whose wide-ranging intelligence was matched by his infectious enthusiasm. Under his guidance, the prize began to show flair and gather momentum. To increase the quality and quantity of the submissions, the 2008 award was opened to all travelogues published in the UK, not only first efforts in the genre. This immediately brought some highly acclaimed works, including Robert Macfarlane's *The Wild Places* (Granta) and Tim Butcher's *Blood River* (Vintage), into the contest. Yet the surprise winner – not least to its author – was a debut, *92 Acharnon Street* (Eland), the poet John Lucas's charming and idiosyncratic account of a year in Athens in the Eighties.

The Banister Fletcher Prize was also in need of reinvigoration, and in 2007, the committee informed RIBA that the Authors' Club would take over sole administration of the award. A new and generous sponsor was found in the French businessman Henri Beaufour. Instead of alternating yearly between art and architecture, the prize would now go to the best book on either field published in the previous year, at the discretion of the judges. The art historian, curator and former director of the Dulwich Picture Gallery, Giles Waterfield, agreed to chair a distinguished panel of judges that included the historian and television presenter Dan Cruickshank, and Anna Somers Cocks, the founder of *The Art Newspaper* and chair of Venice in Peril. The guest speaker at the presentation was the artist and ceramicist Grayson Perry.

In May, the *Independent* columnist, literary journalist and restaurant reviewer John Walsh spoke to a club lunch about his novel *Sunday at the Cross Bones* (4th Estate), based on the life of the controversial Rector of Stiffkey. The writers who most influenced him, he recalled, were A, B, C, and D. A for Martin Amis, B for Anthony Burgess ('I interviewed him twice,' Walsh revealed. 'Asking him a question was like putting sixpence in a jukebox and getting out a whole oratorio'), C for Angela Carter, and D for J.P. Donleavy. All these writers enthralled him with their energy, erudition and verbal dexterity. 'And so,' he concluded with exquisite bathos, 'I became a journalist.'

One of the most memorable events of 2007 was the lunch on 23 October to celebrate the publication of the author and photographer Mark Crick's book *Kafka's Soup* (Granta). This elegant literary pastiche purported to be a history of world literature in 14 recipes. Each dish was described in the style of a writer such as Borges, Márquez and the Marquis de Sade ('Now, my chicks... how about a little stuffing?'). Graham Greene recounted the preparation of Vietnamese chicken for an unnamed female visitor, while dabbing glumly at a spreading stain on his shirt as the twilight congealed. Each recipe was illustrated by Crick in the style of an artist such as Warhol, De Chirico, Hogarth and Henry Moore, but the real joy of this little book was Crick's ear for literary parody. Marvellously, the recipes actually worked, and the chef and his staff excelled themselves in reproducing several of the dishes. The lunch was so well attended that we were moved from the Bronze Room into the main body of the restaurant, with Crick's artwork displayed around the dining area. The icing on the metatextual cake, however, was the readings from two fine actors: Sian Thomas, who recited the Jane Austen pastiche with delightfully mischievous irony, and Simon Green, who brought a sense of growing existential panic to the textual insecurities of 'Moules Marinières à la Italo Calvino'.

In 2008, as Dinah Wiener's term in the chair was nearing its end, she and Stella Kane (much to my surprise) asked me if I wanted to stand for the post. Brian Marsh had also expressed his desire to retire as President, as his charitable work was demanding more and more of his time. At the AGM on Monday 7 July, which was held immediately before the garden party, John Walsh was voted in as President, and I was elected Chairman. Michael Lindsay, a member since 1959, rejoined the committee.

In the event, I found Dinah and Stella's assurances that the role of Chairman was largely a ceremonial one to be a little optimistic. I had inherited a club whose predominantly elderly membership was sadly dwindling. Barbara Whelpton had died in 1995; Russell Foreman in 2000, and Lesley Weissenborn in 2001, in her 90th year, after succumbing to Alzheimer's disease. Kevin Laffan died in 2003; Reay Tannahill, Dermot Englefield and Edwin Robertson – a few months after celebrating his 95th birthday at the club – in 2007; and Norman Marsh in October 2008, also at the age of 95. New members were badly needed to keep the club going, and recruitment was clearly the top priority. Fortunately, we were soon joined by a wave of new members, including the literary editor and broadcaster Suzi Feay, the writer, artist and oral historian Rachel Lichtenstein, the literary agent Oliver Munsen, the writer and human rights activist Lucy Popescu, that intrepid publisher of European literature in translation Meike Ziervogel, and the Indian-born novelist and academic Sunny Singh, all of whom brought energy and enthusiasm to the club and helped to modernise its outlook. Yet again, the Authors' Club was demonstrating its ability to renew itself.

The 2008 Banister Fletcher Award dinner was held on 10 November. Andrew Saint overcame strong competition, including the third volume of John Richardson's monumental *Life of Picasso* (Cape), to claim the prize for his *Architect and Engineer: A Study in Sibling Rivalry* (Yale). The guest speaker, Brian Sewell, gave a characteristically entertaining and provocative talk, culminating in a heartfelt plea that two Titians on loan to the National Gallery, which their owner wished to sell, should be kept in this country. Out of a strong shortlist that included Dervla Murphy's *The Island that Dared* and Grevel Lindop's *Travels on the Dance Floor*, the 2009 Dolman Award was won by Alice Albinia for her impressive debut *Empires of the Indus* (John Murray), which also won the Guardian First Book Award.

In many respects, the club was going from strength to strength. It was achieving a higher profile in the world of literature, publishing and the media, developing a strong online presence with a new website, and had recruited the services of the specialist literary, arts and cultural PR agency Flint Media to promote the Dolman Award. Flint's CEO, Wol Balston, joined the club and proved a creative, enterprising and popular member. His efforts paid off in terms of greatly increased press coverage for the award. Michael Jacobs was joined by a distinguished panel of judges including the television presenter, author and travel adventurer Ben Fogle, Candida Lycett Green, the author and editor of her father John Betjeman's letters, Brett Wolstencroft co-founder of Daunt Books, Dan Linsted of *Wanderlust* magazine and Jonny Bealby of Wild Frontiers. At the ceremony on 6 July, the award was presented to Ian Thomson for *The Dead Yard: A Story of Modern Jamaica* (Faber).

The Banister Fletcher dinner, on Monday 9 November, was also a success. Waterfield, joined that year by Iwona Blazwick, director of the Whitechapel Gallery, and the architectural historian Steven Parissien, presented the award to Bruce Altschuler for his book *Salon to Biennial* (Phaidon), a timely history of the public exhibition. The artist Tom Phillips proved a charming, knowledgable and thoroughly entertaining guest speaker. The Best First Novel Award was also thriving. In March, all six shortlisted authors took part in a lively and well-attended reading chaired by Suzi Feay at Waterstone's flagship branch in Piccadilly. All the authors were also present at the awards dinner on Wednesday 7 April, when the novelist Amanda Craig graced the top table as an incisive yet thoughtful and considerate adjudicator, taking pains to praise each of the shortlisted books. Her choice of the winner, Anthony Quinn's *The Rescue Man* (Vintage), was a popular one despite strong competition from Evie Wyld, who went on to win a Betty Trask award for her extraordinary debut *After the Fire, A Still Small Voice* (also published by Vintage).

The monthly lunches were well-attended, with an exceptional run of guest speakers, including Robert Macfarlane, the novelist and biographer D.J. Taylor, and – thanks to Jeanne Laffan – the veteran comedy actress June Whitfield. The biographer Miranda Seymour held the club spellbound with details from her jaw-droppingly frank memoir *In My Father's House* (Simon & Schuster); Rachel Lichtenstein, the author of *Rodinsky's Room* and *On Brick Lane* (Hamish Hamilton), spoke with deep knowledge and feeling about researching her Jewish roots in London's East End; Susie Boyt entertained members with an account of her *Judy Garland Life;* and Michael Jacobs recounted the epic journey along the entire length of South America that had provided the material for his book *Andes* (Granta). In February, Daniel Snowman returned to the club to discuss his brilliant social history of opera, *The Gilded Stage* (Atlantic).

The Arts Club treated us very well in many respects, funding dinners and generously giving out honorary memberships at our suggestion, and we were deeply indebted to the kindness of its staff, especially Giuliano Carra (who had been with the club for 25 years), Joan Dineen in the front desk, Tino Moussaoui, Isaac Opoku-ababio, Suna Sulaiman and Anna Piwowar. Increasingly, however, Dover Street came to seem like a gilded cage. In common with my predecessors, I found myself struggling to maintain the independent identity of the Authors' Club and prevent it becoming just another interest group within the Arts Club, like the Opera Circle or the Book Group. Successive increases in subscriptions, over which we had no control, made it hard to recruit new members. It was becoming clear that, after a long and mostly happy association, we would have to move – but none of us could have anticipated how abruptly it would happen.

In the autumn of 2010, early in the third year of my chairmanship, I was on holiday with my astronomical telescope, wife and mother-in-law at a remote lodge in the Kielder Forest, where mobile phone and internet connections were non-existent. As I drove into a nearby market town for groceries, my phone pinged to display a text message from Stella Kane asking me to ring her urgently. Even in the town, though, I could not get a strong enough signal to make a call. Driving back across high moorland, I was overtaken by a sudden, violent thunderstorm and took refuge in an isolated pub. Cramming all the change I had into the payphone on the wall, I called Stella, and was informed that the new owners of the Arts Club were insisting that it close for major refurbishments, which would take at least six months.

On my return, I had a meeting with Brian Clivaz, the manager of the Arts Club, to discuss the future. He told me that as far as he was concerned the Authors would be very welcome to return when the Arts Club reopened, but hinted in a friendly way that we might not want to do so. I understood this to mean that neither the prices nor the ambience would be to our liking. I could appreciate his position: in 21st-century London, no one could afford to run a large Mayfair townhouse as a shabby-genteel refuge for low-spending artists and writers.

After 34 years of relative stability at Dover Street, the Authors' Club was once more in search of a home. We had no premises, no money, and were not even sure how many members we had, since the distinction between Arts and Authors' members had become blurred. But I was determined that a literary club approaching its 120th anniversary, which had numbered Oscar Wilde, Thomas Hardy, Arthur Conan Doyle and Graham Greene among its members and which still had a great deal to offer the literary life of the nation, was not going to fizzle out while I was its Chairman. We did have one advantage: unlike our friends in the Arts Club, we owned our name and our history. The Authors' Club had moved home before and could do so again. I reassured myself that the Club had faced, and survived, such crises throughout its history. This was nothing new: we had been here before in 1908, 1923, 1952, 1968 and 1976. Every time, the energy and determination of the Committee and the members had ensured that it survived.

The Authors' Club's belongings that had survived our previous moves were parcelled up. The fine mahogany chest that the Marsh Christian Trust had donated to house our archives was dispatched with its contents to the house of the Honorary Secretary, Margaret Barnard, for storage until we found a permanent home, along with the portrait of Algernon Rose, signed photographs of Arthur Conan Doyle and Compton Mackenzie, the billiards and cricket shields, and four landscapes by Hellmuth Weissenborn. A quantity of recent novels and art books submitted for our awards were bought by a Greenwich bookseller, providing a helpful cash injection. There were administrative and financial issues to be resolved: would members who had recently paid a whole year's subscription to the Arts Club, for example, get any of it back?

With the assistance of Jean-François d'Or, we and our fellow exiles from Dover Street, the Danish Club, found a temporary perch at St Stephen's Club in Queen Anne's Gate. This allowed us to continue our lunches without interruption, though it would clearly not be a permanent base, as it consisted of little more than a small bar and a pretty dining room, and was closed in the evening. In March 2011, after visiting a number of clubs in central London, we settled on Blacks in Dean Street. This small, privately owned club in the heart of Soho offered a relaxed and cultured ambience in a beautiful Grade II* Georgian house, one of a row built by John Meard, after whom the adjacent street is named, in the 1720s. Its atmospheric warren of wood-panelled rooms was lit by candles and warmed by well-stoked log fires. The food and wines, imported from small organic producers in Italy and France, were excellent and affordably priced. In November, members and guests filled the rooms and spilled out on to Dean Street to celebrate the Authors' Club's 120th anniversary.

One drawback, however, was the size of the building. There was no one room large enough to hold a prize reception, so the 2011 Best First Novel Award took place in the Champagne Bar at Waterstone's bookshop in Piccadilly. The adjudicator, Joanne Harris, awarded the prize to Jonathan Kemp for his *London Triptych* (Myriad Editions), a novel that charted the lives of three gay men from the time of Oscar Wilde to the present, and her choice was vociferously endorsed by a contingent of supporters from Brighton's LGBT community. The Dolman Prize that year was presented at Hatchards, a few doors down Piccadilly, in November. Michael Jacobs had stood down as chair of judges because his own book *Andes* was in contention; in the event, the panel, chaired by Giles Foden, awarded the prize to Rachel Polonsky for *Molotov's Magic Lantern* (Faber), a haunting investigation of Russia's communist past prompted by the discovery that her Moscow apartment was once occupied by Vyacheslav Molotov.

A further problem we now faced was that without the support of the Arts Club, we had no paid secretary, so many of the administrative tasks necessary to the running of the club had to be undertaken by committee members on a voluntary basis. To some extent this was made easier by the electronic media now available, though updating the website, sending out email newsletters and maintaining a presence on social media required much time and effort. Yet, with our future uncertain, these tasks were more vital than ever.

On 12 January 2012, just two months after last visiting the club, Dawn Lowe-Watson died following a short illness. Her last play, *Fog and Shifting Pebbles*, an atmospheric drama set on Romney Marsh, was broadcast on Radio 4 in 2005. Her funeral was held on Friday 27 January, a crisp, sunny winter's day, at St. Andrew's, Bishopstone, an ancient parish church nestling into the South Downs and overlooking the English Channel. The warm yet dignified Anglican ceremony included a tribute from her friend Jean Mallows, and her Sussex neighbour Dame Felicity Lott sang from Handel's *Messiah* and Fauré's *Requiem*. Michael Godbee and I attended on behalf of the Arts and Authors' Clubs respectively.

In September 2013, the presentation of the Dolman Award was

once again held at Hatchards. 'We felt that we had been offered up the strongest shortlist since the Dolman Prize was inaugurated,' said the chair of judges, the publisher Barnaby Rogerson. 'Judging was very animated,' he added, before presenting the award jointly to Kathleen Jamie for *Sightlines* (Sort Of Books) and Robert Macfarlane for *The Old Ways* (Hamish Hamilton). It was a bold, some would say contentious decision given that, five years previously, Jamie had savaged Macfarlane's *The Wild Places* in the *London Review of Books*.[2]

While Jamie was there to collect her prize in person, Macfarlane was climbing in the Cairngorms and sent a friend in his stead. It was indeed a powerful shortlist, including as it did *Looking For Transwonderland: Travels in Nigeria* by Noo Saro-Wiwa; A.A. Gill's *The Golden Door: Letters to America*; Jeremy Seal's *Meander: East to West Along a Turkish River*; and Michael Jacobs's *The Robber of Memories,* which combines an exhilarating journey up the Rio Magdalena in Colombia with a moving meditation on the nature of forgetfulness and forgetting.[3] Sadly, this was to be Jacobs's last completed book. The following January, we were shocked to learn of his death, at just 61, after the rapid onset of cancer. The obituaries published in the *Daily Telegraph, The Times,* the *Guardian,* the *Observer,* the *Independent,* and the leading Spanish newspaper *El Pais* were eloquent testimony to the affection and esteem in which he was held. His genial and invigorating presence in the club will be missed for many years to come.

Thanks to the film critic Peter Cargin, a member of both the Authors' and National Liberal Clubs, the Best First Novel Award was held in the latter's elegant Lady Violet Room from 2012. As the limitations of Black's became more and more apparent, it occurred to us that a return to the NLC might offer the club a better future. With Peter's help, we entered into negotiations with the management of the NLC, and arrived at a deal that was acceptable to both parties. In November 2013, at the AGM, we put the proposal to the members, who voted overwhelmingly in favour. The following January, we returned to the National Liberal Club.

The NLC of 2014 was a very different club from the one the Authors' Club had left in 1976, and had long since been returned to a sound financial footing. Although this had been achieved at the cost of selling its second-floor and basement function rooms to the neighbouring hotel, the club was still vast. Its elegant, comfortable rooms, panelled restaurant and bar, magnificent pillared Smoking Room with open fires and deep Chesterfields, and the terrace garden overlooking the Thames seemed entirely in keeping with the history of the Authors' Club. The spacious reception rooms, moreover, allowed the club to launch an ambitious programme of evening panel discussions, readings and other events.

The move represented a historic homecoming, not only to the NLC, but to Whitehall Court, the building in which the Authors' Club was located in the days of Conan Doyle and Rider Haggard, where Robert Sherard stepped across the road to Charing Cross Station to catch the Calais boat train, and a stone's throw from Villiers Street where the young Kipling once lodged. One memorable afternoon I was delighted to find the silver inkwell and quill that Barrie had once used to terminate his own speech in a glass cabinet in the Smoking Room, amid a collection of other trophies and ornaments. Our predecessors must have forgotten to take it with them when they moved out of the NLC in 1976.

The reasons for the return were not only historical, however, but practical, and most of the anticipated benefits have materialised. Full members have the use of all the facilities of the NLC and its many reciprocal clubs overseas. With a viable base and efficient administrative backup, it has become possible to focus on developing the club. We have launched a strong programme of evening events, and the club lunches have begun to attract NLC members in addition to our own. After a very precarious three years, the Authors' Club was back on an even keel, and membership was slowly increasing again.

By 2014, I had exceeded my term as chairman, and felt I had achieved much of what I had set out to do in raising the profile and membership of the club. To smooth the transition to the NLC, however, John Walsh and my colleagues on the committee asked me to stay on for a further year. I agreed to do this on the understanding that Sunny Singh would take up the post of deputy chair so that, after a year of joint planning, she would succeed me. Sunny assumed the chair in 2015 and, as I leave the Authors' Club in her capable hands it only remains for me to pay tribute to our excellent president John Walsh, our committee and our members. May the next 125 years be prosperous ones for the Authors' Club.

Not Quite an Afterword

The Authors' Club has been a cornerstone of my social and creative life for much of my stay in London. I had few friends in the city when I moved here, and London – even in those heady, Blairite, pre-economic crisis days – was not the easiest of cities to meet people. So when my agent invited to me to join her for one of the club's drinks evenings, I was sceptical and interested in equal parts.

The club was still in Mayfair then and the grand stairwell, sparkling chandeliers and polite tinkling of glasses didn't promise a place where I'd make friends. Walking up the stairs, I was already calculating how quickly I could leave. But then I ran into a man with a spectacular shock of silvering hair. Precariously balancing a very full glass of wine and crutches, he still managed to offer me his hand and a warm welcome. Throughout the evening, that glass never emptied and, as he somehow negotiated that packed room on those unwieldy crutches – the temporary result of renovations to a Victorian fireplace – not a drop was spilled. He introduced me to a dizzying range of people and told me about others in the room in gently amusing terms. I have little memory of the conversation but I do remember that it was one of the first in Britain where a stale whiff of Empire did not hang over us. And that I laughed a lot. By the end of the evening, Chris Schüler – the author of this volume, a former chair of the club and now a dear friend – had convinced me that I had found a place in the city that I could call my own.

Other friendships grew out of that evening and ensuing years at the club, too many to name here. However to not name Michael Jacobs, the travel writer, bon vivant, gourmet and a fellow lover of Latin America would be too great an omission. Until his untimely death, we would meet every time he returned from his travels or his home in Spain. We alternated meeting at the club and one of his preferred restaurants, El Moro in Exmouth Market. It was over tapas and a Catalan Prioritat that he told me of his poignant meeting with Gabriel García Márquez, a favourite writer of us both, by then already nearly lost to Alzheimer's. It is my great regret that Michael never won the club's travel book award, as his books on Latin America are among the most insightful about the region.

Over the years, memories have piled up: of literature, writing, passionate discussions, heated political debates ended at times by someone stomping off in fury, including – quite often – yours truly. Some of my favourites include a conversation about growing up with state surveillance – bugs in the house and tapped phones – with Melissa Benn; learning what really goes on inside a papal conclave from Cardinal Cormac Murphy-O'Connor (yes, someone asked him if he had picked out his papal name and no, I still won't share his answer); hearing the fiery Egyptian writer and activist Mona Eltahawy's account of the uprising against Hosni Mubarak; and an insider's view of the phone hacking trial by Peter Jukes. The spirit of the original Uncut Leaves sessions lingers over our evenings reading and discussing works still unpublished or at the cusp of publication. There have been long summer afternoons on the terrace and winter evenings by a cosy Smoking Room fire where no topic is ever off limits. If these lunches, dinners and drinks have seamlessly included literature, politics and way too much food and drink, I like to think that is precisely what the club's founders would have wanted.

Yet the club has also grown in ways that perhaps they would not recognise. In 2016, and partly in response to the dismal findings of the *Writing the Future* report about the lack of diversity and inclusivity in publishing, the club chose to support the newly launched Jhalak Prize for Book of the Year by a Writer of Colour. Given our contentious history, as a club and a nation, it is a step in the right direction. At the same time, we continue to administer two of the oldest literary prizes in Britain: the Best First Novel Award and the Art Book Prize (formerly the Banister Fletcher). The Dolman Travel Book of Year has now attracted additional sponsorship from Stanfords, the Covent Garden-based travel book and map shop, and a heightened profile as the Stanford Dolman Award.

For a club that only began accepting women members in my own lifetime, it is telling that we are particularly welcoming to women writers. The first woman chair was elected just a decade after women were admitted, and women make up a majority of the current committee. It is a reflection of how far we have come from that cold November night in 1891. For me, there is also a quiet satisfaction that the old contentions of genders have been finally – correctly – settled. Even that Victorian tussle between aesthetes and hearties seems to have been put to rest with a lively 2015 dinner when the revived Authors' Cricket XI gathered in our clubhouse.

At the same time, I am keenly aware that other questions are not so easily resolved. This club history has brought home once again that each generation must make its choice between right and wrong, exclusion and inclusion, looking towards our past or our futures. Over the course of this summer, debates have raged among members about Britain's referendum on the European Union, and over the fallout from that vote. It is heartening that the club remains as passionately involved with the larger world as at any time in our past. It is also sobering, however, to realise that our safe haven remains so because we must work tirelessly to maintain it while also remaining firmly engaged with the troubles outside our doors.

One year ago, I was elected Chair of the Authors' Club. As the first woman of colour and the first writer from a former colony to hold this office, I still grapple with the full import of our contentious, destructive, intimate history. While I find solace in noting that Archibald Grimké was an early member and that the club invited W.E.B. Du Bois to join a century ago, I am also acutely aware of the many exclusions practised during much of its history. While Frances Hodgson Burnett's 1895 speech to the club gives me goose bumps, I also must recognise that she most likely did not imagine someone like me when she spoke of that future woman who would be 'so much wiser and more stately of mind'.

The ghosts of all those who excluded and were excluded stand at my two shoulders each time I stand to address a club event, and they are both encouraging and terrifying. Together, they push me to take forward the best of the Authors' Club traditions and yet break, rebuild and renew when those traditions become a burden. It is clearer to me than ever before that, even as the world around us is gripped by some strange nostalgia, the club must look forward and into the unknown if we are to thrive, even survive. To quote Edwin Robertson, who helped negotiate the club through particularly tumultuous times, 'Besant, I feel sure, would have approved.'

Sunny Singh

ACKNOWLEDGEMENTS

First and foremost I would like to thank my wife, Geraldine Beattie, for her insightful comments and careful reading of this manuscript. Special thanks are also due to Miranda Seymour and Sunny Singh for the elegant essays which bookend this history.

I am grateful to all the past and present members of the Authors' Club who gave generously of their time in talking to me: Margaret Barnard, Peter Cargin, Ann de la Grange, Bill Dolman, Richard Gardner, Jeanne Laffan, Michael and Diana Lindsay, Brian Marsh, Lucy Popescu, John Walsh and Dinah Wiener. At the National Liberal Club, I owe a debt of gratitude to Janet Berridge, Michael Meadowcroft, Seth Thévoz and Simon Roberts.

Thanks are also due to Bill Grimké, Henry Hemming, Ruth Heredia (Secretary of the Rafael Sabatini Society), Anna Nyburg and Vivien Whelpton; to Tom Holland and Charlie Campbell of the Authors' Cricket XI; and to Simon Rigge, Simonne Waud and Kezia Bayard-White at Sheldrake Press.

I would also like to thank Cherry Mosteshar of Oxford Editors for her skilful copy-editing, John Macphail for the index, Sarah McElroy Mitchell at the Lilly Library of the University of Indiana, and the staff of Richmond Local Studies Library, the British Library and, as always, the inimitable London Library. Where else would one find the histories of gentlemen's clubs shelved under 'Science: Clubs'?

And of course, profound thanks to all our backers, who made the production of this book possible. Their names are listed on the facing page.

NOTES

Chapter 1

1. 1891 Census
2. *New York Times*, 17 July 1891
3. *Hansard*
4. Stashower, *Teller of Tales*
5. *The Author*, 1 Aug 1891; 1 April 1893
6. BM Add. Ms. 56868
7. *The Author*, 15 Dec 1890
8. *The Author*, 16 Feb 1891
9. *Manchester Guardian*, 25 Sept 1891
10. *Manchester Guardian*, 3 Nov 1891
11. *Manchester Guardian*, 1 Feb 1894, 6 May 1894
12. Gribble, *Seen in Passing*
13. Room, *Dictionary of Pseudonyms*
14. Sladen, *Twenty Years of My Life*
15. *Lloyds Weekly*
16. *The Author*, 1 Dec 1891
17. *Daily News*
18. *Victoria County History*
19. *Bookman*, March 1893
20. *Daily Graphic*, 28 May 1892
21. *The Author*, 1 Aug 1891
22. Friswell, *In the Sixties and Seventies*
23. Waller, *Writers, Readers, and Reputations*
24. *Birmingham Post*, 7 Jan 1893
25. *Birmingham Daily Post*, 27 June 1892
26. Phillpotts, *From the Angle of 88*
27. Lycett, 2007
28. *Illustrated London News*, 19 Nov 1892
29. Richmond Library, SLA 22
30. Pearson, *Conan Doyle*
31. Blumenfeld, *RDB's Procession*, 1935
32. Lellenberg, *Arthur Conan Doyle*
33. *Western Daily Mercury*, 3 Jan 1893
34. SLA 21, p. 209
35. *Daily News*, 31 Jan 1893
36. *Birmingham Daily Post*, 11 Jan 1893
37. *Dundee Courier*, 17 Jan 1893
38. Sladen; *Birmingham Mail*, 13 Jan 1893
39. *The Times*, 4 Feb 1958. This historic curiosity was finally abolished by the reform of local government licensing in 2004.
40. *Daily News*, 24 March 1893

Chapter 2

1. Powys, *The Verdict of Bridlegoose*
2. Bibliographical note in Rodd, *Rose Leaf and Apple Leaf.* The publisher did not comply with Rodd's request; Mosher's note makes it clear that he thought that Wilde's essay was of greater value than the poems themselves.
3. *The Academy*, 11 Nov 1882
4. Watson, *Lectures to Living Authors*, 1925. The author of several historical romances, E.H. Lacon Watson (1865–1948) joined the Authors' Club in 1897.
5. *The Times*, 29 Sept. 1893
6. *Times Literary Supplement*, 29 July 1920
7. Lellenberg, *Arthur Conan Doyle: A Life in Letters*
8. Skilton, David, Introduction, in: George Moore: *Esther Waters* (Oxford World Classics, 1983)
9. Coustillas, Pierre, 'A Forgotten Anecdote', *The Gissing Newsletter*, Vol XIII, No. 2, April 1977
10. *The Times*, 10 July 1894
11. *The Author*, 1 Dec 1894
12. Kernahan, *In Good Company*
13. Stashower, *Teller of Tales*
14. Ricketts, *The Unforgiving Minute*
15. Harris, *Oscar Wilde*
16. *Pall Mall Gazette*, 12 Nov 1895
17. *Morning Post*, 7 Nov 1895
18. Haggard, *Days of My Life*
19. *Pall Mall Gazette*, 2 Sept 1895
20. Jerome, *My Life And Times*

Chapter 3

1. *New York Times*, 16 Aug 1896
2. *The Sketch*, 12 June 1895
3. *New York Times*, 16 Aug 1896
4. *New York Times*, date
5. Wodehouse, *Letters.*
6. *Illustrated London News*, 18 Dec. 1897
7. *The Times*, 13 June 1901
8. Gribble, *Seen in Passing*
9. SLA 21/488
10. Christies' auction catalogue, 1991
11. AGM Minutes, 8 April 1908
12. Horace Cowley Wyndham (1873–1970), novelist and biographer of Speranza Wilde

13 Gribble, *Seen in Passing*
14 Swinnerton, *Arnold Bennett: A Final Word*
15 *The Times*, 18 Sept 1934
16 Sladen, *Twenty Years of My Life*
17 Authors' Club Rules and Regulations, 1923
18 Leuliette, Vol I
19 Annual Report, 1914–15
20 In 1914, Algernon Rose sent Du Bois an Authors' Club prospectus with an invitation to join; he does not appear to have taken up the offer.
21 *New York Times*, 2 March 1909
22 *The Times*, 24 May 1909

Chapter 4
1 Higgins, *Rider Haggard*
2 www.lewismasonic.co.uk/blog/authors-lodge-authors-lodge-no-3456.htm [accessed 23 April 2016]; www.freemasonrytoday.com/news/lodges-chapters-a-individuals/item/400-authors%E2%C3%AF%C2%BF%C2%BD%C3%AF%C2%BF%C2%BD-lodge-a-history [accessed 23 April 2016]
3 Annual Report, 16 Feb 1911
4 Annual Report, 14 Feb 1912
5 Meudell, *My Pleasant Career*
6 Langmore, Diane, 'Meudell, George Dick (1860–1936)', Australian Dictionary of Biography, National Centre of Biography, Australian National University, http://adb.anu.edu.au/biography/meudell-george-dick-7564/text13201 [accessed 11 Sept 2011]
7 Meudell, *Pleasant Career*
8 *Hobart Mercury*, 2 Feb 1911.
9 Nicolson, 'Post-Impressionism and Roger Fry'
10 Woolf, 'Mr Bennett and Mrs Brown'
11 Bennett, *Journals*.
12 Wilson, *Arnold Bennett and H.G. Wells*
13 Ford, *The Good Soldier*, Dedicatory letter to Stella Ford, 1927 ed.
14 I am indebted to Aldington's biographer Vivien Whelpton for this information.
15 Jerrold, *Georgian Adventure*

Chapter 5
1 Annual Report, 1914–15
2 Annual Report, 1915–16
3 Lellenberg, *Arthur Conan Doyle: A Life in Letters*
4 *Who Was Who*
5 Jerrold, *Georgian Adventure*
6 Annual Report, 1914–15

7 Kingsmill, *Behind Both Lines*
8 Bennett, *Journals*.
9 Aldington, *Life for Life's Sake*
10 Mizener, *The Saddest Story*
11 Ford, *Letters*
12 Saunders, *Ford Madox Ford: A Dual Life*
13 Dunsany, *Patches of Sunlight*
14 Leuliette, Vol. III
15 greatwarlondon.wordpress.com/2014/01/31/temporary-housing-for-the-government-in-great-war-london [accessed 6/4/16]
16 Typewritten membership list, c.1938–39
17 Jones, *Whitehall Diary*
18 Annual Report, 1918–19
19 Lewis, *Blasting & Bombardiering*

Chapter 6
1 Annual Report, 1919–20
2 Saunders, *Ford Madox Ford: A Dual Life*
3 Annual Report, 1920–21
4 Annual Report, 1919–20
5 The 23rd, as announced in the Annual Report for 1919–20 and not, as incorrectly stated in the 1920-21 report, the 29th, which was in fact a Sunday. The confusion may have arisen because 1920 was a leap year.
6 Annual Report, 1920–21
7 Minutes of EGM, 29 March 1922
8 Annual Report, 1922–23
9 Executive Committee Minutes 1932–53
10 Annual Report, 1922–3; Hansard, HL Deb 17 Nov 1920 vol 42 cc293-317; HL Deb 28 July 1921 vol 43 cc68-80
11 Annual Report, 1922–3
12 *The Times*, 30 Oct 1956; *Manchester Guardian*, 14 Oct 1958
13 Typewritten memoir in the Authors' Club archive, signed 'E.G.C.'. The only person in the members list with these initials is Edmund George Cousins, 'contributor to the film and lay press'. His statement that he was a member for eight years before the outbreak of the Second World War must be a mistake – maybe he meant to write 'eighteen'. Had he joined in 1931 or 1932, he would not have remembered Gilbert Parker, who died in 1930, or Squire Bancroft, who died in 1926.
14 1911 Census
15 http://www.aucklandmuseum.com/war-memorial/online-cenotaph/record/C41141
16 Annual Report 1923–4, 1924–5

17   Annual Report 1923–4,

18   *ibid.*

19   Haggard, *Diaries*

20   *Yorkshire Post,* 10 Jan 1922

21   *Manchester Guardian,* 6 Oct 1925

22   Friedman, *The Hyde Park Atrocity*

23   *Manchester Guardian,* 7 Oct 1925

24   Friedman, *The Hyde Park Atrocity*; *The Times,* 23 Nov 1925

25   *The Times,* 7 April 1926

26   *The Times,* 10 April 1926

27   Miller, *Adventures of Arthur Conan Doyle*

28   Bennett, *Journals*

29   Mackenzie, *My Life and Times: Octave Six*

30   Annual Report, 1925–6

31   Annual Report, 1926–7

32   Annual Report, 1927–8

33   *History Today* 22 (12), Dec 1972

34   *The Times,* 13 Jan 1928

35   University of Sussex special collections: Papers of John Lockwood Kipling and Mrs. J.L. Kipling. Correspondence 21/22

36   *West Australian,* 12 May 1928

37   *Manchester Guardian,* 4 September 1928

38   *The Times,* 24 June 1910

39   *Manchester Guardian,* 4 Sept 1928

40   Annual Report, 1928–9

41   *The Times,* 11 Dec 1928

42   Souhami, *Trials of Radcliffe Hall*

43   Pollnitz, 'Censorship and Transmission'

44   Annual Report, 1931–3

45   BM Add. MS 88924/8/11

Chapter 7

1   *Manchester Guardian,* 9 March 1937

2   BL Loan 96 RLF 1/2990

3   BL Loan 96 RLF 1/2765

4   BL Loan 96 RLF 1/2804

5   Jameson, *Morley Roberts*

6   BL Loan 96 RLF 1/2804

7   Jameson, *Morley Roberts*

8   *The Times,* 8 October 1935

9   BL Loan 96 RLF 1/2804

10   BL Loan 96 RLF 1/2956

11   BL Loan 96 RLF 1/2848

12   BL Loan 96 RLF 1/2888

13   *The Times,* 22 March 1939

14   Linklater, *Compton Mackenzie*

15   *Manchester Guardian,* 13 Jan 1931

16   *The Times,* 7 Oct. 1931

17   David Howell, 'Alexander, Albert Victor, Earl Alexander of Hillsborough (1885–1965)', *Oxford Dictionary of National Biography,* OUP, 2004; online edn, Jan 2008 [http://www.oxforddnb.com.ezproxy2. londonlibrary.co.uk/view/article/30368, accessed 4 June 2016]

18   Robert Crossley, 'Stapledon, (William) Olaf (1886–1950)', *Oxford Dictionary of National Biography,* OUP, May 2006; online edn, Oct 2007 [http://www.oxforddnb.com. ezproxy2.londonlibrary.co.uk/view/article/38876, accessed 4 June 2016]

19   Elaine Kaye, 'Micklem, Nathaniel (1888–1976)', *Oxford Dictionary of National Biography,* OUP, 2004 [http://www.oxforddnb. com.ezproxy2.londonlibrary.co.uk/view/article/31443, accessed 4 June 2016]; Micklem, *The Box and the Puppets*

20   *Manchester Guardian,* 6 Jan 1951; *The Times* 6 Jan 1951

21   *Manchester Guardian,* 2 Oct 1930

22   Annual Report, 1936–37

23   Annual Report, 1937–38

24   *Manchester Guardian,* 9 Feb 1937

25   Committee Minutes, 3 May 1937

26   Jerrold, *Georgian Adventure*

27   Lehmann, *Authors Take Sides*

28   Takehiko Honda, 'Garratt, Geoffrey Theodore (1888–1942)', *Oxford Dictionary of National Biography,* OUP, 2004 [http:// www.oxforddnb.com.ezproxy2.londonlibrary.co.uk/view/article/39642, accessed 16 April 2016]

29   Petrie, *A Historian Looks at his World*

30   *The Times,* 2 June 1937

31   Both Schlottman and Thadden were hard-line Nazis. Schlottman was interrogated after the war, and his evidence helped to convict Ribbentrop at Nuremberg. Thadden was later involved in the deportation of Jews to concentration camps; after he gave evidence at Eichmann's trial in 1961, his own role in the Holocaust came under investigation, but he was killed in a car crash before he could face trial.

Chapter 8

1   As reported by Michael Korda, *New Yorker,* 25 March 1996

2   Muggeridge, *Chronicles of Wasted Time*

3   Typewritten memoir, Authors' Club archive

4   Annual report 1940-41
5   BL Loan 96 RLF 1/2956
6   *Oxford DNB*
7   Myres, 'Stanley Casson'
8   Sparrow, *Words on the Air*
9   *Burlington Magazine 61* (357), Dec. 1932
10   Cooper, *Patrick Leigh Fermor*
11   *Listener*, 21 March 1940
12   Petrie, *A Historian Looks at his World*
13   *The Times*, 7 Feb 1941
14   Edwards, *Victor Gollancz*
15   *Manchester Guardian*, 9 April 1941
16   Annual Report 1943-3; Oxford DNB
17   http://www.chch.ox.ac.uk/fallen-alumni/
     chaplain-4th-class-joseph-edward-gough-
     quinn#sthash.D085r9uc.dpuf
18   *Manchester Guardian*, 26 Oct 1943
19   Memorandum, General Meetings 1943
20   Powell, *Faces in my Time*
21   Pearson & Kingsmill, *Talking of Dick
     Whittington*
22   Greene, *The Lost Childhood*
23   Jerrold, 'Graham Greene, Pleasure-Hater'
24   Powell, *Faces in my Time*
25   Ingrams, *God's Apology*
26   Petrie, *A Historian Looks at his World*
27   *New York Times*, 2 Sept 2002
28   Ingrams, *God's Apology*
29   Sherry, *Life of Graham Greene*
30   Executive Committee Minutes 12 Oct
     1948, 16 Nov 1948, 8 June 1953
31   Ellis, *Death and the Author*
32   Minutes, 17 May 1949
33   Hunter, *Nothing to Repent*

Chapter 9
1   Annual Report, 1950–51
2   *The Author*, Summer 1976
3   Minutes, 4 March 1952
4   *Evening Standard*, 24 Sept 1953
5   *Sketch*, 26 Aug 1953
6   Fraser, *My History*
7   *New York Times*,
8   *Daily Express*, 8 April 1954; *Daily Telegraph*, 8
     April 1954; *Guardian*, 13 April 1954
9   *Manchester Guardian*, 1 April 1955
10   *Times Literary Supplement*, 6 May 1955
11   *Evening Standard*, 26 Nov 1955
12   *The Times*, 18 May 1955
13   *Spectator*, 21 Jan 1955
14   *Manchester Guardian*, 14 Oct 1958

15   'BONHAM-CARTER, Victor', *Who Was
     Who*, A & C Black, an imprint of Blooms-
     bury Publishing plc, 1920–2016; online edn,
     OUP, 2014; online edn, April 2014 [http://
     www.ukwhoswho.com/view/article/oup-
     ww/whowaswho/U8059, accessed 16 July
     2016]; *Daily Telegraph*, 20 March 2007
16   'THURSTON, Gavin (Leonard Bour-
     das)', *Who Was Who*, A & C Black, an
     imprint of Bloomsbury Publishing plc,
     1920–2016; online edn, OUP, 2014; online
     edn, April 2014 [http://www.ukwhoswho.
     com/view/article/oupww/whowaswho/
     U160312, accessed 28 May 2016]
17   *New York Times*. 2 Dec 1996
18   Richard Davenport-Hines, 'Russell, (Ed-
     ward Frederick) Langley, second Baron
     Russell of Liverpool (1895–1981)', *Oxford
     Dictionary of National Biography*, OUP, 2004
     [http://www.oxforddnb.com.ezproxy2.
     londonlibrary.co.uk/view/article/31636,
     accessed 2 Aug 2016]
19   *The Times*, 28 Feb 1959
20   *The Times*, 14 Nov 1956
21   *Evening Standard*, 14 Jan 1957
22   Annual Report, 1957–58; *The Times* 31 Oct
     1957
23   *The Times*, 1 Sept 1959

Chapter 10
1   *The Times*, 11 March 1960
2   *Observer*, 27 March 1960
3   Minutes, 15 Nov 1960
4   *The Times*, 16 Feb 1961
5   Forster, *Diaries*, Vol. 2
6   Williamson wrote in his diary that he was
     in London on the 15th and had dinner
     'with' Forster; henrywilliamson.co.uk/
     bibliography/a-lifes-work/the-inno-
     cent-moon [accessed 14 Aug 2016]
7   *The Times*, 14 Dec 1961
8   *The Times*, 11 Oct 1962
9   Petrie, *A Historian Looks at his World*
10   *The Times*, 11 Dec 1962
11   *Tatler*, 2 Jan 1963
12   *The Times*, 12 July 1962
13   *The Times*, 29 March 1962. Thurston would
     subsequently officiate at the inquests on
     Cass Elliot, Jimi Hendrix and Sandra
     Rivett, Lord Lucan's nanny.
14   *Guardian*, March 23 1963

15 *The Times,* 10 Dec 1963
16 Paul Baker, Typewritten obituary, Authors' Club archive
17 *Arts Club Journal,* Spring 1981
18 *The Times,* 1 Aug 1964
19 *Guardian,* 24 July 1964
20 *The Times,* 8 July 1964
21 *The Times,* 26 Feb 1965
22 *The Times,* 27 May 1965
23 *Illustrated London News,* 1 Jan 1966
24 Authors' Club archive. Correspondence: Victor Bonham-Carter
25 *The Times,* 12 Jan 1967
26 Brophy MSS VI, 7, Indiana University
27 Boll, 1981
28 Michael Lindsay, personal communication
29 Petrie, *A Historian Looks at his World*
30 *Ibid.*
31 *The Times,* 21 March1968
32 Annual Report, 1969
33 *The Times,* 13 Feb 1969
34 *The Times,* 23 April 1969; Trevelyan, *What the Censor Saw*
35 *The Times,* 19 March 1970
36 *Arts Club Journal,* Autumn 1981
37 *Guardian,* 15 Jan 2011
38 During these years, the award was given biennially.
39 *Arts Club Journal,* Autumn 1981
40 *The Times,* 30 Mar 1972.
41 *Glasgow Herald,* 5 Dec 1972

Chapter 11
1   Centenary speech, Authors' Club archive

2   *Guardian,* 23 March 1977; *The Times,* 28 July 1977; *The Times,* 21 Oct 1982
3   *Arts Club Journal,* Autumn 2006
4   *The Times,* 20 Jan 1978
5   *The Author,* 1976
6   Boll, 1981
7   Typewritten obituary, Authors' Club Archive
8   Obituary by Brian Bagnall, Authors' Club Archive; *Guardian* 22 Nov 2000
9   *Ibid.*
10 *Guardian,* 12 Aug 2000
11 *Daily Telegraph,* 9 Aug 2000
12 *Arts Club Journal,* Autumn 1981
13 *Arts Club Journal,* June 1983
14 *Arts Club Journal,* April 1983
15 *Arts Club Journal,* June 1983
16 *The Times,* 18 July 1991; 16 June 1994
17 *The Times,* 5 Dec 1983
18 *The Times,* 10 Jan 1983
19 Minutes, 17 July 1984
20 Cousins, typescript in Authors' Club archive
21 Annual Report, 1987–88; Minutes, 3 May 1988
22 Min Liu was subsequently released after three years in jail
23 *Arts Club Journal,* Spring 1993
24 *Arts Club Journal,* Spring 1997

Chapter 12
1   James Burge, *Heloïse and Abelard* (Profile)
2   *London Review of Books,* 6 March 2008
3   *Condé Nast Traveller,* 25 Sept 2013

BIBLIOGRAPHY

Primary sources: memoirs, journals and letters

Aldington, Richard, *Life for Life's Sake: A Book of Reminiscences.* New York: Viking, 1941.

Bennett, Arnold, *The Journals of Arnold Bennett,* ed. Newman Flower. London: Cassell, 1933.

Blumenfeld, Ralph, *RDB's Procession.* New York: Macmillan, 1935.

Bonham-Carter, Victor, *What Countryman, Sir?* Milverton: Bonham-Carter Press, 1994.

Dunsany, Lord, *Patches of Sunlight.* London: Heinemann, 1938.

Eliot, T.S., *Poetry and Drama.* London: Faber, 1951.

Fraser, Antonia, *My History: A Memoir of Growing Up.* London: Weidenfeld & Nicolson, 2015.

Friswell, Laura Hain, *In the Sixties and Seventies: Impressions Of Literary People and Others,* H.B. Turner & Co., Boston 1906

Garrett, Geoffrey T., *The Shadow of the Swastika.* London: Hamish Hamilton, 1938.

Gates, Norman T., *Richard Aldington: An Autobiography in Letters.* University Park, PA: Pennsylvania State University Press, 1992.

Gissing, George. *The Collected Letters of George Gissing,* ed. Paul F. Mattheisen, Arthur C. Young and Pierre Coustillas. Athens OH: Ohio University Press, 1994.

Greene, Graham, *The Lost Childhood and other Essays.* London: Eyre & Spottiswoode, 1951.

Greene, Richard (ed.), *Graham Greene: A Life in Letters.* London: Little, Brown, 2007.

Gribble, Francis, *Seen In Passing. A Volume of Personal Reminiscence.* London: Ernest Benn, 1929.

Haggard, H. Rider, *The Days of My Life.* London: Longmans, 1926.

Hart-Davis, Rupert and Merlin Holland (eds), *The Complete Letters of Oscar Wilde* (New York: Henry Holt, 2000), Oscar Wilde to R.H. Sherard, 16 October 1897, p. 963

Jerome, Jerome K., *My Life And Times* (pub details)

Jerrold, Douglas, *Georgian Adventure.* London: Collins, 1937.

——————— 'Graham Greene, Pleasure-Hater'. *Harper's Magazine,* August 1952.

Jones, Thomas, *Whitehall Diary, Vol. I 1916–1925,* ed. Keith Middlemiss. London: Oxford University Press, 1969.

Kernahan, Coulson, *In Good Company.* London: John Lane, 1917

Kingsmill, Hugh, *Behind Both Lines.* London: Morley & Mitchell Kennerley, 1930.

Lehmann, John (ed.), *Authors Take Sides on the Spanish Civil War.* London: Left Review, 1937.

Lewis, Wyndham, *Blasting & Bombardiering.* London: Calder & Boyars, 1967.

Ludwig, R.M., ed., *Letters of Ford Madox Ford.* Princeton University Press, 1965.

Meudell, George Dick, *The Pleasant Career of a Spendthrift.* London: Routledge, [1935].

Micklem, Nathaniel, *The Box and the Puppets.* Geoffrey Bles: London, 1957.

Muggeridge, Malcolm, *Chronicles of Wasted Time: Vol. 2, The Infernal Grove*. London: Collins, 1973.

——————— *Like It Was: The Diaries of Malcolm Muggeridge*. London: Harper Collins, 1981.

Nash, Eveleigh, *I Liked the Life I Lived: Some Reminiscences*. London: John Murray, 1941.

O'Sullivan, Vincent, *Some Letters of Vincent O'Sullivan to A.J.A. Symons*, with an introduction by Alan Anderson. Edinburgh: Tragara Press, 1975.

Pearson, Hesketh, *Hesketh Pearson by Himself*. London: Heinemann, [1965].

Pearson, Hesketh and Kingsmill, Hugh, *Talking of Dick Whittington*. London: Eyre & Spottiswoode, 1947.

Petrie, Sir Charles, *A Historian Looks at his World*. London: Sidgwick & Jackson, 1972.

Phillpotts, Eden, *From the Angle of 88*. London: Hutchinson, [1951].

Powell, Anthony, *Faces in My Time*. London: Heinemann, 1980.

Powys, Llewellyn, *The Verdict of Bridlegoose*. New York: Harcourt, Brace & Co., 1926.

Rodd, Rennell, *Rose Leaf and Apple Leaf*. Portland: T.B. Mosher, 1906.

Ryan, W.P., *Literary London, Its Lights & Comedies*. London: Leonard Smithers, 1898.

Sherard, Robert, *Oscar Wilde: The Story of an Unhappy Friendship* (1905; rpt. 1970).

Sladen, Douglas, *Twenty Years of My Life*. London: Constable, 1915.

Swinnerton, Frank, *The Georgian Literary Scene, 1910–1935: A Panorama*. London: Hutchinson, 1950.

——————— *Arnold Bennett: A Last Word*. London: Hamish Hamilton, 1978.

Watson, E.H. Lacon, *Lectures to Living Authors*. London: G. Bles [1925].

Wilson, Harris, ed., *Arnold Bennett and H.G. Wells: A Record of a Personal and a Literary Friendship*. London: Rupert Hart-Davis, 1960.

Wodehouse, P.G., *A Life in Letters*, ed. Sophie Ratcliffe. New York: W.W. Norton, 2013.

Secondary sources

Adams, Jad, 'Kipling's Dilemma: Decadent or Hearty?' *The Kipling Journal* 82 (325), 2008.

Adams, John Coldwell, *Seated with the Mighty: A Biography of Sir Gilbert Parker*. Ottawa: Borealis Press, 1979.

Allen, Walter, *As I Walked Down New Grub Street: Memories of a Writing Life*. London: Heinemann, 1981.

Alpert, Michael, *A New International History of the Spanish Civil War*. Basingstoke: Palgrave Macmillan, 1994.

Amory, Mark, *Lord Dunsany: A Biography*. London: Collins, 1972.

Authors Cricket Club, *The Authors XI: A Season of English Cricket from Hackney to Hambledon*. London: Bloomsbury, 2013.

Belford, Barbara, *Violet: The Story of the Irrepressible Violet Hunt and her Circle of Lovers and Friends – Ford Madox Ford, H.G. Wells, Somerset Maugham, and Henry James*. New York: Simon and Schuster, 1990.

Boege, Fred W., 'Sir Walter Besant, Novelist,' *Nineteenth-Century Fiction*, March 1956, pp. 249–80; June 1956, pp. 32–60.

Boll, Theophilus E.M., 'The Authors' Club of London'. *English Literature in Transition* XXIV (2), 1981, pp. 99–107.

Bonham-Carter, Victor. *Authors by Profession. Vol.2. From the Copyright Act 1911 until the end of 1981*. London: Bodley Head/Society of Authors, 1984.

Cheng, Vincent J., 'The "Zeppelin Nights" of Ford Madox Ford'. *Journal of Modern Literature* 15 (4) Spring 1989, pp. 595–597.

Cooper, Artemis, *Patrick Leigh Fermor: An Adventure*. London: John Murray, 2012.

Coustillas, Pierre, 'A Forgotten Anecdote', *The Gissing Newsletter*, XIII (2), April 1977.

Day, Peter, *Franco's Friends*. London: Biteback Publishing, 2011.

Denvir, Bernard, *A Most Agreeable Society: 125 Years of the Arts Club*. London: Arts Club, 1989.

Edwards, Ruth Dudley, *Victor Gollancz: A Biography*. London: Victor Gollancz, 1987.

Ferrall, Charles, & McNeill, Dougal, *Writing the 1926 General Strike: Literature, Culture, Politics*. New York: Cambridge University Press, 2015.

Ford, Brian J., 'Surprising Insights into H.G. Wells'. *Bulletin of the Friends of Cambridge University Library* 25, 10–14, December 2004.

Freidman, Terry, *The Hyde Park Atrocity: Epstein's 'Rima' – Creation and Controversy*. Leeds: Henry Moore Sculpture Trust, 1988

Goldring, Douglas, *The Last Pre-Raphaelite: A Record of the Life and Writings of Ford Madox Ford*. London: Macdonald, 1948.

Greene, Richard (ed), *Graham Greene: A Life in Letters*. London: Little, Brown, 2007.

Hale, Frederick, 'The Formation of a Conservative Catholic Intellectual: Douglas Francis Jerrold as a Disciple of Hilaire Belloc'. *Heythrop Journal 54* (3), pp. 397–413, 2013.

Hardwick, Joan, *An Immodest Violet: The Life of Violet Hunt*. London: André Deutsch, 1990.

Harris, Frank, *Oscar Wilde: His Life and Confessions*. New York: Brentano, 1916.

Harrison, Gilbert A., *The Enthusiast: A Life of Thornton Wilder*. New York: Fromm, 1986.

Haslam, Sara, *Fragmenting Modernism: Ford Madox Ford, the Novel and the Great War*. Manchester: Manchester University Press, 2002.

Heldman, James M., 'The Last Victorian Novel: Technique and Theme in Parade's End', *Twentieth Century Literature 18* (4), 1972, pp. 271–284

Higgins, D.S., *Rider Haggard, The Great Storyteller*. London: Cassell, 1981

Hughes, Linda, 'A Club of Their Own: The "Literary Ladies," New Women Writers, and "Fin-de-Siècle".' *Victorian Literature and Culture 35* (1), 2007.

Hunter, Ian, *Nothing to Repent: The Life of Hesketh Pearson*. Hamish Hamilton: London, 1987.

Ingrams, Richard, *God's Apology: A Chronicle of Three Friends*. London: André Deutsch, 1977.

Jameson, Storm, *Morley Roberts: The Last Eminent Victorian*. London: Unicorn, 1961.

Linklater, Andro, *Compton Mackenzie: A Life*. London: Chatto & Windus, 1987.

Lycett, Andrew, *Conan Doyle: The Man Who Created Sherlock Holmes*. London: Weidenfeld & Nicolson, 2007.

Macklin, Graham, 'Major Hugh Pollard, MI6 and the Spanish Civil War'. *Historical Journal 49* (1), 2006, pp. 277-280.

Masters, Anthony, *The Man Who Was M: Life of Charles Henry Maxwell Knight* Wiley-Blackwell; 2nd edition. 1984.

Messinger, Gary S., 'An inheritance worth remembering: The British approach to official propaganda during the First World War'. *Historical Journal of Film, Radio & Television 13* (2), 1993, p.117.

Miller, Russell, *The Adventures of Arthur Conan Doyle*. London: Pimlico, 2009.

Mizener, Arthur, *The Saddest Story: A Biography of Ford Madox Ford*. London: Bodley Head, 1972.

Myres, John L., 'Stanley Casson: 1889–1944'. *Annual of the British School at Athens* 41 (1940–1945).

Nicolson, Benedict, 'Post-Impressionism and Roger Fry', *The Burlington Magazine 93* (574), Jan 1951.

Nyburg, Anna, *From Leipzig to London: The Life and Work of the Émigré Artist Hellmuth Weissenborn*. New Castle, DE: Oak Knoll Press, 2012.

Pollnitz, Christopher, 'The Censorship and Transmission of D.H. Lawrence's "Pansies": The Home Office and the "Foul-Mouthed Fellow"'. *Journal of Modern Literature 28* (3), Spring 2005.

Ricketts, Harry, *The Unforgiving Minute: A Life of Rudyard Kipling*. London: Chatto & Windus, 1999.

Room, Adrian, *A Dictionary of Pseudonyms and their Origins: With Stories of Name Changes*. Jefferson, NC: McFarland, 1989.

Sanders, M.L., 'Wellington House and British Propaganda during the First World War'. *Historical Journal 18* (1), March 1975, pp. 119-146

Saunders, Max, *Ford Madox Ford: A Dual Life*. Oxford: Oxford University Press, 1996.

Schaffer, Talia, 'A Wilde Desire Took Me: The Homoerotic History of *Dracula*', *English Literary History 61* (2), Summer 1994, pp. 381–425.

Sherry, Norman, *The Life of Graham Greene*. London: Cape, 1989–2004.

Souhami, Diana, *The Trials of Radclyffe Hall*. New York: Doubleday, 1999.

Spilka, Mark, 'Henry James and Walter Besant: "The Art of Fiction" Controversy', *NOVEL: A Forum on Fiction* 6 (2), Winter 1973, pp. 101–119.

Stashower, Daniel, *Teller of Tales: The Life of Arthur Conan Doyle*. London: Allen Lane, 2000.

Trevelyan, John, *What the Censor Saw*. London: Michael Joseph, 1974.

Turner, John, *Lloyd George's Secretariat*. Cambridge: Cambridge University Press, 1980.

Waddington, G. T. 'An idyllic and unruffled atmosphere of complete Anglo-German misunderstanding: Aspects of the Operations of the Dienststelle Ribbentrop in Great Britain, 1934–1938'. *History 82* (265) (January 1997), pp. 44-72

Waller, Philip, *Writers, Readers, and Reputations: Literary Life in Britain, 1870–1918*. Oxford: Oxford University Press, 2006.

West, Nigel, 'Fiction, Faction and Intelligence', in P.D. Jackson and L.V. Scott (eds.), *Understanding Intelligence in the Twenty-First Century: Journeys in Shadows*. London: Routledge, 2004.

White, Winifred M., *Hubert W. Peet*. London: Friends Home Service Committee, 1952.

Whittington-Egan, R. & Smerdon, G., *The Quest of the Golden Boy: The Life and Letters of Richard Le Gallienne*. London: Unicorn Press, 1960.

Wiegand, Wayne A, 'British Propaganda in American Public Libraries, 1914–1917'. *Journal of Library History 18 (3),* Summer 1983, pp. 237–254.

Winter, J. M., 'R.H. Tawney's Early Political Thought', *Past & Present 47,* May 1970, pp. 71–96.

Index of Names